THE MODERN
SEAFOOD
COOK

THE MODERN SEAFOOD COOK

New Tastes, New Techniques, New Ease

By Edward Brown and Arthur Boehm
Foreword by Pierre Franey

Illustrations by Leland Burke
Technical Drawings by Laura Karp

Clarkson Potter/Publishers
New York

Published by Clarkson N. Potter, Inc., 201 East 50th Street, New York, New York 10022. Member of the Crown Publishing Group.

Random House, Inc. New York, Toronto, London, Sydney, Auckland

CLARKSON N. POTTER, POTTER, and colophon are trademarks of Clarkson N. Potter, Inc.

Manufactured in the U.S.A.

BOOK DESIGN BY RENATO STANISIC

Brown, Edward.
    The modern seafood cook : new tastes, new techniques, new ease / by Edward Brown and Arthur Boehm.
        p.   cm.
    Includes index.
    1. Cookery (Seafood)   2. Seafood.   I. Boehm, Arthur.   II. Title.
TX747.B653   1995
641.6'92—dc20   95-31150
                                                                    CIP

ISBN 0-517-70241-X

10 9 8 7 6 5 4 3 2 1

First Edition

For Kelley Wade Brown
and
Janet and Albert Brown
and for
Leonore Boehm
and
Richard Getke

Acknowledgments

Both authors with to thank their agent, Anne Edelstein, whose ongoing commitment to the book brought it to safe shore, and Pam Krauss, their editor, whose infallible eye, steady hand, and ready ear made mutual collaboration a joy. We cannot imagine two people with whom we would rather go fishing. Thanks also to Ann Cartwright, our vigilant recipe tester, and to the many hands at Clarkson Potter who have made this book so much better than it might have been otherwise.

My love and thanks above all to my wife, Kelley Wade Brown, for her support and for having more confidence in me than I had in myself. My deepest love and gratitude to my mother, Janet Brown, who taught me how to cook, and to my father, the late Albert Brown, who taught me everything he knew about business while showing me how to be a decent man.

To my mentors Werner Herble, Christian Delouvrier, Pierre Franey, and all the wonderful cooks I've worked with in the past, who have inspired me as greatly as anyone—many thanks. My gratitude also to those other cooks who have unselfishly helped me in my work by their expertise or by simply lending a hand.

I thank also my good friends John DiLeo, Albert DeAngelis, and Bobby Flay. My deep appreciation to Restaurant Associates for always supporting my work and making it possible for me to discover my own culinary talent while working within a wonderful organization.

I thank particularly Nick Valenti, chief executive officer of Restaurant Associates, for his patience and generosity.

I would also like to acknowledge especially the efforts of Louis Rozzo at F. Rozzo & Sons, seafood purveyors, without whose marvelous fish and shellfish it would not be possible for me to cook as I do.

And lastly to Arthur Boehm, a great friend and talented writing partner, thanks for contributing the patience, diligence, and words to make this book possible.

E.B.

My deepest love and thanks for the patient friendship and editorial discernment of Judy Fireman and Judy Gingold, both of whom tirelessly read and reread the manuscript. To Judy G., a hug far bigger than the Ritz; to Judy F., an endless fax full of kisses. Thanks, also, to Geila Hocherman for her support and keen judgment in so many matters.

The late Peter Kump provided continuous support and a happy place for me at Peter Kump's New York Cooking School. I am very grateful.

Above all, my appreciation to Edward Brown, who fed me his extraordinary food and became my friend, and to Richard Getke, the best of all dining partners.

A.B.

Contents

Foreword

Let me say right away that I love Ed Brown's cooking.

I got to know him years ago, when he was chef at Marie-Michelle, a small and thoroughly delightful Manhattan restaurant no longer in existence. At the time Bryan Miller and I regularly visited restaurants we thought might be eligible for review in the *New York Times*. I don't remember exactly what we ate that night, but it was clear from the moment we tasted our meals that there was a presence in the kitchen. The food had a finish and its own very distinct—and delicious—personality; it was good cooking. At this time Ed was, I think, freshly returned from France, where he had worked with Chef Alain Senderens at the three-star Lucas-Carlton. I remembered that we had first met through Christian Delouvrier, the chef at Manhattan's much-esteemed Restaurant Maurice, under whom Ed had apprenticed.

As I followed Ed and his cooking, we became good friends. Though we have never actually worked together, Ed was kind enough to make several extraordinary seafood dishes for my son's wedding reception. That was an event! At the time Ed and I talked a good deal about fish and shellfish, and we were in complete accord on several important points: that there is no good seafood cooking if your fish and shellfish aren't absolutely fresh; that you must always avoid overcooking; and that the best seafood dishes are very simple, very light.

In this last respect particularly, Ed has become a master. I enjoyed recently at the Sea Grill, Edward's new "home" in Rockefeller Center, a small, absolutely succulent soft-shelled crab. The crab was lightly breaded, quickly and cleanly fried, and served with soy sauce. That's all. There was just enough crisp breading, and the crab burst with sweet juices—the dish was to my style and absolutely to my liking. It was, I feel, what cooking should be about.

When Ed was the chef at Tropica, a very successful restaurant with an island theme, he created his first menu. By that I mean he was able to devise a consistently delicious and completely personal homage to tropical cooking while avoiding pastiche—those dishes, too common these days, that feel invented. I could see that Ed was sensitive to the unique demands of every kind of seafood he approached. Ed has had enough experience over the years to make the rules work for him, and—as I've observed firsthand—to teach them to others. What that says to me is that he is passionate about his subject, about all seafood.

Cooking changes all the time. When I was a young chef we learned by the book the dishes of Escoffier and the other great cooks. In the 1950s, when I worked in America at Le Pavillon, things were as rigid in fine food service as they were elsewhere in the culture. We had to follow the rules, and they were very strict indeed. But even Escoffier had gone to Russia and returned with many new culinary ideas with which he infused his cooking—cuisine evolves. In the 1970s nouvelle cuisine opened the minds of cooks everywhere. The trick to nouvelle cuisine was, of course, to have a firm grounding in classical technique, to have a base. In this regard, Ed is on the most solid ground. As all true artists do, he uses the rules to set himself free—to create his own good food. Look through the pages of this book and you will see how he has masterfully reconciled the old and the new to devise dishes everyone can make and enjoy. That is what makes his cooking—and this book—so special.

There is no question in my mind that seafood is more popular than ever before. When Bryan Miller and I wrote our own seafood cookbook a few years ago, people were just beginning to appreciate the joys (including the health-promoting qualities) of fresh seafood. Now the dam has burst! Of the many books I have read devoted to seafood preparation, the book you now hold in your hands is among the very best. Ed Brown and Arthur Boehm have created a book that all cooks can use. I will cook from it often, as I know you will once you try Ed's special recipes and techniques. With the book in your kitchen, and Ed Brown at your side, you will make the best and most delicious seafood imaginable!

Pierre Franey

Introduction

I hated fish as a child. My mom was a fine cook, but the halibut, fluke, or sole she served us weekly were definitely in the backseat-to-meat category. Maybe growing up you felt the same way about fish. I wanted no part of it.

But we lived near the New Jersey shore. Fresh fish were good and plentiful there, and when I was seventeen, I got my first restaurant job unloading the fishing boats that docked near our house. The fish I hauled off the day boats gleamed like the brightest new coins. Their smell was intoxicating—sweet and salty and green, like a windy day by the shore. Readied for the restaurant kitchen, their pearly flesh was mouthwatering raw and astonishing to eat when prepared. At the restaurant I feasted on perfectly sautéed fillets, whole fish steamed to melting tenderness, soul-satisfying chowders and stews. I tasted fish again and again. It didn't take me long to become seriously hooked.

I had always loved to cook. Even as a kid of eight or nine, I loved turning ingredients into dishes that excited and satisfied people, that made them happy. I wasn't more than sixteen when, inspired by a restaurant dish I liked, I devised a fish cooking technique I still use and that I now call moist-broiling. I took a fillet of sparkling snapper and covered it with a moisture-protecting layer of onions. The onions caramelized deliciously and the fish tasted perfectly of itself.

I felt like I'd invented the wheel, but what I'd really done was find my own way to preserve all the sweet goodness—the pure taste—of fresh snapper. And friends to whom I served my creation agreed. To my great pleasure, one of them, older and sophisticated, said, "Well, Edward, I've finally *tasted* fish."

1

That's the point of what I do now—and of this book: to help even old seafood hands enjoy fish and shellfish as if for the first time. To give you a repertoire of great original dishes and reborn classics that will put seafood cooking into your life once and for all. To provide you with great restaurant techniques I've made sure you can use, and guide you to experiment with your own variations of my recipes. If you've ever thought about making seafood but gave up because you were self-conscious about buying it or were sure you'd over- or undercook it—even if you're timid about fish because of all the bones— this is the book for you.

Of course, it took a while for me, an aspiring cook, to find my own way with seafood. I did my classical professional training both here and in France, practicing my *sole normande* and *pompano en papillote*. It's hard for me to believe now that as late as the mid-eighties we apprentice-chefs were being taught to poach a fish for a half hour or more, and then let it cool in the poaching liquid. We then paired these poor victims of our culinary attention with butter-drenched sauces. Disaster! It wasn't until I returned from cooking in France and worked as chef at the restaurant Maurice in Manhattan that I truly "got it"—the more gently I cooked the fish, the better it tasted. The lighter the accompaniment, the more delectably the fish flavor came shining through.

The Japanese approach to seafood has had the biggest impact on my thinking. Spending some time with Japanese cooks in the early 1980s, I saw firsthand their devotion to total seafood freshness and to the inherent goodness of ingredients. Their joy in presentation—itself a reflection of a love for those ingredients—was contagious. I started to cook seafood the way I do now: with respect for the pure taste and succulent texture of all fresh seafood; with a love of simple, intense flavors captured as they are.

I want to pass my love of seafood on to you. The recipes here teach you the very best methods for making fish and shellfish sing with natural flavor. (For a test, try my fresh seared tuna, grilled crusty on the outside, rosy and melting within.) I've also provided a full range of delicious dishes that can be put on the table fast, often within minutes. Whether making a quickly assembled after-work meal like the Shallow-Poached Snapper with Baby Shrimp, Thyme, and Lime or a company dish like my Sautéed Cod with Sake and Chinese Black Bean Sauce, you'll find yourself eating luscious, healthful seafood in less time, often, than it takes to put together a hamburger plus salad. You'll see that seafood can work for you and everyone in your family, every day.

Of course, great seafood cooking begins with wise seafood shopping. I've made sure, first of all, that the recipes in this book call for seafood that is readily available to you. Because seafood freshness is so important to the success of all fish and shellfish cooking, I will tell you everything you need to know about how to recognize it. The most important thing is to establish a relationship with your fish seller. The more demanding you are, the more responsible your fish seller will be. And investigate ethnic seafood markets. Here in New York City the best place for the noncommercial shopper to buy fish is Chinatown. So in the book I take you on a tour of Chinatown fish stores (and other representative markets) to help you learn to identify freshness. With freshness on your side, you're well on your way to great seafood cooking. Then just follow my rules for cooking fish, outlined specifically in Chapter 4, "A Note on Undercooking and Overcooking." With some practice, you'll make vibrant, perfectly done seafood every time.

I can't mention seafood freshness without praising those twin culinary wonders, sushi and sashimi. I'm very excited to make the preparation of these supreme Japanese treats accessible to every home cook. Sashimi is one of the great fish experiences. You dip a piece of sparklingly fresh raw fillet into a dish of pungent wasabi-laced soy sauce and pop the fish in your mouth. The taste is clean and briny, pure and sweet; the texture velvety. Sashimi and sushi are transporting, addictive—the real thing. If I do nothing else but put sushi and sashimi into your home repertoire, even as special-occasion treats, I'll be happy.

I've been cooking seafood now for most of my life, making and serving it as chef of three Manhattan restaurants, including the Sea Grill. And as much as I've learned, I feel as if I've only begun to explore the incredible range of seafood preparation. I can be a virtuoso with fish—and so can you. It's the best possible canvas.

I've designed this book to be your own personal guide to seafood cookery. It's a tool that I guarantee will rid you of your fear of fish. Please accept my invitation to cook, taste, and learn with me.

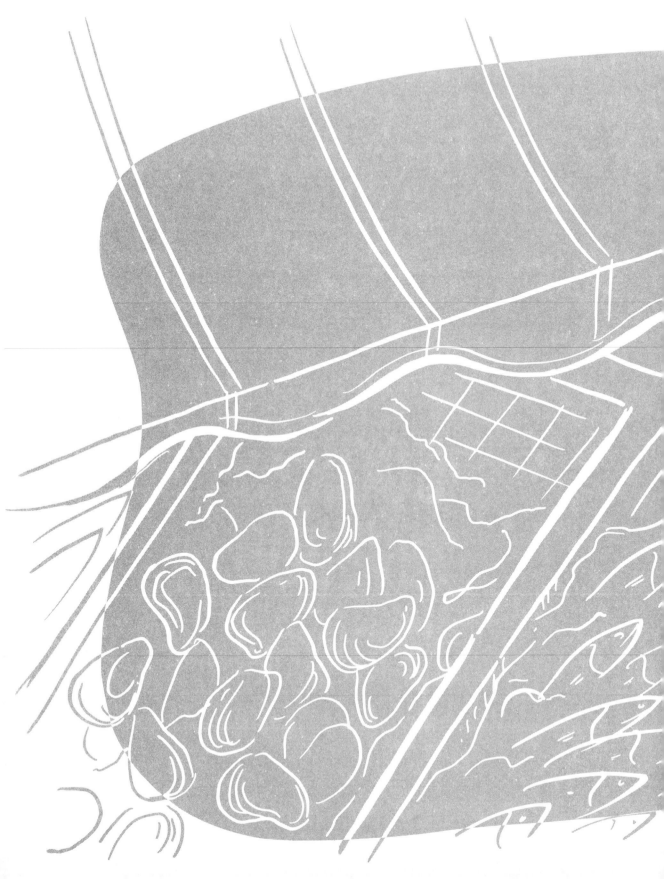

Getting Ready

1. BUYING CONFIDENTLY

The last few years have brought about an enormous improvement in seafood quality. When I step into a fish store these days I'm delighted to find a vastly increased selection of fish and shellfish and, overall, more consistent attention paid to handling the catch. Chalk this up to a greater demand for topnotch seafood, resulting in wider variety and higher quality. Improved transportation methods (including flash-freezing) have also done their share to help deliver pristine seafood to our tables, as has seafood farming.

Still, the burden of selecting the very best our waters have to offer falls squarely on the cook. You can't begin to enjoy the good seafood cooking and eating you deserve if the fish and shellfish you choose aren't fresh. Freshness is important in the selection of any food you prepare, but when it comes to seafood, freshness is *all*.

To select the freshest possible seafood, you must first know what to look for. Fortunately, there's no mystery involved; fish and shellfish are books that *can* be read by their covers.

THE BASIC RULES

More people are insecure about buying seafood than any other kind of food. But these anxieties can be allayed right away once you realize that there's little fundamental difference between buying fresh fish or shellfish and choosing good-quality produce. You buy fruit only if it looks, feels, and smells right. If the tomatoes in one market seem substandard, you shop elsewhere, or change your menu to accommodate what is freshest. And experience has undoubtedly taught you which markets can be relied on. All these rules apply to shopping for fish and shellfish.

Following are the five most important criteria for buying fish and shellfish:

1. *Use all your senses.* The freshest seafood *looks* fresh. Colors are bright and true, skins have a sheen. Crustaceans are visibly lively; bivalves glisten; squid, scallops, and octopus shine. Everything appears brand-new.

Take a sniff. Fresh seafood *smells* sweet and clean—nearly odorless or briny like the sea itself. There should be no noticeably fishy smell, which is a sign of decomposition or unsanitary market conditions, anywhere near the display. Stores should be spotless and the displays themselves should help sustain freshness. Whole fish and fillets should be on top of—not concealed under—lots of ice; lobsters should be in tanks of running water;

clams, mussels, and oysters (among other sea creatures sold live) should be refrigerated or displayed on ice.

If you are able to, *touch*. Fish should feel firm or slightly springy (natural firmness varies from species to species), and your finger should confirm the presence of a light natural slime. If you buy packaged fish, look, sniff, and touch. You can detect bad-smelling or pulpy specimens through a layer of plastic.

2. *Buy from a popular merchant who cares.* The seafood seller is a specialty merchant dealing in a highly perishable commodity—one well known for its variable quality. Presumably he wishes to please. Establish a relationship with him; tell him when you are satisfied and when you are not. Getting to know him and showing that you appreciate quality will create a sense of accountability on his part; he'll try harder. If you must buy your seafood in supermarkets, be particularly fussy about what you get. None of us likes to complain to overworked counter people, but managers do listen. You can create a demand that may well result in higher quality.

Busy seafood stores are usually the best—the more turnover, the greater the likelihood of really fresh seafood. If sales in your local market seem slow, find out when your dealer receives his shipments. In New York City, fish arrives in the wholesale market Monday and Thursday mornings. It should be in retail stores by the afternoons of those days. Similarly, Sunday afternoon is unlikely to yield a pristine piece of sole at the supermarket counter. Speak to your fish seller and ask him when he shops.

3. *Choose seafood yourself.* I'm tempted to make this rule number one. Develop your buying skills and use them. Never just ask for a fillet of this or a fresh piece of that. Counter people may care, but you're sure to care more. Inspect your selections carefully and choose every piece of seafood you buy. Go further—ask your fish seller to cut fillets from whole fish or to slice steaks to order. If a fish is buried beneath ice, ask your seller to show it to you. Ask him to hold a fish (which he should do with two hands) so that you can gently lift a gill cover to look within. The more active you are in selecting seafood, the greater likelihood of your getting the freshness you want.

4. *Be flexible about your menu.* I've often seen people approach the seafood counter with a fixed idea about what they will have for dinner. If you feel like a salmon steak, but the fish on display seems somewhat questionable (and you haven't time to shop elsewhere), change your plans. What you want to buy is the freshest seafood available. The difference between eating seafood that was caught within two days and that caught a day earlier, or improperly handled in shipment (not carefully gutted or chilled), can be immense.

5. *Buy in season.* Eastern oysters are available year-round, but they're best from September through April. A majority of fish is available frozen, but fresh is always best. Check the chart at the end of the book for guidelines on when each variety is at its best, and if necessary use the information about substitutions.

FRESHNESS — THE SIGNS AT A GLANCE
WHOLE FISH

Whole fish are fish sold as they come from the water with their gills, fins, and scales intact. They are often but not always gutted.

They should never smell fishy. Skins and gills should be almost odorless or smell like fresh seawater.

The whole fish should look bright, as if lit from within. Skin should be covered with a light, natural slime and without wrinkles. Scales, if any, should be moist, shiny, and intact. If the fish is gutted, the body cavity should show signs of fresh blood.

Gills should be deep red when lifted—literally blood-filled—with no visible mucous or slime. As a fish ages, gill color fades to light pink, to gray, and finally to a dull brown. Always check the gills; they are a primary indicator of freshness.

The body should be firm to the touch, giving elastically when you press it and bouncing back when released. Beware of ungutted fish with soft bellies—fish viscera decay first.

Eyes are not always a reliable sign of whole fish freshness; in some species they can cloud right after death, in others they can remain clear even when the fish has decayed. In addition, eyes may be damaged from rough handling with no effect on overall quality. If undamaged, eyes should protrude slightly. (The eyes of most flatfish are more flush with the head than those of roundfish.)

Whole fish provide you with the greatest opportunity for determining fish freshness, so buy "on the bone" whenever you can. Once you've assured yourself of the freshness of a given specimen, you can have the fish cleaned and prepared to your specifications by the fish seller, or do it yourself.

FILLETS AND STEAKS

Fillets are the sides of a fish that have been removed from it lengthwise. Steaks, also called *darnes*, are unboned crosswise cuts taken from larger varieties of round- and flat-fish like tuna, salmon, swordfish, or halibut. Steaks are generally cut 2 to 3 inches thick.

Fillets and steaks should never smell fishy. They should appear bright, firm, and translucent. Their flesh should be moist to the edges.

Color should be true and consistent—two-tone flesh means that melted ice has leached away blood—and flavor with it.

There should be no gaping or cracking flesh, an indication of overlong storage. Reject fish with blood spots, a sign of rough handling.

Do not buy fillets or steaks if they are sitting in a pool of liquid.

PACKAGED FISH

Avoid packaged fish if at all possible. Otherwise, apply the same criteria as you would when buying unwrapped fish. Your eyes are your most valuable tool, but give the package a sniff; the smell of bad seafood can be detected through the wrapping or in its folds.

Check absorbent pads beneath the fish. If they appear to retain a good deal of liquid, chances are the fish has been around for a while.

FROZEN FISH

Everyone should eat fresh fish—and on both coasts, most everyone can. Once inland, however, or away from airfreight traffic in fresh seafood, the likelihood of encountering frozen fish increases. If frozen fish is the only kind available to you, here's what to look for.

Whole fish freeze better than fillets; firm-fleshed varieties like salmon, snapper, and swordfish are more successfully frozen than flaky fish like cod. Make sure you can see the flesh throughout the package. If you can't, the fish has been improperly handled; visible ice crystals indicate refreezing or temperature fluctuations while holding.

Check for freezer burn—milky white or opaque flesh. The package itself should be undamaged, without water stains on the tray or ice crystals adhering to the inside of the plastic, both signs of thawing.

Always thaw frozen fish in the refrigerator. Never leave it on a counter to defrost or you risk the possibility of spoilage.

SHELLFISH

Northern Lobster

These inhabitants of the Atlantic Coast must be lively. When removed from the tank, a lobster should wave its claws and antennae; its tail should be tightly curled.

Touch the shell—it should be hard and thick. Soft shells mean that a lobster has recently shed its shell (it's growing a new one) and its meat may be skimpy and/or mealy. A soft shell may also indicate that a lobster comes from warm waters. Generally speaking, the colder the water, the tastier the lobster.

Lobsters are sold by size, which has nothing to do with the quality of their meat. The smallest are called *chicken lobsters* and run about 1 pound each; *quarters* weigh in at about 1¼ pounds; *large* or *selects* are 1½ to 2½ pounds; *jumbo* designates any lobster at over 2½ pounds. Lobsters with one claw are called *culls* and those with no claws *bullets.*

Female lobsters are more tender than males and contain coral—dark green eggs that turn bright red when cooked. If you care to, check the gender by turning a lobster on its back and looking at the point where the head and body meet. You will see small, spiny "feet." Touch them; if they're hard, the lobster is male; if soft, female. Females are particularly desirable for bisques or stews, as their coral colors the dish a lovely orange-pink and flavors it deliciously.

Spiny Lobster

Spiny lobsters come from warm waters primarily, including those of the Florida Keys, Southern California, Brazil, and the Mediterranean. They are clawless and have large tail sections—the only part of the creature that can be eaten. The tails have delicious sweet meat, which is often sold frozen and graded by size, usually about 1½ pounds. Spiny lobsters are unrelated to crawfish, which they resemble but which inhabit fresh waters.

Hard-Shell Crabs

Blue and Dungeness crabs, from the East and West coasts respectively, are those most likely to be sold live. They should be extremely active.

Weight is an important test of freshness for Dungeness crabs—they should feel heavy for their size. You may also determine crab freshness by squeezing the third leg from the front. The shell should give; if it doesn't, its meat may be skimpy.

Packaged crabmeat, which is sold cooked, should be white and somewhat translucent. Avoid any meat that looks cottony or smells of ammonia. Crabmeat taken from cooked crab is sold in various grades as follows, from most to least desirable:

- *Jumbo lump* or *backfin* is meat picked in whole lumps from the crab's body or backfin.
- *Lump* contains whole lumps and some smaller pieces of meat taken, like jumbo lump, from the body or backfin. It can cost up to 30 percent less than jumbo lump or backfin.
- *Special* consists of some lumps and flakes from the remaining parts of the body.
- *Flake* or *regular* contains no lump meat and is taken from the whole body.
- *Claw* is meat picked from the claws only.

All crabmeat grades are sold by the pound, fresh or pasteurized and canned. Fresh is best, but the canned meat is very good; there are times of the year when it is the only kind available. Canned meat is sometimes sold chilled—redundant, as the meat once pasteurized and canned cannot spoil.

Soft-Shell Crabs

These are blue crabs caught in their molting or soft-shelled stage. Sold usually on beds of seaweed, they should be alive. Check their small appendages, which should move periodically. If they do not, determine freshness by making sure the bodies are plump and shiny. Never buy crabs that appear dried out.

Mussels and Clams

Mussels and clams should have uncracked, tightly closed shells. (Geoduck, razor, and soft-shelled clams have protruding siphons so the shells never close completely.) If an open bivalve does not close when its shell is tapped, or its siphon does not react when touched, it's dead. Don't buy it.

Bivalves should glisten. If surfaces appear dried out, the shellfish is at least not being kept or displayed properly and may be past its prime. Don't select mussels and clams that feel heavy for their size—they may be filled with sand or mud.

Bivalve shells should be reasonably free of dirt and debris, with the exception of cultivated mussels, whose shells are usually clean. Cultivated mussels have a high meat to shell ratio and require rinsing only. Their quality is excellent.

Mussels and clams that are sold shucked should lie plumply in plenty of their own clear liquid. Fresh or cooked, shell meat should have a sweet odor, or none at all.

Oysters

All the rules that apply to buying mussels and clams pertain to oysters. If an oyster remains open after a sharp tap, it's dead—don't buy it. Oysters should be displayed with their rounded shells down so the liquid that keeps the oyster alive doesn't drain out. Some oysters may be covered with green algae—an indication that they come from pure waters, as pollution kills sea moss. Shucked oysters should glisten prettily in a shallow pool of their own clear liquor. Raw shucked oyster meat is available in plastic containers. Canned oyster meat is cooked and therefore best used in stuffings or for frying. It should never be eaten as is.

The commonly obtainable species are the Atlantic or Blue Point; the Pacific or Japanese from the West Coast; the Olympia, indigenous to the Northwest; and the European flat oyster, usually referred to as a Belon. An increasingly wide variety of oysters are available to us, most commercially grown.

Shrimp

Most of the shrimp we buy has been flash-frozen and thawed at the retail market. Shrimp do very well frozen if they've been carefully handled. Look for full-fleshed bodies without any freezer burn.

If you have the good fortune to find shrimp with their heads still on, buy them. As the heads deteriorate rapidly, almost all shrimp are beheaded (and frozen) at sea. If head-on shrimp have reached the market and are fresh, they're *really* fresh.

Depending on their place of origin, raw shrimp come in a variety of colors, including bright pink, reddish brown, and gleaming gray. Whatever their color, shells should be deeply hued and unslippery.

Neither raw nor cooked shrimp should have a strong smell; any that are ammoniated should be avoided.

Shrimp are categorized and sold by size. *Colossal* are the largest available at 8 to 10 per pound; *jumbo* shrimp, sometimes called prawns, come 11 to 15 to the pound; 16 to 20 per pound are *extra large*; 21 to 30 are *large*; and 31 to 35 are *medium*. More shrimp than that—up to 45 a pound—are *small*. *Tiny ocean shrimp*, which are sold shelled and cooked, come 50 to 70 per pound. The smallest variety, called *titi*, weigh in at 400 to the pound, and are always sold peeled, cooked, and frozen. Bags of frozen medium, small, or titi shrimp, known as *IQFs*—instant quick frozen—are available widely.

Scallops

The large, drum-shaped scallops most regularly sold in our markets are sea scallops. Bay scallops are smaller and tend to be sweeter than other varieties. Deep water calicos are sold unshelled seasonally, in bags, and are the least desirable among available species.

Because whole scallops die quickly after harvesting, only the adductor muscle, which is the part of the scallop people in the United States eat, is retained at the time of harvesting; rarely are scallops sold in the shell. (In some states it's illegal to gather scallops in their shells, which can hold bacteria.)

Scallops should look brilliant and be sweet smelling, with just a slight characteristic odor. Avoid scallops that smell sulphurous, seem unusually white, bulge, or are shrunken.

Unpackaged scallops are usually sold in buckets. They should lie in a minimum of liquid. Reject any swimming in a milky bath. Try asking your dealer for "dry" scallops, which have not been subject to the preserving solution too often used to prolong freshness.

Scallops in the shell are naturally open. They are bad if they emit a strong odor. Packaged scallops should be sniffed carefully.

Be aware that there are fake scallops on the market usually composed of a mixture of ground pollack and skate. These "scallops" are good only for giving the real thing a bad name—don't buy them.

Squid

Squid are considered shellfish because of the transparent, quill-like cartilage inside their bodies.

They should look bright and firm and have creamy white flesh under their mottled brown or mauve "skin."

Squid should smell fresh. Tentacles should be firm and whole and eyes should be distinct. Squid are covered with a light, natural slime. They are sold both raw and cooked but raw is preferable as you can better determine freshness and cook the squid to *your* specifications. Small squid are the most desirable.

Conch

Conch can be purchased live in its shell, but the meat is most often extracted—a laborious process—and sold frozen, partially or fully cooked. I have never found fresh conch meat in the marketplace; buy it if you can find it. Since fresh conch spoils rapidly, unless you are certain of its provenance, frozen meat is safest. *Number 1 white* is the best grade; avoid flesh that appears gray or beige. Ethnic markets are more likely to carry conch meat than fish stores. Conch from the Bahamas or Ecuador is particularly desirable.

Octopus

As with squid, look for shining flesh. The skin should be gray and the flesh beneath it a creamy white. It should smell sweet and fresh.

Octopus can be bought fresh, precooked, and/or frozen. Buy domestic octopus fresh if you can; precooked and frozen varieties are also good. Precooked and frozen imported Japanese octopus, whose skin is red and which weigh about three to six pounds each, are best.

Caviar

All fish roe is caviar, but not all may be so labeled. Only the eggs of the sturgeon may be designated simply "caviar" on a jar or tin. Costly and precious, sturgeon eggs are available in several varieties: *beluga*, which is gray and has the best quality, mildest-flavored eggs; *osetra*, intensely flavored, with large golden brown, gray, dark green, or blue-white grains; and *sevruga*, small-grained with dark gray or black eggs and lovely flavor. *Malossol* is the best and least salty grade. Other roes—which must be labeled with the name of the fish preceding the word "caviar"—include *keta*, large-grained, bright red salmon eggs; and *tobiko*, Japanese flying fish roe, which is crunchy and has a definite but pleasing fish taste. No caviar should smell or taste truly fishy or be excessively salty. Buy caviar from a reputable seller only and read labels well; taste, if at all possible.

Canned Fish

Canned tuna, salmon, sardines, and anchovies have been tasty mainstays since preservation in tin began. Like canned asparagus or peas, canned fish are virtually a different species than their fresh counterparts—and not necessarily undesirable for it. They have their place. People will always eat canned fish (sardines and anchovies are rarely available fresh)—and I myself love a good tuna salad sandwich or salmon cake made with canned fish.

The best canned tuna to buy is the darkest. Depth of color indicates the presence of fat and fat equals flavor. Americans have long been told that the lighter the flesh, the better; this is a marketing ploy. Have your canned Albacore if you wish, but realize that darker varieties taste better.

Canned salmon also has merit. The best variety is King salmon or any labeled Alaskan. "Extra fancy" or "fancy," however, are meaningless designations. Water-packed canned salmon and tuna are not only fine for sandwiches or in dishes like croquettes but excellent from the point of view of health as they have less fat than oil-packed varieties. As with all canned food, try different brands, as they vary in quality.

A Word about Seafood and Health

I've always enjoyed the sign on a truck that delivers fish around New York City. It says, in its entirety, "Eat Fish—Live Longer."

All of us can profit by eating seafood. Low in calories (lean species such as flounder, cod, or sole contain fewer than 100 calories in a 3-ounce cooked portion; even fattier varieties, like salmon or mackerel, have no more than 200 calories in a similar serving), saturated fats, sodium, and cholesterol (for most species, less than 100 milligrams of cholesterol in that 3-ounce portion before cooking), seafood is also rich in vitamins and minerals. In short, it is a splendid protein source, and may actually reduce the incidence of heart disease. Though no scientific data have established the fact conclusively, studies seem to show that the omega-3 fatty acids found in seafood benefit those who eat it regularly. (We do know that there are no properties in seafood that tend to block arteries.) It's been noted that the Japanese, Eskimos, and Greenlanders—all large consumers of fish and shellfish—have a low incidence of heart disease; and that as the Japanese diet has begun to approximate our own, the incidence of heart problems in that country has risen. In any case, the relative fatlessness of seafood means less cholesterol production in our bodies. Add the beneficial effects of omega-3s (which our bodies do not produce in sufficient quantities), and seafood eating seems positively advantageous.

Of course, most of us consume seafood primarily because we love it. We should know, however, that because of its particularly perishable nature, there are certain health precautions we need to note and observe to assure seafood wholesomeness:

• Be sure to eat only seafood that is pristinely fresh. Follow all the rules concerning freshness listed on pages 8 to 15. In a nutshell, do not buy any seafood that smells, or appears even slightly over the hill. Buy whole fish when you can. Generally speaking, there's no way a whole fish can sit around too long and *not* reveal its age.

• Be extra careful when buying fish and shellfish to be eaten raw or partially cooked. If you have any doubt about bivalves, ask to see the tag your dealer receives that certifies the waters of origin are safe. It's wise to give every oyster you eat a sniff. Cultivated oysters are your safest bet, whether harvested in a controlled natural resource or a completely controlled environment.

• Make sure fish and shellfish caught or gathered privately are properly handled. Some of the most dangerous fish to eat are, unfortunately, those given as gifts by fisherman friends. Ask (discreetly, of course) where the angling has been done and how the fish has been handled once caught. Dispose of gifts you suspect have stayed too long in the bottom of a boat, sat in the sun, or have otherwise not been overseen properly. (For general information about handling and storing seafood, see pages 47 to 51.) When fishing or gathering shellfish yourself, check with fish and wildlife authorities to make sure waters are safe.

• When possible, don't buy prewrapped fish or shellfish you cannot touch and smell. If you buy frozen fish, make sure you can see it through the package to assure yourself it's in good shape.

• Know that some fish can occasionally contain parasites. Saltwater species that are sometimes infected with tiny worms of the *Anisakis genus* include herring, rockfish, cod, haddock, and sole; freshwater species such as salmon, pike, and perch can harbor other parasites. While fish fillets are routinely candled—inspected with blue light to detect lurking infestation, owing usually to mishandling—a quick visual check of your food before preparing it makes sense. In any case, it is reassuring to know that all parasites are killed by cooking seafood to 145°F. (for at least 1 minute) or by freezing, preferably at subzero temperatures for two days. I must emphasize that very few people are affected by seafood infestation. The National Academy of Sciences has found that parasitic infection is rare in America, and as yet there is no evidence of a significant increase owing to the growing consumption of raw-fish dishes like sushi and sashimi. While we're on this unpleasant but important topic, I must mention that fish are very occasionally contaminated by certain toxins that are resistant to heat. Scombroid or saurine poisoning may occur in swordfish, mahi-mahi (dolphinfish), mackerel, and jack—again, mostly when the fish have not been chilled when caught, and then stored in warm places. Fish with scombroid poisoning (which causes an allergic response) smells bad. Ciguatera poisoning, which is undetectable normally, affects jacks, snappers, groupers, and parrot fish, among others. It is mostly a problem in the Caribbean and Hawaii, where fish feed on coral reefs. Commercial fisherman know what areas of the sea to avoid; people visiting tropical places should be prudent about eating fish they have caught themselves.

• Recreational anglers, in particular, should be aware of potential health risks from chemical contaminants like PCB (polycholorinated biphenyl), mercury, and pesticides. Though there is no hard and fast evidence of the long-term effects of these pollutants, data indicate that exposure to them over long periods may affect reproduction and development of children and poses the risk of cancer. The good news is that the FDA sets action and tolerance levels for suspect chemicals; federal and state governments monitor contaminant levels in seafood and "close" waters or ban individual species from the commercial marketplace when acceptable levels are exceeded. Those of us who fish regularly (and high-risk individuals, such as pregnant women) should be aware that health authorities issue advisories against potentially dangerous fish from specific bodies of water. Waters are also tested regularly for red and brown tide, a natural pollution caused by toxic algae that affect bivalves in particular. Raw shellfish pose the greatest potential danger, but advisories are issued constantly.

To repeat—very few people get sick from fish and shellfish. Most waters are monitored often and fish and shellfish are constantly being tested. That truck I mentioned earlier really has it right: fish and shellish are not only wonderful to eat but if selected carefully can help to ensure our well-being.

CAN SOME FISH BE TOO FRESH?

You may have read about the fish freshness theories of Jon Rowley, a Seattle-based seafood expert. Rowley (and others) maintain that fish cooked less than one day after being taken from the water will be poorer eating than fish that has had a chance to go through its rigor mortis slowly—a five- to six-day process. How long a fish remains in rigor (the period of muscle stiffening that begins shortly after death) depends on the manner in which the fish was killed and how it was treated once dead. Properly killed fish that is immediately iced down will stay in rigor for the requisite period; improperly killed fish will go through rigor in just a few hours, resulting in cooked flesh that is mushy or grainy or that lacks full flavor, according to Rowley. In other words, some fish *can* be too fresh.

I don't agree that a five- or six-day period of rigor is needed before we can enjoy the best fish eating. My experience tells me otherwise. I spend a good deal of time and money to ensure that the fish I serve at the restaurant arrives there no later than thirty-six hours after it is killed because I want fish with only the most impeccable taste and texture. That is what I get.

Of course, any improperly killed or poorly handled fish—fish that has not been stunned, bled, gutted, and iced down immediately, then kept cold and well drained—will yield poor flesh. But even large fish like giant grouper, which must be held past rigor so their flesh will be tender, don't require more than a 2½-day postmortem period.

So do search out the very freshest fish you can find. If it has been well treated and carefully cooked it is unlikely that you will enjoy anything less than superb eating.

To Market . . .

It's one thing to learn signs that indicate fish and shellfish excellence, another to apply that knowledge when you're seafood shopping. How do real-world market selections measure up to ideal standards of freshness? How can you take best advantage of what your own local seafood market (or supermarket seafood department) actually has to offer?

To help you choose only the highest-quality fish and shellfish available to you, I visited several different kinds of seafood markets and shopped them with a critical eye. Because I live in Manhattan, with its many neighborhoods attuned to the culinary and financial requirements of diverse populations, I was able to explore a wide range of stores. Together, they covered every buying issue I've discussed.

THE TOP-OF-THE-LINE FISH STORE

My first stop took me to a highly regarded "gourmet" seafood market, one that's esteemed for its quality, presentation, and diversity of catch. Although its prices aren't in the stratospheric range of some of the city's ultra-ritzy seafood stores, it isn't cheap. High price, however, is not always indicative of best quality. Even though you pay top dollar and have an up-to-the-minute selection, you still have to shop thoughtfully, as my visit here confirmed.

My days of marketing for fresh fish have taught me that you can get an excellent sense of the quality of a store's merchandise by sniffing the air as you enter. Here, all was well, as only a slight scent of brininess emanated from the fish—displayed properly *on* and not under ice in a spotless environment. One exception was a large loin of tuna that sat on a foil-covered tray. Tuna is a popular fish and merchants can become careless about preserving its freshness. The tuna should have been on ice or refrigerated; left this way, it can deteriorate rapidly. In addition, cooked shrimp were displayed next to raw with only a plastic divider separating the two; bacteria from the raw shrimp could contaminate the cooked. Fresh and prepared seafood should always be well separated.

I preach endlessly about not buying ready-cut fillets if at all possible. Choose instead whole fish personally inspected for freshness and have them filleted, or do the filleting yourself (see pages 26 to 35). Fillets-to-go are undoubtedly convenient, but they've often been around, especially those in packages. Even fine fish stores like this one purchase fillets from wholesalers who have in turn gotten them from a fillet house; fillets from popular fish like sole, scrod, and flounder, and supermarket fillets are usually prebutchered as a matter of course. You, the retail customer, are thus three distributive steps away from the whole fish. When handling has been careful and swift, ready-cut fillets can be choice, but you must really check for any negative signs like dryness, inconsistent color, lack of translucence, or cracking. For example, the salmon fillets I saw here had problems—the thinner part near the tail had begun to turn gray. Here is the perfect opportunity to ask if the seller doesn't have a whole fish he can cut for you. Alternatively and if practical, buy a whole fish, cut what you need, and freeze the rest.

What about the freshness of the whole fish? In general, skins of the whole fish offered here were properly bright and gills were red. (I asked one of the rubber-gloved countermen to pull back the gill covers on several whole fish for inspection.) An exception was the condition of a batch of John Dory, which were wet and wrinkled. John Dory is an excellent fish, but it comes from European waters, and can take as many as five days to get here. The John Dory had been out of water too long, and in an attempt to spruce them up had been bathed repeatedly. What you want is shiny, firm flesh that glistens from a coating of natural slime, *not* water.

I noticed that a number of the whole fish here had not been gutted. This is a tricky matter. On the one hand, all whole fish are best eviscerated when caught, as the guts spoil first. On the other hand, many markets, assured of the tip-top freshness of their merchandise, display ungutted fish. Here is a case in which it really helps to know the reputation and popularity of the seller. If in doubt, ask your fish seller to gut the fish and allow you to sniff its interior. You'll know immediately if you have a desirable specimen or not. (Or feel the fish's belly; if it is soft, the guts have begun to go.) Most merchants, however, are conscientious in this department. The ungutted whole fish at this store allayed suspicion by the visible signs of their freshness—and I trusted the seller.

Nearby I noticed a section of carp without the head, ready to be cut into steaks. I wondered if there would be fresh blood along the center bone or wetness where the head had been removed. In both cases, these sure signs of freshness weren't evident.

While inspecting the carp, I overheard a typical exchange between a customer and one of the counter men. The customer comes in and asks for a fillet of sole. The counter man smiles at the customer, reaches into the display, and pulls out the most undesirable piece of fish. From my point of view, this is the fish-buying nightmare. Unless you have reason to trust a particular counter man, choose your own piece of fish, always. If you've read this far you have a good idea of what to look for. At the risk of repeating myself, freshness is indicated by no single sign alone, but by a combination of sensual clues.

Freshness is the issue for fish, shrimp, squid, octopus, and scallops, but shellfish like lobster, crabs, mussels, oysters, and clams must show actual signs of life. Of all the shellfish in our markets, mussels are probably the most popular, a happy phenomenon of fairly recent origin. There were two kinds here—cultivated local and green-lipped from New Zealand.

The cultivated mussels here looked bright and were almost all tightly closed, a sure indication of liveliness. I tapped a partly open mussel and the shell obligingly shut—the mussel was alive. The New Zealand mussels were impressively large and, with their kelly green shell edges, wonderful to look at. They can be deliciously sweet, but as with any imported variety of seafood, be on guard. On your first try, don't buy a carload. Get a few and see if you're pleased. What you're really attempting to determine is how reliable your market is with imported or unconventional kinds of seafood.

Like mussels, clams and oysters should also be tightly closed. Of the several varieties of oysters offered here, including Belons, Wellfleets, and Apalachicolas, the Cape Blue Points looked particularly bright and appetizing, as did the littleneck and cherrystone clams, the only kinds offered. All were well iced and without odor. This market sold shucked oyster meat—is it a compromise? Give it the smell test; if its scent is fresh and sweet, you're probably safe. There were no hard-shell crabs in the market, but hard-shell crabmeat was on hand. The three grades sold here are the most typically available: jumbo lump or backfin, flake, and claw. Whichever grade you buy, open the plastic container in which the meat is usually packed and sniff. When buying lump crabmeat, turn the container upside down to see if the bottom pieces are as large as those on the top, just like checking strawberries in their basket.

Lobster is ideally sold from a fresh water tank. When buying it live there's really one primary thing to look for: the creature must be *kicking*. When the counter man removed two of the lobsters from the tank, one splayed its legs and claws, the other curled its tail, all signs of liveliness.

Soft-shell crabs were also active. They should be packed in sea grass or their shells will dry out, and displayed directly on ice. Here, they were displayed in the wax-coated boxes in which they were shipped, which itself sat on ice. Their shells were moist, however, and the crabs properly plump.

Bay and sea scallops are almost always sold from plastic tubs. (Unshucked scallops are occasionally available; if you find them, enjoy their beautiful coral roe and save the wonderful shells for serving seafood gratins or for decoration.) The shucked scallops here were just fine—surfaces,shone and there was none of that sulphurous, "scalloppy" odor that characterizes specimens past their prime. Make sure the bay scallops you buy are not afloat in the milky liquid they exude if left around too long. Squid must also shine, as it did here. In raw shrimp, what you want to look for are deeply colored, odorless specimens with shiny—not slimy—shells. When I bent over the shrimp display here and took a sniff I was satisfied to find that nothing was ammoniated.

The market offered a number of prepared items, among them seafood sausage. They looked appetizing, but what was in them, I wondered? Were they made on the premises or bought from a supplier? Before buying anything already prepared, ask about ingredients and sources. As always, homemade is best.

I've pointed out a number of common problems at this market, proving that buyers in upscale markets must still be alert. Nevertheless, I'd give it a good grade. Overall, customers here got the quality they were paying for. The store and its merchandise were in general well kept and the merchandise fresh. There was abundant selection. This is a busy place with an obvious commitment to making its customers, many of them devoted, return again and again. If you have such a fish market in your neighborhood you can consider yourself fortunate and shop there with confidence.

THE NEIGHBORHOOD FISH SELLER

Those living outside a major metropolitan area may have more modest options. I'm thinking about the local fish market, perhaps the only one in town devoted solely to selling seafood. Its selection is limited, its commitment to quality, though pure in intention, may not always be reflected in the merchandise itself. How can you shop such a place to best advantage?

I didn't have to look far to find such a store in Manhattan. The market in question has a reputation for good seafood at fair prices. It is in a neighborhood that boasts a "seafood row"—a series of no-frills markets that often find themselves praised in guidebooks for their freshness and low prices. The fact that the store I visited fell below this standard made it that much more useful as a reflection of the challenges that shoppers are often faced with.

The small store was dominated by a marvelous old display case, a charming artifact long removed from commercial circulation. There's nothing wrong with an old case if the seafood it contains is properly kept and in fine shape. The manager-proprietor, a third-generation family owner, was immediately friendly, explaining his policy of filleting to order rather than displaying large numbers of prebutchered parts. The fillets I did see were buried in ice, which could wash away flavor as it melted and make flesh soggy. Of the whole fish on display—bluefish and porgy among them—many had eyes that were shrunken, and appeared to have been watered down. The cod, mackerel, and salmon looked fine, as if they had been bought that morning, but the shellfish—other than some sparkling scallops—appeared tired. True, the prices would have been excellent if the seafood had been up to par, but poor quality seafood at cut-rate prices is no bargain.

What if a store like this is your only nonsupermarket seafood buying option? Suppose your own fish market, usually reliable, seems to be having a bad day? Here are some useful strategies:

- It may sound obvious, but buy what *is* fresh. Change your menu if necessary.

- As a general rule, buy whole fish rather than fillets. If you need fillets or steaks, buy a whole fish personally inspected for freshness, and have it filleted for you, or have steaks cut to order.

- If most of the fish are buried in ice, ask your fish seller to extract individual fish for your inspection. Always make your own selection. The more discerning you are, the more particular your fish seller will be in what he chooses to show you.

- When confronted with a problematical selection, don't attempt dishes that require pristine freshness like seviche or carpaccio. Instead serve soups or stews in which the seafood is helped by vegetables and herbs.

- Talk to the store manager. If you determine that he really wishes to please his clientele, find out when his fish and shellfish come in. You're much more likely to get decent seafood if you know when fresh arrivals are scheduled to make their appearance. It is, in fact, remarkable how well you can do in situations of variable quality when you shop by the calendar.

THE SUPERMARKET

It is possible to get good seafood at your supermarket, often better than that at a poorly run fish store, if you know what to look for.

Chain supermarkets have someone who does the buying for all the stores in a particular area. What you want, therefore, is a seafood department that someone seems to care about—a *department*, preferably, rather than a single case, which can discourage rapid turnover of merchandise. In many cases, you will do better buying frozen seafood than the "fresh" supermarkets offer if you observe the rules about buying frozen fish and shellfish (page 9).

I live near one of a large chain of upscale supermarkets that makes a point of quality and diversity in its stock. It includes a lobster tank, a setup that raises hopes. Conditions are extremely sanitary—there isn't the faintest scent of fishiness anywhere near the seafood display. The lack of scent, however, can sometimes be deceptive. I don't recommend buying packaged fish, but if you have absolutely no access to unwrapped whole fish or fillets, and you must have seafood, pick up the package and examine its contents carefully. Expiration dates are relevant, of course, but you must investigate further. Are colors true and eyes bright? Are fillets moist-looking and without cracks? Sniff the package. Fish that is off can often be detected through plastic or in its folds. If visible, observe the condition of the absorbent paddding under a piece of wrapped fish or other seafood. If the padding seems saturated or plump, or if the package itself seems wet, avoid buying the seafood. Here, the flounder fillets passed muster, as did packages of whole trout. On the other hand, the flesh of cod fillets was dried and discolored, almost brown, and the belly edges of a whole scrod had begun to wrinkle. An unpackaged chunk of tuna, on ice too long, was multicolored, but the fresh salmon and shark steaks looked fine. Bluefish was glossy and appetizing, and lobsters in their tank of clean water were lively.

What about already prepared seafood—packages containing "clams oreganato" or "marinated catfish"? Avoid these convenience concoctions. Thick breadings often conceal what's underneath; you have no idea of what you're getting. Raw clams sitting under a bread-crumb covering for any length of time are in themselves a potential health problem.

My supermarket department had a courteous crew behind its counter of unpackaged seafood, but don't trust counter people to make decisions for you about freshness. They're simply too far removed from the original product and may not always be knowledgeable or well trained when it comes to seafood. The supermarket, whatever its advantages, represents the disappearance of the specialty market—an unhappy fact of life. This reality need not, however, prevent you from finding fresh seafood on the other side of the check-out counter.

CHINATOWN

If we adopted the buying requirements of the Chinatown seafood shopper, we would enjoy the freshest possible seafood as a matter of course. The Chinatown clientele demands nothing less than perfect quality, and that is what it gets.

Because freshness is so highly prized, Asian shoppers usually prefer whole fish. In fact, in Chinatown many whole fish are sold still swimming in tanks. Failing this, fish are laid out in such a manner as to allow the shopper to take a good look at eyes and gills and to touch flesh for firmness. This results in discerning shopping and best seafood eating.

If you have a local Chinatown or Asian marketplace that sells fish, by all means take advantage of it. You will see what freshness is all about—a concerted effort to keep fish and shellfish alive, or at its prime, for as long as possible. In New York's Chinatown I saw tanks filled with catfish and buffalofish; plastic bins loaded with flopping tilefish, sole, and baby shark; sidewalks traversed by skittering crabs, only to be stopped by fast-fingered merchants. Everything said "alive." And prices were unbelievable—often half of what is common in other neighborhoods, and sometimes even less.

Chinatown shoppers do not hesitate to take an active role in making their seafood selections. Working my way through more than twenty retail seafood markets, most spotless and with gleaming, well-iced displays, I came upon an old man picking through a basket of blue crabs. "All female," said the seller. The old man, unimpressed, demanded a pair of tongs, which the seller quickly produced. One by one the prospective customer went through the bucket, turning over every glistening crab until he found two or three that suited him. What was he looking for, I asked. "Big," he said with an any-fool-knows expression on his face. "And fine." His devotion to quality in no way reflected his total expenditure—less than one dollar!

My trip to Chinatown reminded me of the need to be bloodthirsty when it comes to buying fish. Here gills routinely showed fresh blood; chunks of silver carp were bright red along the cuts as were the cavities of glistening sardines. Other indications of freshness abounded. The center bone "pockets" of swordfish steaks were still filled with pools of proteinous liquid; squid were beautifully clean and plump; blue-black eels nestled against one another in naturally shining coils. Elsewhere, I was delighted to see picture-perfect Spanish mackerel (a sensationally beautiful fish whose silver-bright skin is dotted with gold) and live shrimp in tanks, maneuvering their almost transparent bodies with fluttering leglets.

Frankly, I don't know where, on the wholesale level, all these creatures come from. The Chinese merchants have established their own network of suppliers. The customer always benefits from such arrangements, which encourage accountability, but ultimately it is the consumer who makes the difference. Our modern fragmented families no longer include an on-the-premises grandmother, skilled in shopping, who buys fresh food in the morning for lunch, then returns to the market to get more for dinner. But why not make it our business to shop and cook with a similar eye? A trip to Chinatown should show us the way.

2. PREPARING FISH AND SHELLFISH FOR COOKING

Even though you are probably used to having your fish seller butcher your seafood for you, there are many rewards for doing it yourself.

The better you know the anatomy of a fish or shellfish, the easier and more pleasurable its preparation. Mastering preparation techniques boosts confidence and enables you to better maintain freshness—the name of the game in seafood handling. When you know how to fillet a flounder or clean a crab, you help yourself to better eating.

These things aren't hard to do. My grandmother had no special training yet she could fillet a fish with flair. All you need are the proper tools, the desire to learn, and a little patience. In no time you'll reap the benefits of buying the whole fish: fresher fillets, bones for the stockpot, a delectable result.

ROUNDFISH AND FLATFISH

Almost all the world's fish are divided into two categories: roundfish and flatfish. Roundfish, such as salmon or trout, have rounded or oval bodies, swim in a vertical position, and have one eye on each side of their heads. Flatfish, such as flounder, are indeed flat—their bodies are platelike. They swim horizontally and have both eyes on only one side of their heads. (An interesting fact: a flatfish begins life just like a roundfish does, with an eye on each side of its head. When it reaches a length of 1½ inches, however, one eye migrates toward the other, joining it on one side of the fish's newly flattened head.)

Both roundfish and flatfish may be served whole, in which case they are first cleaned or dressed (the terms are interchangeable), then scaled. They may also be filleted or cut into steaks or portions.

CLEANING A WHOLE FISH

When you select a whole fish at the market, chances are it has already been gutted to remove the viscera, the most perishable part of the fish. However, you should know how to do the job yourself, especially if you fish or unexpectedly find yourself the recipient of a friend's skillful angling. Note that a fish is gutted before sealing, which, if done too vigorously, can rupture the entrails and spread bacteria.

Note: All directions that follow are for a right-handed cook; reverse the procedures if you are left-handed.

ROUNDFISH
Gutting and Removing the Gills

1. Place the fish on your work surface with its head to the right. With a sharp knife, split the whole length of the fish's belly from behind the pelvic fins to the anal vent. Cut shallowly to avoid piercing the entrails, which lie within the belly.

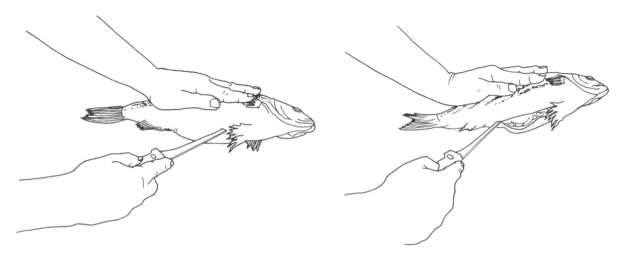

2. Reach into the cavity and pull out the entrails, severing them from the point near the head where they're attached. Discard.

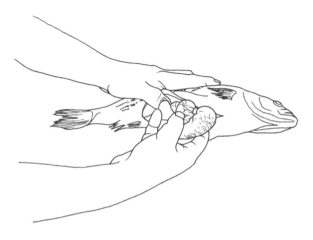

3. Lift a gill cover with one hand. Using a sharp, heavy scissors, snip out the reddish gills underneath. Repeat on the other side.

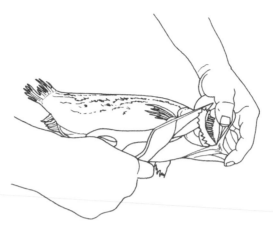

4. For neatness, trim the edges along the opened belly, reserving them for stocks, salads, or sashimi. (Discard the trimmings from smaller fish.)

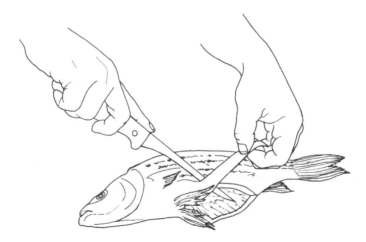

5. Rinse the cavity and gill openings well with cold running water. Remove the fins with a scissors, if you like.

Scaling

1. Place the fish in a sink to contain loosened scales.

2. Grasp its tail and using a fish scaler or butter knife, scrape the fish gently toward its head. Use long, strong strokes—this keeps the scales from flying about. (Don't worry about scaling the head; it won't be eaten.) To avoid scales sticking to work surfaces, wash up immediately.

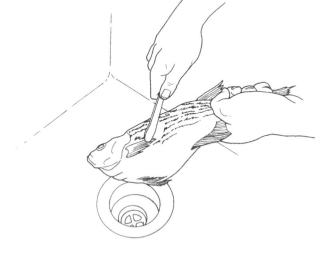

Removing the Head

Although I like the way a fish looks served with its head on, you can remove it. Place the fish on a cutting board, belly away from you. With a sharp chef's knife, cut behind the head in back of the pectoral fin and through the center bone, below left. *For a large fish*, below right, cut through the flesh only, on both sides. Pull the head away from the body and cut it free.

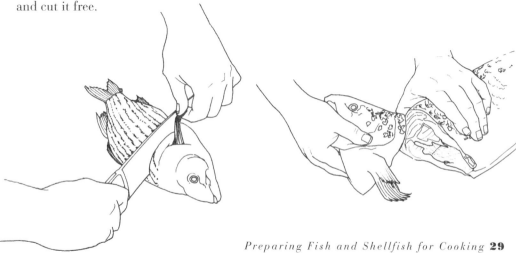

Filleting for a large fish

1. Remove the head as directed above. Place the fish on your cutting board with the tail to the left and the belly away from you. Insert a filleting knife into the flesh at the headless end as shown, just above the backbone.

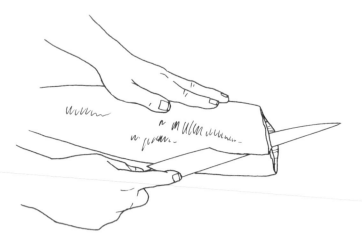

2. Resting the knife against the backbone for support as you proceed, cut toward the tail. Saw in even motions. Keep the knife angled slightly downward, but be careful not to cut through the rib cage. Remove the top fillet.

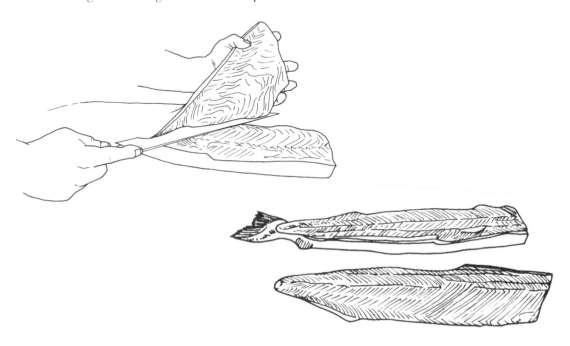

3. Flip the fish. The tail is still to the left. Hold the tail and make an incision directly in front of it, as shown. Keeping the knife angled downward almost parallel to the body, work the knife toward the head end. Free the fillet from the skeleton.

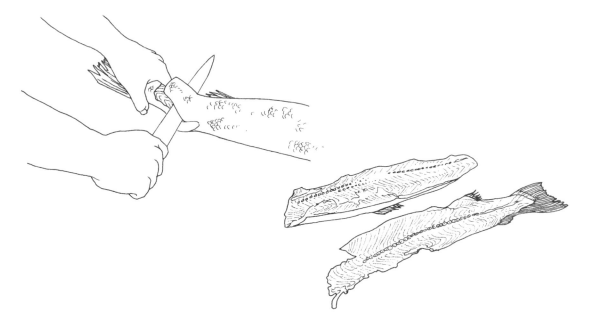

4. With the back of a knife, stroke the center of each fillet to locate any remaining pin-bones (found perpendicular to the fish's body along the middle of the fillets). Using a needle-nosed pliers, remove the bones. Or press the tip of a knife against the flesh at the base of each bone and pluck it out with your fingers.

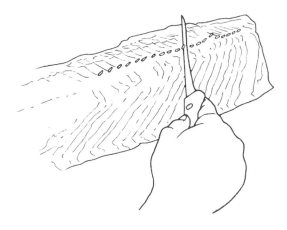

Filleting for smaller fish

1. Do not remove the head. Place the fish on your cutting board with the tail to the right and the belly away from you. Position a filleting knife directly behind the gills and pectoral fin, as shown. Angling the knife toward the head, make a shallow incision toward the tail. Insert the knife fully and using the center bone for support, slice toward the tail. Saw in even motions. Keep the knife angled downward, but be careful not to cut through the rib cage. Detach the fillet.

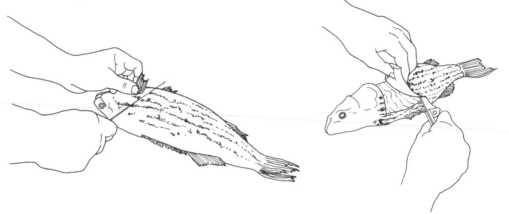

2. Flip the fish and repeat the procedure. Remove any pinbones, as instructed above.

Skinning a fillet

1. Place the fillet skin side down on your cutting board.

2. Holding the tail end, slip a thin-bladed flexible knife at a slight angle between the skin and flesh. Grasping the cut-away skin, continue to separate the flesh from the skin

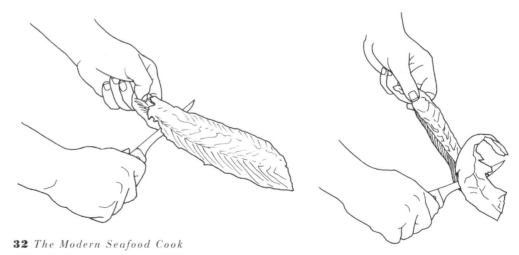

along the length of the fillet using long, sweeping strokes. Keep the skin taut, wiggling it to help separate it from the flesh. (When skinning salmon or other oily fish, make sure not to cut too close to the skin—you want to remove as much fat as possible, which may be bitter when cooked.)

3. Trim off any bits of skin you may have missed. The skin of nonoily fish can saved and used for stock making.

Steaks

Large roundfish, such as salmon, tilefish, and cod, can be cut into steaks. Using a serrated knife, remove the head and tail. Cut through the fish at 1- to 2-inch intervals. For particularly large fish, hold the knife in the cut and hit the back of the blade with a mallet.

FLATFISH
Gutting

1. You need not gut a flatfish if you intend to fillet it. Otherwise, place the fish dark skin up and head to the right on your cutting board. Insert the tip of a boning knife into the fish just behind the pectoral, as shown.

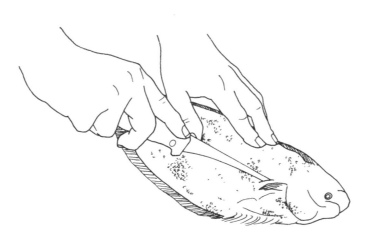

2. Cut a short diagonal incision; you have opened the visceral cavity. Remove the entrails with your fingers. Discard, and rinse the visceral cavity well.

Scaling and Removing the Head

The scales on a flatfish aren't large; on a small fish they are virtually nonexistent. Scrape gently to remove what scales there are following the method used for roundfish.

It is not necessary to remove the head of a flatfish; you risk cutting away too much of the flesh if you do so.

Filleting

1. Place the fish on your cutting board with the dark side upward and the head to the right.

2. With a filleting knife, make a horizontal cut in back of the pectoral fin, as shown. Cut along the lateral line toward the tail. Because the bone is rounded, your knife will fall to one side or the other of the bone.

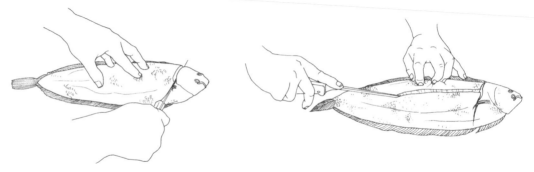

3. Make an incision at the point where the tail joins the body, as shown. Staring at the head and holding your knife almost parallel to the skeleton but not cutting into it, work the blade along the left side of the fish to the tail. Detach the "left-handed" fillet. Trim the fin flesh from the fillet.

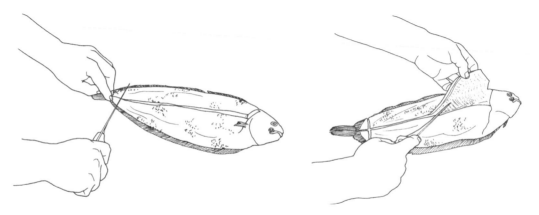

4. Turn the fish so its head is to the left. To remove the remaining fillet, insert the knife at the tail as shown, and work it against the skeleton toward the head. Aim at all times to cut hard against but not into the skeleton. Remove the second fillet.

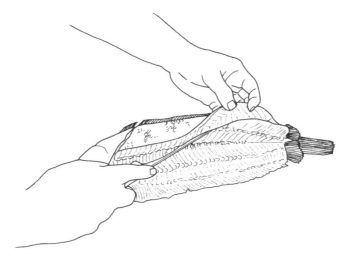

5. Flip the fish. Repeat the procedure. Be careful when removing fillets from this side—the belly flesh is thinner than that on the top.

6. Trim any bones that have adhered to the flesh.

Skinning a Fillet

Proceed in the same manner as you would for skinning a roundfish fillet.

Steaks

Large flatfish such as halibut can be cut into steaks following the same method used for roundfish. Smaller flatfish, such as flounder, sole, or turbot, should be cut into steaks about ½ inch thick.

PREPARING WHOLE COOKED FISH AT TABLE

Knowing how to "carve" a whole fish at table not only provides a sense of accomplishment but guarantees a neat, plentiful presentation.

ROUNDFISH

1. With a knife, make an incision along the back of the fish. Using a fork for support, work a spatula or turner under the fillets, as shown. Your objective is to loosen the fillet from the skeletal structure.

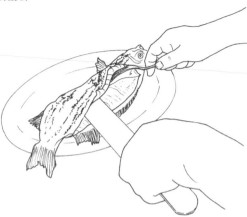

2. Using the spatula, lift off the top fillet. Starting with the head and holding down the bottom fillet with the back of a fork, lift away the whole skeletal structure. The second fillet is ready to be eaten.

FLATFISH

Flatfish are easier to fillet at table because their flesh is firmer than that of roundfish.

1. Make an incision along the lateral line. Using a fork for support, slide the spatula or turner under one section of the fillet at a time, as shown. Using the spatula, lift off the two top fillets, one section at a time.

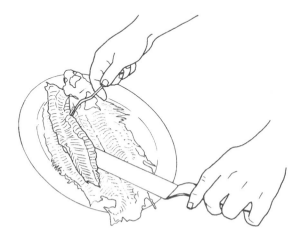

2. Remove the skeletal structure, discard, and enjoy the "bottom" fillet whole.

CLEANING SHELLFISH
Cleaning and Shucking Oysters

1. Using a vegetable brush, scrub oysters well under running water to remove any sea debris.

2. Place an oyster in a heavy cloth with its larger, more rounded shell down. Arrange the oyster so its hinge side faces away from you. Bunch the cloth around the top of the oyster to protect the holding hand.

3. Insert an oyster knife into the apex of the hinge as shown, then push, twist, and lift it to loosen the top shell. Run the knife along the top of the shell, severing the muscle that holds the meat in place.

4. Discard the top shell. Be careful to retain the oyster's liquor.

Cleaning and Shucking Cherrystone and Littleneck Clams

1. Rinse the clams under running water.

2. Place a clam in a small towel and cradle it in the palm of one hand, hinge inward.

3. Position the thin edge of a clam knife in the groove between the shells. Twist the knife to pry open the shells. (Sometimes it's difficult to insert the knife into the clam. If so, turn the clam around so that the hinge faces you. Push the knife into the crack at the hinge—you're not trying to open the hinge, only to loosen it. Now reverse the clam, and proceed as above.)

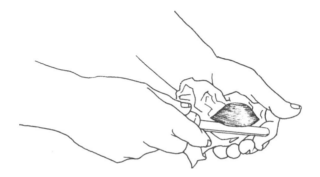

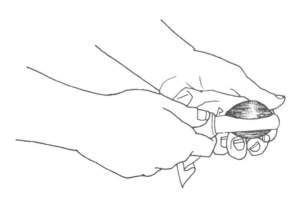

Cleaning, Bearding, and Shucking Mussels

Most of the mussels sold today are farmed and come fully cleaned. They need only be rinsed and bearded. Wild mussels should be scrubbed well with a stiff vegetable brush. I've never felt the barnacles that sometimes attach themselves to the shells need to be removed; they do no harm. However, if you find them unsightly, pry them off with the back of a knife.

As mussels die shortly after their beards are removed, do not beard a mussel until right before you intend to cook it. To beard, use your fingers to pull out the clump of hairlike strands that protrude from the shells. If the beard is difficult to remove, use a pliers, but don't be too forceful lest you pull the mussel apart. If the whole beard won't emerge, remove what you can and let the rest stay in the shell.

Cleaning Squid

1. Pull the head and intestines from the body cavity or mantle. Discard the intestines.

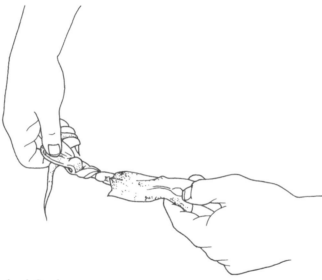

2. With your fingers, remove the translucent cartilage or "pen" from the body. Cut off the tentacles above the eyes. Discard the head. The tentacles may be fried or poached for use in a salad.

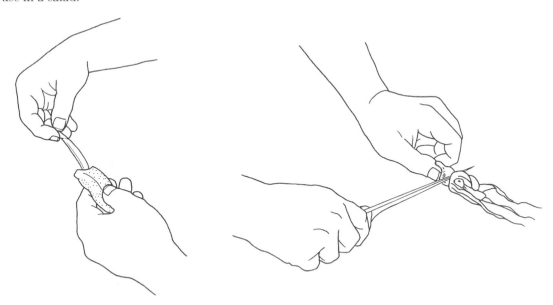

4. For aesthetic reasons you may peel away the spotted membrane from the body. Rinse the body and its cavity well. The winglike projections can be removed and reserved for frying. You may keep the body whole for stuffing, slice it into rings for frying or poaching, or split it open, scrape the interior, and cut it into halves. The halves can be grilled.

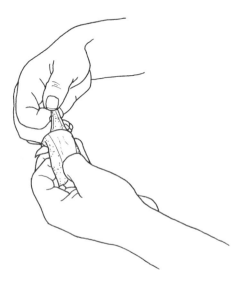

Cleaning Octopus

1. Using your fingers, remove the slimy membrane that covers the body. Rinse well.

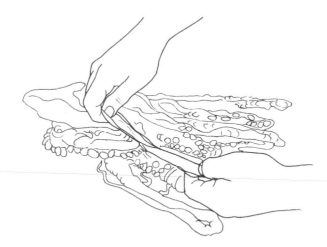

2. Turn the head inside out and flush the water. If present, carefully remove the delicate ink sac from inside the head and save. (The ink is excellent for sauces, risottos, or for making squid-ink pasta.) It is unnecessary to remove the other organs if present. Turn the head right side out.

Killing, Splitting, or Sectioning a Lobster

1. To kill a lobster instantly, place it on your cutting board and insert the tip of a large chef's knife just behind the head. To avoid muscular contractions, you can put the lobster in the freezer for a few minutes before dispatching it. This will slow down postmortem movement. In any case, allow the lobster to become still before preparing it further.

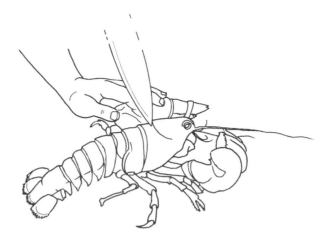

2. *To split a lobster for broiling or grilling,* cut through the underside from head to tail. Make sure you do not cut all the way through the back shell.

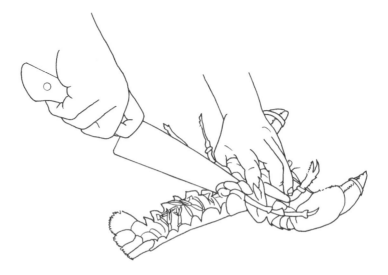

3. Spread the halves apart. With your fingers, or using a paring knife, remove and discard the veinlike intestinal tract that runs along the length of the lobster. Remove the small sac from behind the eyes. Do not remove the tomalley—the greenish-gray pancreas and liver—or the dark green coral (present if the lobster is female).

4. *To section a lobster* into six or eight pieces for cooking, first twist off the claws. Place the lobster belly side up on your cutting board. Using a sharp, heavy knife, split the lobster in half from head to tail. Split each half crosswise at the point where the body meets the tail. You have now cut the lobster into six pieces. If you wish to have eight, split the body pieces crosswise once again.

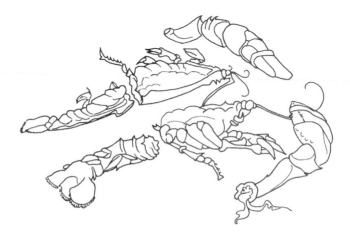

Cleaning Shrimp

1. With a small knife, split the shrimp along their underside. Peel from the bottom, starting with the head section. Leave on the section nearest the tail and the tail shell. (Save the shells for making bisques or shell-infused oils; see page 60.)

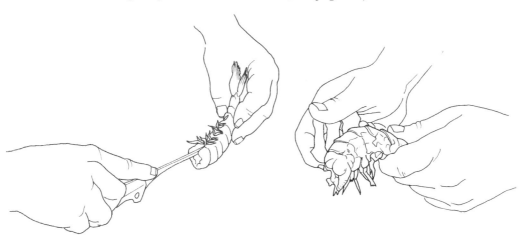

2. If you want to remove the intestinal vein, a purely aesthetic decision, cut shallowly into the shrimp along the back and pull out the vein.

3. *To prepare shrimp for stir-frying*, cut halfway through the back, and fan out. This will help to avoid contraction of the meat when the shrimp is added to the wok and also speeds cooking. *To butterfly shrimp for broiling and grilling*, split the unshelled shrimp deeply through the underside, spread open, and remove the vein.

Cleaning Soft-Shell Crab

1. With a scissors, cut off the face, as shown, below left. Apply pressure on top of the crab near the cut until the bubblelike bile sac emerges from the opening, below right. Though entirely edible, the sac can burst during cooking, causing unnecessary splattering.

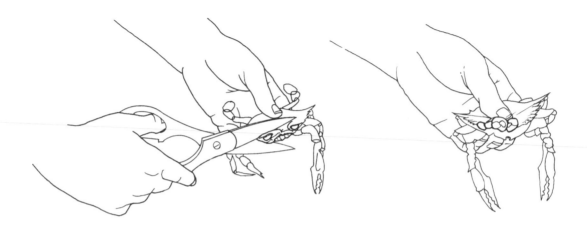

2. Turn the crab over. Lift up its triangular tail, below left, or apron and remove. Lift the flaps on each side of the crab and remove the feathery gills with your fingers, below right.

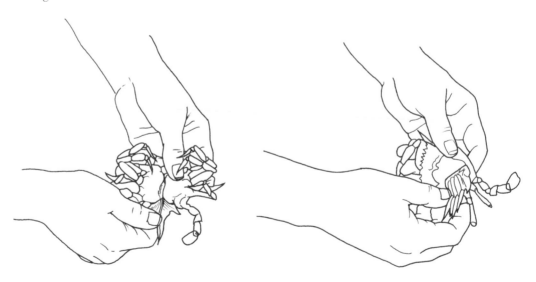

To Section a Live Hard-Shell Crab

1. Holding the crab down with a hand over its upper shell, quickly twist off the claws.

2. With a cleaver, cut the body into four sections, as shown. Gill removal is not necessary, as you will be eating the meat only and not the entire crab.

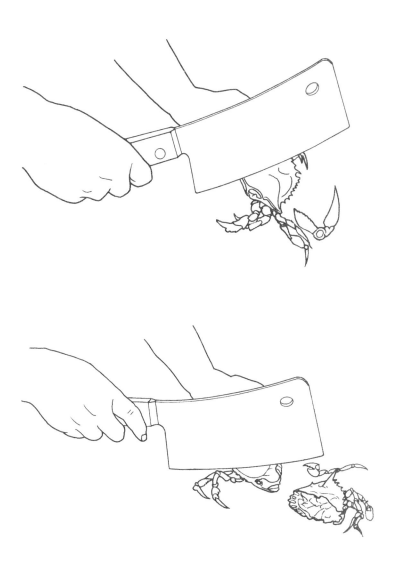

Storage Guidelines

In a world more perfect than ours, you would have assured access to freshly caught fish and shellfish, which you would then rush to the table. Unfortunately, unless you do your own fishing, you have no way of knowing exactly how long the seafood supply has been out of the water. This is due to the vagaries of distribution.

Ideally, a day's catch arrives at the wholesale market within twenty-four hours after being fished. But boats can linger at sea, causing weeklong delays, and not-so-fresh catch can be mixed with seafood that has gone directly to the market. So you must do your best to ensure freshness, not only through vigilant marketing but by storing your purchases carefully. I've already gone into what to look for at your fish seller's, and Chapter 3, "The Working Seafood Kitchen," will provide you with special storage strategies to ensure delicious eating when shopping is a problem or time is tight. Here, then, is the remaining storage information.

The Basic Rules

1. Seafood, and fish in particular, deteriorates rapidly. Try always to prepare it as quickly as possible after buying or catching it. Unless you have done the fishing yourself, your fish has most probably been gutted by the time you get it. If you fish, get the guts out on the boat or at the dock. If you buy fish that hasn't been eviscerated, gut it at home immediately, and rinse the cavity well.

2. Shop, if possible, just before going home, and make sure your seafood has been packed properly. Fresh fish, whether whole or filleted, is usually wrapped in paper by your fish seller. Paper is an *adequate* insulator only—refrigerate your purchases as soon as possible. Seafood doesn't wait happily on the back seat of a car or, needless to say, in a shopping bag at the office. If you can't get your seafood to a refrigerator quickly, ask that it be packed in ice and double-bagged. Use frozen gel packs or coolers for longer hauls.

Storing Fish

As a rule, really fresh fish of one to three pounds can be stored in your refrigerator for up to three days. Wrap whole fish in moist paper toweling and then in plastic wrap.

Your refrigerator can dry things out. To avoid circulating air, store fish in refrigerator produce drawers. Fillets and steaks should also be wrapped in wet toweling and plastic wrap and stored in vegetable bins. Change the toweling daily. Check the freshness of your stored fish every twenty-four hours to make sure everything is as it should be—a sniff should tell the whole story.

STORING BIVALVES

Oysters and other bivalves need air as well as moisture to stay alive. Store them in bowls or oyster baskets, if you can get them, buried in seaweed (available from your fish seller) or wrapped in wet newspaper. (Oyster baskets, which look like children's pails made of a widely open mesh, allow air to circulate freely.) Don't put bivalves in fresh water or on ice, and don't beard mussels—all these things will cause bivalve demise. Oysters should last about a week, clams and mussels a couple of days. Put a weight—a head of iceberg lettuce or a can—on top of stored oysters after two days. This will help to keep them closed. Check daily to make sure your bivalves are alive—the shells should be closed. If a clam, mussel, or oyster is open, tap the shell gently. If it doesn't close, throw it away.

STORING CRAB

Hard-shell crabs should be eaten immediately after they're bought. Soft-shells will keep for a day or so refrigerated in a container lined with moist seagrass, seaweed, or moist shredded paper toweling.

STORING LOBSTER

It's best to eat lobster the day you buy it. However, it can be stored in the fridge, buried in seaweed or wet newspaper for about three days.

STORING SHRIMP

The best way to store shrimp is to buy them frozen and keep them that way until ready to use. If you can, buy shrimp frozen in a solid block. Run the block under cold water until you can just barely break it apart, removing the still-frozen shrimp one by one. Place the shrimp in a plastic bag and store in the freezer. They will keep for four to six weeks. To store unfrozen shrimp, place the shrimp on a rack in a shallow pan. Drape the shrimp with a damp towel and cover it with ice. Refrigerate. The shrimp will last about three days.

STORING SQUID

Cleaned fresh squid can be held for a day or two in a tightly covered plastic container. Sniff the squid every twenty-four hours to make sure everything is as it should be. Don't worry if slime develops—it's characteristic, and can easily be washed off before the squid is prepared for cooking.

STORING OCTOPUS

Octopus is best stored after preliminary cooking. Clean the octopus if necessary and boil it until tender, about 40 minutes. Cool and then refrigerate or freeze (see page 51). The head may be removed and only the tentacles stored in resealable plastic bags.

FREEZING

Of course, it's best not to freeze fresh seafood at all. But there are times when you have a windfall of freshly caught fish or know you won't be using all the fresh squid you've bought right away. How then do you use the freezer most productively?

Know first that your home refrigerator freezer, unlike the ultra-cold commercial variety, doesn't bring food much below 10° F. It cannot, therefore, freeze fast enough to make long-term storage of fresh or frozen seafood desirable. However, lean fish and some cooked shellfish may be kept for up to two weeks. Fatty fish deteriorate more rapidly—their fat is polyunsaturated, which is more vulnerable to spoilage than the saturated fat of, say, meat or poultry. Do not hold fatty fish in the freezer for more than one week. *Do not freeze uncooked lobster or soft-shell crabs or any bivalves.* Frozen lobster meat will be mealy when defrosted; crab and bivalve flesh also degenerates when frozen. Freeze only cooked lobster, crab, or bivalve meat, then use it for salads. Do not refreeze any previously frozen fish or shellfish.

Freezing Fresh Fish

The most successful way I've found to freeze fresh whole fish is to create a moisture-protecting frozen environment around the fish that is similar in some ways to its natural home.

Fill a shallow pan just large enough to hold the fish with water. Add kosher (coarse) salt until the water tastes noticeably salty. Place the fish in the pan and freeze.

Whole fish freezes most successfully, but you may also freeze fillets or steaks. Wrap fresh fillets (preferably unskinned) or steaks in a triple layer of plastic wrap and freeze.

Fillets and steaks will keep for six to eight weeks.

To defrost whole fish, fillets, or steaks, allow the fish to thaw slowly in the refrigerator over a twenty-four-hour period. In a pinch, you can run packaged frozen fish under cold—not tepid or warm—water to defrost it. This method leaches away some flavor, so it's for emergencies only.

Freezing Cooked Hard-Shell Crab and Lobster Meat

Hard-shell crabs and lobster should not be frozen live. Instead, put the cooked meat in a plastic bag, squeeze out as much air as possible, then freeze. Defrost slowly in the refrigerator for about twenty-four hours, never at room temperature.

Lobster shells, and those of other crustaceans, should always be saved to make bisques or shell-infused oils. Freeze the shells in a plastic bag; they will keep for four weeks and usually do not need to be defrosted before use.

Freezing Shrimp

Never refreeze frozen and defrosted shrimp. To freeze previously unfrozen fresh shrimp, place them in a shallow pan of salted water sufficient to cover them and freeze. Once frozen, they will keep for four to six weeks.

To defrost individually frozen shrimp, place them in a colander that you have put into a deep pan. Place the colander and pan in the refrigerator and allow the shrimp to thaw, which will take about twenty-four hours. As the shrimp defrost, excess water will drain into the pan. Another good method is to put frozen shrimp in a resealable plastic bag, force out excess air, and defrost in the refrigerator for three to four days. In an emergency you can run the bagged shrimp under cold water until thawed, but be aware that there will be some loss of flavor and texture if you use this method. Don't run individual shrimp under water to defrost them; the water will leach away flavor. Don't forget to freeze shrimp shells for future preparations.

Freezing Squid and Octopus

Place well-cleaned raw squid or parboiled octopus in a small pan of salted water and freeze in a block, as you would fish. Or freeze them in resealable plastic bags from which you've squeezed as much air as possible. Defrost in the refrigerator for about twenty-four hours, never at room temperature.

3. THE WORKING SEAFOOD KITCHEN

As a chef who must oversee the preparation of many meals a week under the tyrannical eye of the clock, I'm painfully aware of the necessity of finding ways to shorten the distance between kitchen and table. Like me, you probably have little time or inclination to fuss in the kitchen, but still want to put terrific food on the table for yourself, your family, and your guests. Many recipes in this book are particularly fast or easy to prepare (see the list on page 304), but there are tricks that can make virtually all your seafood cooking less time-consuming and more enjoyable. These include creating a seafood pantry, learning prepreparation strategies, and organizing the cooking process itself. Master these and you're on your way to having a working seafood kitchen. In a nutshell you should:

- Make sure your pantry supplies are complete.
- Prepare component parts of a recipe ahead of time, storing core ingredients like stocks, shells, seafood butters, and oils as a professional kitchen does.
- Do much of the preparation or cooking beforehand so that the actual assembly of a dish is a matter of minutes, not hours.

These strategies make otherwise time-consuming or special-occasion efforts reasonable options for any cook, no matter how busy.

THE SEAFOOD PANTRY

I confess—I sometimes check out people's kitchen cupboards the way other people peek into a friend's medicine cabinet. What I often find duplicates the sad state of my own pre-enlightenment pantry: the staples, a few cans of soup, cookies, the usual spices and dried herbs, often past their prime. The freezer isn't much more encouraging—ice cream, packages of frozen vegetables, a small store of poultry trimmings held against the day when someone might make a stock. Creating a working seafood pantry begins with a well-outfitted cupboard and the freezer, and this means a trip to the market. I needn't tell you to buy staples like flour, bread, or sugar, or where to find them. But some of the ingredients I call for may be unknown to you or seem to require "special" shopping.

Always check your supermarket first. I've been delighted to find such items as couscous, balsamic vinegar, even Chinese chili paste on the shelves of my local supermarket. If you can't find what you need, or the high quality you require, a trip to the gourmet shop, Asian market, or health food store is in order. (A shopping hint: make a *month-to-month* list of things you'll need and plan to do all your shopping on a single, nonbusiness day—remember, you're focusing on the future and want to save as much legwork as possible.)

Here's a rundown of the things your cupboard, refrigerator, and freezer pantry should contain with notes about each ingredient and where to get it, or how to make it.

THINGS TO BUY

OILS

Because of its transparency of flavor, seafood seems to demand the best tasting and lightest of accompanying ingredients, olive oil paramount among them.

Olive oil. Our markets are now so full of olive oils—"pure," "blended," "virgin," and "extra-virgin," not to mention those carrying confusing brand designations such as "classico" or "lite"—that you may be tempted to grab the first bottle you see. Olive oil grading has to do with the method by which the oil is extracted from the fruit and the amount of oleic acid it finally contains. "Extra-virgin," "superfine virgin," "fine virgin," and "virgin" oils—the best kinds you can buy—come from fruit that has been "cold pressed," or extracted without the use of heat or chemicals. By Italian (and Californian) law these oils must not contain more than a designated amount of acid: 1 percent for extra virgin oil; 1½ percent for superfine; 3 and 4 percent for fine virgin and virgin, respectively. Oils with more than 4 percent oleic acid are derived from successive pressings of the olive and may be extracted by the use of heat or chemical solvents. Their flavors may be "improved" by chemical correctives or by blending with oils of a higher grade. These oils are labeled "pure" (or "Olio d'Olivia"). They are utilitarian, without good flavor.

Though the taste, color, mouth feel, and lightness of olive oil varies across the board, and from country to country, the best oils are always clean tasting and have a definite and delicious fruit presence. "Pure oils" (that misleading adjective!) are usually yellow in color (as opposed to the straw-green to green color of higher-quality oils) and are universally bland. They are adequate for use when the flavor of the oil doesn't matter much—for sautéing or in some marinades, for example—but should not be used when flavor counts. Other designations such as "classico" are commercial inventions that usually connote "pure" oils. You should taste and taste again. You'll find that you prefer certain oils to others, not only from category to category but within a particular classification.

My own seafood pantry contains several olive oils—from top-of-the-line to lesser-but-true-tasting, which I use as a recipe and my needs (or budget) dictates. (I *don't* use olive oil when vegetable oil will do just as well or better.) Though I call for olive oil in most of the recipes here, leaving the choice up to you, I advise you to use the best olive oil you can afford, depending on the role the oil will play. Your pantry should contain at least one Italian (or Spanish or Tunisian) extra-virgin oil, if only for salad making.

Vegetable oils. As you undoubtedly know, not all vegetable oils are equal. Because I use vegetable oil most often for sautéing and deep-frying, an oil with a high smoking point is desirable. Unless a specific flavor is required, vegetable oil should be just about anonymous, permitting other tastes to shine through. Most supermarket oils—corn, cottonseed, soy, canola, and peanut, among them—are chemically refined; this helps to strengthen their cooking stability and adds to shelf life. Cold-pressed oils, the kind you see most often in health food stores, often taste more definitely of their source, and should be used when flavor is desirable. (Cold-pressed oils also burn more quickly and keep less well than their refined cousins—check them regularly for rancidity.) Most supermarket oils smoke at about 440° F.—higher than the temperature required for deep-frying. My preference is for canola oil, which is clean tasting and monounsaturated—it may, in other words, be effective *against* high cholesterol levels in the blood. Other vegetable oils I recommend include soybean and cottonseed oil, both of which are neutral in taste and nongreasy.

Asian sesame oil. Not to be confused with the light-colored refined oil of the same name, Asian sesame oil has a nutlike hue and the delicious taste of freshly roasted sesame seeds. It is not used for cooking but as a flavoring, and as such is added to a dish at the last minute. Sesame oil is a staple of both Chinese and Japanese cooking, and there are many imported brands to be found on both supermarket and Asian grocery shelves. I prefer Japanese oils, which in my experience are more likely to be sold fresh, neither rancid nor burnt tasting. Here is another case where you should sample available brands. What you want is a clean-tasting oil that is nonetheless full flavored and highly aromatic. Store sesame oil in a cool place away from the light.

Hot chili oil ("dragon oil"). Another staple of Chinese and Japanese cooking, this is sesame or vegetable oil that has been infused with red chili pepper. Because of its fire, it is never used for cooking but is added in small quantities to dishes as a seasoning. I like Chinese or Thai chili oil. As with sesame oil, rancid oil appears too frequently in the marketplace; shop for chili oil in stores with a rapid turnover of Asian products. The quality of hot chili oil varies widely—some brands are coarse tasting, others offer only heat.

VINEGARS

When I was growing up, the only vinegar on our pantry shelf was made from cider and used, if at all, for salad dressings that were definitely mouth-puckering. Today's repertoire of vinegars provide a range of subtle tastes and are used much like salt or fresh lemon juice are, as a seasoning. Like fresh lemon juice, vinegars enliven other flavors, providing "backbone"; those of us on low-salt diets know that vinegars can add zip.

Fermented wine is the basis of most of these vinegars. Once opened, most varieties will keep for two to three months before their flavors change. Keep this and other vinegars tightly sealed in a cool dark place after opening.

Champagne vinegar. Made from fermented Champagne, this is a delightfully mild wine vinegar. As with any vinegar, some brands are better than others. One I like particularly is La Marne, which is never harsh or thin tasting. Champagne vinegar isn't usually available at supermarkets; try gourmet shops. Any light white wine vinegar will do as a substitute, if necessary.

Sherry vinegar. I'm a devotee of this vinegar, which is fuller flavored and less acidic than many other wine-based varieties. Try to find a sherry vinegar whose tartness is well rounded by "sweet" sherry notes. A brand I like is Don Bruno, which is made in Jerez, Spain.

Balsamic vinegar. It would be a better world if we all had access to artisan-made balsamic vinegar. Produced solely in Modena and Reggio, where it originated nearly a thousand years ago, this complex sweet-tart vinegar made from the must of the white Trebbiano grape is pure nectar and is treated as such. It is used by the dropful to season meat, fish, or fruit (it is amazing on strawberries), or served traditionally as a *digestif* (the name derives from "balm," or curative).

Unfortunately, true artisan-made balsamics, aged for up to a century in casks made from woods including oak, cherry, mulberry, and chestnut, are relatively rare and expensive—it's possible to spend $100 for a small bottle. Get some if you can afford it; if not, buy commercial balsamic vinegars from Modena and Reggio (the ones used for testing the recipes in this book), which do wonderfully blended *into* dishes,.

The best of these vinegars are produced along traditional lines—though they're made of a blend of wine vinegar, must, and caramel and receive an abbreviated period of aging. The finest commercial brands balance sweet and tart into a unified whole. A brand I like is Monari Federzoni. Keep trying them until you find one you like; price is often not a guide to quality. By the way, I've come up with the following method for enhancing ordinary balsamics. It rounds off the edges of many too-rough vinegars and adds texture, which recalls the syrupy Aceto Balsamico Tradizionale di Modena. Place 2 cups of ordinary balsamic vinegar in a medium nonreactive saucepan with 2 tablespoons of sugar. Reduce the mixture over high heat by one-third, 4 to 5 minutes. Cool and bottle.

THE ETHNIC SHELF

My seafood cooking uses flavors from around the world. Besides the customary spices and condiments, your pantry should contain these multinational items, which will quickly become part of your home cooking.

Supermarkets are the first place to look for many of these ingredients; otherwise, try gourmet shops or Asian markets. Stores that ship a wide range of Asian food products include Asia Food Market in New York City at (212) 962-2020; Thai Grocery in Chicago at (312) 561-5345; and Ann's Dutch Import Co. in Studio City, California, at (818) 985-5551.

Ketjap manis. This Indonesian soy sauce is dark, sweet, and syrupy, unlike most of the Chinese and Japanese kinds we know. It is used extensively in Indonesian recipes and as a table condiment; by itself it makes an excellent marinade for seafood that is to be grilled. The word *ketjap*, incidentally, is the root for our own *ketchup*, and means "an addition that provides extra taste." My favorite brand is Conimex. Ketjap manis will last indefinitely if stored in a cool, dry place.

Hoisin sauce. Sweetish and vaguely fruity, this Chinese sauce is made from a base of fermented wheat or soybeans. Its name means "sea freshness," a description contradicted by its taste and texture. Hoisin is used as an ingredient or a jamlike condiment, as with Peking Duck, and comes in cans and bottles; a brand I like is Koon Chun.

Hoisin is sometimes confused with hot bean paste or sweet bean paste. Though they all share ingredients and flavors, hoisin has its own particular character. Check labels carefully to make sure you're getting the genuine article.

Chinese chili paste (hot bean paste). When I first started to cook I often confused the various Chinese bean pastes. There is one common denominator: they are all made from soybeans. Of these, the two most popular are sweet bean paste and hot bean paste, the latter usually called Chinese chili paste. This condiment and sauce ingredient is available in cans and bottles and varies in color along the red-brown spectrum. It is very hot, and should be used judiciously.

Once opened, cans or jars should be stored in the refrigerator. The paste will last for at least two months. Taste it after a bit—it looses its power on standing.

Sambal. Sambal—the name itself sounds exotic. And in fact *sambal* refers to a raft of Southeast Asian red chili pastes and condiments, as well as the accompaniments served with the famous Indonesian rice dish, rijsttafel. For our purposes sambal is *sambal oelek*, a mixture of chilies, salt, and sometimes tamarind; a brand I like is Conimex. Sambal is used as an ingredient and table condiment. Try it on grilled fish or mixed into soups or marinades. Store opened bottles in the refrigerator, where it will keep indefinitely.

Lemongrass and lemongrass powder. Lemongrass is a wonderfully aromatic tropical ingredient with a citrus taste and a scallionlike base. Gray-green in color and resembling the smallest of leeks, it is among the preeminent flavorings of Thai cuisine. Look for lemongrass in the produce section of Asian markets. If it is not available, lemongrass powder, which is made from the dried plant, is an adequate replacement. Sometimes called sereh powder, this ingredient may be found in natural food stores and herb shops. One teaspoon of the powder is equal to one stalk of the grass.

Fresh lemongrass should be stored in moist toweling in the vegetable bin of the refrigerator, where it will keep for up to three weeks. In cooking, use the portion of the stalk from the base to the point where it begins to branch; the leaves should be discarded. In a pinch, lemon peel makes an acceptable substitute for the grass or the powder. Two strips of peel are roughly equivalent to one stalk of the grass.

Harissa. This pastelike Tunisian seasoning made from dried chilies, olive oil, garlic, and salt is bright red and fiery hot. Available in tubes, cans, and bottles, harissa is most notably used to make Moroccan couscous (the dish, not the pasta). Combined with olive oil and preserved lemon, it becomes a table condiment. Some brands of harissa contain starch thickeners or adulterants; check labels carefully. Transfer canned harissa (or any canned condiments, for that matter) to glass or plastic containers; it will keep for at least two months in the refrigerator if any exposed paste is covered with oil or flush with plastic film.

Kaffir leaves. I love this Thai seasoning ingredient, sometimes called kaffir lime leaves. Available in small packages from Asian markets, they exude a delightfully pungent lime aroma. Do your best to find them, but if you can't, you can substitute ½ teaspoon grated lime peel per leaf.

The leaves will last for three weeks in the refrigerator if kept away from light or moisture. They are best kept frozen, however, in which state they will last indefinitely.

Thai fish sauce. This light, mild brownish gray flavoring ingredient, called nam pla in Thailand, plays an important role in the cooking of all Southeast Asia. It is made with dried shrimp and anchovies and/or other dried fish. Though nam pla will keep on the shelf for up to three months, it is best stored in the refrigerator. Make sure the fish sauce you buy is Thai. Burmese and Vietnamese versions may be fermented and unpleasantly strong.

Curry powder. By now most of us know that there is no such thing as curry powder in Indian cooking. The combination of spices that goes by that name is shorthand for individual spices roasted and ground "to order." Nonetheless, fine, fresh, well-balanced curry powders are available.

Most curry powders contain some combination of cumin, coriander, fenugreek, turmeric, and red pepper; because the spices are ground before packing, flavors can disappear quickly. Always sniff curry powder before you buy it, or if this is impossible, check the color of the powder carefully. Dull color means dull taste. Garam masala, a packaged spice blend including cardamom, cinnamon, peppercorn, cumin, and cloves may be a better bet than curry powder itself—if your market carries it, get some. Store powders in a cool, dry place and check their aromas periodically.

Red curry paste. This fiery Thai seasoning, made from red chilies, garlic, ginger, cumin, cinnamon, lemongrass, turmeric, and vegetable oil, is available in jars. It keeps indefinitely refrigerated—I can't imagine any bacterium having the nerve to invade it.

Miso. The principal flavoring ingredient of the Japanese soup that bears its name, miso is a delicious fermented soybean paste that is also used for seasoning. There are two kinds—white and red. White miso, called shiromiso, contains rice; it is light tan and tastes faintly sweet. Red miso, or akamiso, is made with barley; its deep brown color suggests its rich, heady flavor. Both misos are available in jars, bags, and tubs in the refrigerator sections of supermarkets, Asian groceries, and health food stores. It is best to store miso in the fridge, where it will last for up to three months.

Banana leaves. Banana leaves are available fresh or frozen at Latin American markets or specialty produce stores. Fresh are best. The leaves should be rinsed and dried before using, and their fibrous central stems cut away. One-pound packages of frozen leaves are available throughout the year. They are already cut and their veins removed. To use, defrost the leaves at room temperature, unfold them carefully, and cut them to size. Wipe them gently with a damp cloth and proceed with the recipe.

Konbu. Konbu or kelp, which has a delicate sea taste, is more readily available in packages in pliable sheets from Asian markets. (You may be able to get fresh konbu from your fish seller.) The sheets are available packaged in various sizes; the smaller sheets (roughly 6 by 7 inches) are right for the recipes in this book.

Rice paper. A staple of Vietnamese and other Southeast Asian cuisines, rice paper is available packaged in many Asian markets. You'll need the larger round sheets for the recipes in this book. Rice paper keeps indefinitely in a cool, dry place; it's dampened to make it pliable for use in preparing spring rolls and for other recipes. The best-quality paper is the thinnest.

Harusame. A translucent Japanese noodle made from various bean starches, harusame (the name means "spring rain") are available in packages of different sizes. Like Chinese rice noodles, they are soaked before using, or may be fried and used as a crisp garnish. The noodles last indefinitely on the pantry shelf.

Wonton skins. Like pasta dough, wonton skins are made from flour, eggs, and salt. They come packaged in a variety of forms—round or square, thick or thin. For the recipes in this book, thin round skins are needed. They will last refrigerated for about a week, frozen for up to six months.

Things to Make

FLAVORED OILS AND BUTTERS

Homemade flavored oils and butters are wonderful cooking tools to have on hand. I call for them in such recipes as Sautéed Soft-Shell Crabs with Pine Nuts and Scallion Butter (page 220), but they should be part of everyone's seafood pantry. The oils are quickly turned into superior mayonnaises and vinaigrettes. They make great marinades and are wonderful brushed on bread, or used to season soups, vegetables, or grilled fish just before serving. The butters, formed into logs and sliced, make a quick and delicious finish for broiled or steamed seafood, or become the basis for any number of "fast sauces." Softened, they may be spread on bread.

Oils containing fresh herbs are best used within a day or two, but can be stored refrigerated for two to three weeks. Shellfish oils are good for up to one month if kept in a cool place—no more than two to three weeks is best. Store the butters, well wrapped in foil, for up to one week in the fridge or for a month in the freezer.

SHELL-INFUSED OILS

MAKES 3 CUPS

3 cups canola oil

1 pound lobster, crab,
   or crayfish shells, or ¹/₂
   pound shrimp shells, or 1
   pound combined shells

¹/₂ teaspoon salt

Cooked shrimp, lobster, crab, or crayfish shells may be used alone or in combination to make shell-infused oils. Store shells from seafood in resealable plastic bags and pop the bags into the freezer, adding new shells to the bags as you get them. Shells should last from two to three weeks frozen. Use shell-infused oils as you would other seasoned oils. They're especially good as seasonings for simply prepared seafood. Freshly steamed cod sprinkled with lobster oil and coarse salt is fantastic; crayfish oil drizzled on grilled swordfish or marlin makes for really delicious eating. The shell-infused oils bring flavor and richness to a dish without cream or butter.

The basic recipe calls for 1 pound of shells per 3 cups of oil, but you may use more shells for a more intensely flavored oil.

1. In a large, heavy pot over high heat, bring 2 tablespoons of the oil to the smoking point. Add the shells and cook, stirring occasionally, until they are brightly colored, 4 to 6 minutes.

2. Add the remaining oil and salt, reduce the heat to very low, and cook until the oil is deeply fragrant, 30 to 35 minutes. Strain the oil, allow it to come to room temperature, and pour it into glass jars. Seal and store in the refrigerator for up to two weeks.

BASIL OIL

MAKES 1 CUP

1¹/₂ bunches fresh basil leaves

1 cup olive, canola, or other
   vegetable oil

¹/₂ teaspoon salt

Try drizzling this oil, alone, on the top of salads, or on grilled swordfish just before you serve it. It also makes a marvelous seasoning for grilled vegetables of any kind.

Combine the basil, oil, and salt in the bowl of a food processor. Process 2 minutes. Store in a nonreactive container.

CILANTRO OIL

MAKES 2 CUPS

Great added to such soups as Scallop Vegetable Soup with Shiitake Mushrooms (page 105) just before serving. For delicious results, baste scallop brochettes with this oil while they broil or grill.

Combine the cilantro, oil, and salt in the bowl of a food processor. Process 2 to 3 minutes. Store in a nonreactive container.

3 bunches fresh cilantro
(coriander), leaves only
1²⁄₃ cups canola oil
¹⁄₂ teaspoon salt

GARLIC OIL

MAKES 3 CUPS

Brush Garlic Oil on crusty bread or serve it with Caribbean Bouillabaisse with Long Croûtes (page 90). It's also a fine way to store chopped garlic for whenever you need it. Just strain the garlic from the oil in the quantity your recipe requires. It will keep refrigerated for up to two months in sealed glass jars.

1. In a nonreactive saucepan, combine the garlic and oils. Cook the garlic over medium-low heat until it is slightly softened, 12 to 15 minutes. Do not allow the garlic to brown or the oil to color.
2. Remove the oil from the heat and allow it to come to room temperature. Add the peppercorns and season with the salt. Pour into a glass jar, seal, and store in the refrigerator.

Peeled cloves from 2
large heads garlic
1 cup olive oil
2 cups canola oil
6 black peppercorns
¹⁄₂ teaspoon salt

Butters

All my butters are simply made: butter and flavoring ingredients are blended in a food processor, wrapped in a block shape or rolled into logs, and refrigerated or frozen. You can easily cut slices off a refrigerated log to melt on top of cooked seafood. It is also easy to transform flavored butters into a sauce, as follows.

Put 2 tablespoons of water in a small saucepan over medium heat. When the water simmers, turn off the heat and add the butter 4 tablespoons at a time, whisking in each batch before adding the next. The butter should not melt but remain in a creamy suspension. If necessary, season with fresh lemon juice, salt, and freshly ground pepper.

Please remember to wrap all butters well in foil—they can absorb refrigerator odors with alarming speed. Butters will keep for one week refrigerated or for up to one month in the freezer.

SCALLION BUTTER

FOR 8 TO 10, AS A GARNISH OR MADE INTO A SAUCE

½ bunch scallions, green parts only, coarsely chopped
½ pound (2 sticks) unsalted butter
Juice of 1 small lemon
½ bunch fresh Italian (flat-leaf) parsley, coarsely chopped

This butter is delicious when allowed to melt on grilled fish, used in pureed potatoes, or made into a sauce.

1. Combine all the ingredients in the bowl of a food processor. Process until well blended, 45 seconds to 1 minute, scraping down the sides of the bowl as necessary.

2. Remove the butter to a sheet of foil, wrap, and refrigerate. Or shape the softened butter into 2 logs by placing equal portions of butter along the center of 2 sheets of foil. Use the foil to shape the butter into loglike rolls. Seal the foil and refrigerate. These may be sliced and served on top of cooked fish, crabs, or other seafood.

CHIVE BUTTER

FOR 8 TO 10, AS A GARNISH OR MADE INTO A SAUCE

Like Scallion Butter, Chive Butter is delicious served as is on cooked fish, crabs, and other seafood. Or make it into a sauce and serve it on seared tuna. Chive Butter is also a great addition to mashed potatoes.

Follow the instructions for making Scallion Butter, processing the combined ingredients for 45 seconds to 1 minute, scraping down the sides of the bowl as necessary. Form the butter into logs, or make it into a sauce.

2 small bunches chives
1/3 bunch fresh Italian (flat-leaf) parsley, coarsely chopped
1/2 pound (2 sticks) unsalted butter
1/2 teaspoon fresh lemon juice
Salt

RED PEPPER BUTTER

FOR 8 TO 10, AS A GARNISH OR MADE INTO A SAUCE

This butter is especially nice turned into a sauce and served with a lean white fish like cod.

Puree the red peppers in the food processor for 45 seconds. Add the remaining ingredients and proceed as for Scallion Butter.

2 large red bell peppers, roasted and peeled
1/2 pound (2 sticks) unsalted butter
1/2 teaspoon fresh lemon juice
Salt
3 dashes of Tabasco Sauce, or to taste

CILANTRO BUTTER

FOR 8 TO 10, AS GARNISH OR MADE INTO A SAUCE

Particularly good on broiled or grilled fish.

Follow the instructions for making Scallion Butter, processing the combined ingredients for 45 seconds to 1 minute, scraping down the sides of the bowl as necessary. Form the butter into logs, or make it into a sauce.

1 bunch cilantro, leaves only
1/2 pound (2 sticks) unsalted butter
Juice of 1 small lemon
Salt

HAZELNUT-LEMON BUTTER

FOR 10 TO 12, AS A GARNISH OR MADE INTO A SAUCE

1 cup skinless hazelnuts
1/2 pound (2 sticks) unsalted
    butter
2 teaspoons fresh lemon juice
1/4 teaspoon grated lemon zest
Salt and freshly ground black
    pepper

This particularly delicious butter, fragrant with toasted hazelnuts, is terrific served with steamed vegetables or on grilled or barbecued shrimp.

1. Preheat the oven to 375°F. Place the hazelnuts on a cookie sheet and toast them, turning as necessary, until they are golden and very fragrant, about 14 minutes. Allow to cool.

2. Add the nuts to the bowl of a food processor and process until you have a nut butter, 1½ to 2 minutes. Scrape down the sides of the bowl as necessary. Add the remaining ingredients and process until well blended, about 1½ minutes. Form into logs or make into a sauce.

Spice Rubs

These are wonderful to have on hand. They add savory flavor rubbed into fish flesh before broiling or grilling, or may be used as at-table seasonings. Though you may buy prepared rubs, your own are invariably better as you can assure yourself of the freshness of their ingredients. Store all rubs in glass jars or resealable plastic bags in a cool, dark place.

MEDITERRANEAN RUB

FOR ABOUT 1/3 CUP

3 tablespoons herbes de
    Provence
1 tablespoon dried thyme
1/2 tablespoon dried marjoram
1 tablespoon dried oregano
1 tablespoon dried basil

This richly fragrant rub, with its piquant herbiness, is especially good for firm fish like tuna, swordfish, and marlin. You may adjust the quantities to please your palate. Use dried herbs only.

Combine the herbs in a small bowl. Before using, rub between your fingers. Store as described above.

ROSY FISH RUB

FOR ABOUT ⅓ CUP

Perfect for use on mild fish like sole, snapper, or cod, this rub adds appetizing color as well as great flavor.

Combine the ingredients in a small bowl. Store as described above.

4 tablespoons sweet paprika,
    preferably imported
    Hungarian
2 tablespoons celery salt
1 tablespoon garlic powder

MOROCCAN RUB

FOR ABOUT ¼ CUP

This rub, which evokes the sunny, sensual flavors of Morocco, works particularly well on tuna, mackerel, and salmon. It is also good rubbed on fish portions before moist-broiling. If you have a coffee or spice grinder, buy coriander and cumin seeds and grind them before blending.

Grind the spices if using whole. Combine all ingredients. Store as described above.

2 tablespoons coriander,
    ground or seeds
1 tablespoon cumin, ground
    or seeds
1 teaspoon cayenne

PIQUANT ROASTING PASTE

FOR ABOUT ⅓ CUP

The addition of olive oil turns this rub into an easy-to-use paste. Excellent to use on whole fish or large portions before searing, then finishing the fish in the oven. Particularly good on swordfish.

Combine dry ingredients in a bowl and drizzle in oil, stirring. May be stored refrigerated.

2 teaspoons dry mustard
½ teaspoon turmeric
5 bay leaves, ground
1 tablespoon olive oil

Stocks and Broths

Stock in the refrigerator or freezer makes your working seafood kitchen *work*. Please take the little time necessary to prepare these culinary fundamentals. One weekend day spent making stock means many months of fast and delicious seafood cooking.

Stock can be stored in a variety of ways:

- In a bowl, where it will keep for one week refrigerated.

- In 1-cup portions. Fill resealable plastic bags with about 1 cup of cooled stock and squeeze as much air as possible out of the bags. Store the bags in the refrigerator for one week or in the freezer for two months. Or use close-sealing plastic containers of the appropriate size.

- In ice-cube portions, which are especially handy when small amounts of stock are required. Pour cooled stock into the trays, cover them with plastic film to prevent freezer burn, and freeze. Pop the cubes into resealable plastic bags and store frozen. One cube of stock equals 1½ tablespoons of stock; a cup will require 1¼ cubes.

- Reduce the stock to make a glace (page 70).

CHICKEN STOCK
MAKES 2 QUARTS

3½ pounds chicken bones
(preferably necks and backs),
giblets included if desired
2½ quarts water
1 medium onion, cut into sixths
2 carrots, peeled and cut into
2-inch lengths
2 celery stalks, cut into 2-inch
lengths

I'm frequently asked why I use chicken stock in my seafood recipes. The answer is that it gives needed body to sauces and other preparations. A light chicken stock is required for seafood recipes—light, but with depth of flavor and a good amber color. If your completed stock lacks any of these, make certain, first, that you've used a sufficient quantity of bones. Stock that is pallid after the required cooking time can be cooked down to intensify its flavor.

To make life as easy as possible gather bones beforehand and freeze them. Don't throw away those little bags of poultry innards that come with whole birds. Remove livers from the packages (store them separately), then rewrap and freeze the necks and giblets. Unless you're a chicken wing fanatic, remove the wing tips and store them, too. You may also use bones from boning breasts or cooked chicken carcasses (but store cooked and uncooked bones separately to avoid cross-contamination). In no time you'll have all the the chicken parts you require to make a wonderful pot of stock.

1. Rinse the bones and giblets, if using, well under cold running water.

2. In a stockpot, combine the bones and water. Bring to the boil, reduce the heat, and simmer. Remove the scum (blood residue, proteins, and albumin) that rises to the top of the stock with a skimmer. You may have to do this twice. Simmer slowly for 1¼ hours.

3. Add the vegetables and simmer for 45 minutes longer. Strain the stock into a second pot. Fill the kitchen sink half full of cold water and add ice cubes. Place the pot in this ice-water bath to cool the stock quickly (this reduces the possibility of spoilage). When the stock is cool, transfer it to a bowl and refrigerate it.

4. Remove the fat that has solidified on the surface of the stock and store the stock.

FISH STOCK
MAKES 2 QUARTS

Unlike meat stocks, fish stocks, fumets, and court bouillons (concentrated fish stocks and fish-cooking mediums) require little cooking time. Ask your seafood seller for the fish bones you'll need—those from flatfish such as flounder, halibut, or fluke produce the best stock, but bones from nonoily roundfish like tile, cod, or rockfish work well, too. Store them in your refrigerator for two days or in the freezer for up to two weeks. Unfrozen bones are best, as they produce the clearest stock. You can also use shrimp or lobster shells for the stock; store them the refrigerator for at least two months or in the freezer for one month.

3½ pounds fish bones from nonoily roundfish, flatfish, or a combination

2½ quarts water

2 leeks, white parts only, split lengthwise, well washed, and cut into 2-inch lengths

2 celery stalks, cut into 2-inch lengths

2 bay leaves

6 black peppercorns

1. In a stockpot, combine the bones, water, leeks, celery, and bay leaves. Bring to the boil, then reduce the heat and simmer gently for 25 minutes. Remove any scum that rises to the surface with a skimmer.

2. Add the peppercorns and simmer 10 minutes longer. Strain the stock into a second pot. Fill the kitchen sink half full of water and add ice cubes. Place the pot in the ice-water bath to cool the stock quickly. When cool, refrigerate or freeze.

FISH FUMET

FOR 2 QUARTS

1 tablespoon unsalted butter

3 pounds fish bones and
   trimmings from nonoily white
   fish such as snapper, cod,
   tile, or rockfish and/or trimmings from flatfish such as
   flounder, halibut, or fluke

2 leeks, white parts only, split
   lengthwise, well washed, and
   cut into 2-inch lengths

2 celery stalks

2 cups dry white wine

2 quarts water

2 bay leaves

6 black peppercorns

Fish stock is a relatively light cooking medium; fumet is more richly flavored—sometimes concentrated—and therefore best for making sauces or as a substitute for fish stock whenever you want greater depth of flavor. Fumet is prepared with fish trimmings such as belly flaps as well as bones; the trimmings give the fumet extra body and flavor. Store fumet as you would chicken stock.

1. In a stockpot, melt the butter over medium-low heat. Add the fish bones, leeks, and celery and cook, stirring occasionally, until the leeks have softened, 6 to 8 minutes. Do not allow the vegetables to color.

2. Add the wine, increase the heat to medium, and simmer until it has reduced by one-half, 5 to 8 minutes. Add the water and bring to the boil. Reduce the heat and simmer gently for 25 minutes. Remove any scum that rises to the surface with a skimmer. Add the bay leaves and peppercorns and simmer 10 minutes longer.

3. Fill the kitchen sink half full of water and add ice cubes. Strain the fumet into a second pot. Place the pot in the ice-water bath to cool the fumet quickly. When cool, refrigerate or freeze the fumet.

SHELLFISH BROTH

FOR 1 QUART

1 tablespoon olive oil

1 pound shrimp shells, or 2½
   pounds crab or lobster shells,
   or a combination

3 medium shallots, sliced

2 tablespoons tomato paste

This shellfish-based broth is used as a base for soups or in shellfish recipes. Use it in place of fish stock in any recipe that would benefit from the taste of shellfish—in the Risotto with Octopus (page 280), for example, or the All-Seafood Paella (page 278). Make it with stored shells from cooked or uncooked seafood.

1. In a large stockpot, bring the oil to the smoking point over high heat. Add the shells and cook, stirring occasionally, 8 to 10 minutes, or until bright red if uncooked.

2. Add the shallots and tomato paste and cook until the bottom of the pan develops a coating, or *fond*, 3 to 5 minutes. Add the wine, scraping up the *fond*.

3. Add the water or water-stock mixture, herbs, and garlic. Reduce the heat and simmer until the broth is richly flavored, about 45 minutes. Season with the salt. Strain and use or store.

Note: If you're in a hurry, you can make the broth with shells, water, and aromatics (shallots, garlic, and herbs) only. Place all the ingredients in a large stockpot, bring to the boil, reduce the heat, and simmer until the broth has good flavor, about 40 minutes. This broth doesn't have the richness of the full-dress version, but works well to add depth to seafood preparations.

³/₄ cup white wine

5 cups water, or 2¹/₂ cups each water and Fish Stock (page 67)

¹/₃ bunch fresh thyme sprigs

¹/₃ bunch fresh tarragon sprigs

2 garlic cloves, slightly crushed with the flat of a knife

Salt

COURT BOUILLON

FOR 2 QUARTS

A court bouillon is not a stock but an aromatic liquid in which fish is poached or braised. As its name implies (*court* means "short" in French), it is quickly made. It can be prepared beforehand and refrigerated or frozen. If using the bouillon to poach a mild nonoily fish, it may be reused two or three times for any fish; if used for oily fish, it may be reused for the same fish only. Court bouillon that has been used for poaching may be refrigerated for up to five days, or frozen, and then used again.

Having court bouillon on hand makes short work of such dishes as the Poached Joint of Cod (page 196) or the Poached Whole Bass with New Potatoes and Spring Vegetables (page 197).

1. In a stockpot, combine all the ingredients except the peppercorns. Bring to the boil, reduce the heat, and simmer 30 minutes.

2. Add the peppercorns. Simmer 10 minutes longer and strain. The Court Bouillon is ready for use or may be refrigerated or frozen.

2 quarts water

2 cups dry white wine

¹/₄ cup white wine vinegar

1 medium onion, sliced

1 bunch fresh Italian (flat-leaf) parsley

6 fresh thyme sprigs, or 1 teaspoon dried

¹/₂ lemon

2 bay leaves

5 celery stalks, cut into 2-inch lengths

8 black peppercorns

DASHI

FOR 1 QUART

1 quart water

A 2-inch piece of konbu (kelp)

2 tablespoons mirin (sweet sake)

2 tablespoons sake

2 heaping tablespoons katsuo-
bushi (dried bonito flakes)

2 tablespoons soy sauce

Dashi is Japan's all-purpose soup stock and the primary ingredient in the fine soup known as miso. It is easily made. (Information about ingredients may be found earlier in this chapter and in Chapter 7, "Sushi, Sashimi, and Other Raw Specialties.")

In a medium nonreactive saucepan, combine the water and the konbu. Bring to the boil, turn off the heat, and add the mirin and sake. Sprinkle with the katsuo-bushi and allow the mixture to stand for 2 minutes; add the soy sauce. Strain and the dashi is ready to use. Both the bonito flakes and the konbu can be stored for reuse in secondary dashi, a vegetable cooking broth and soup seasoning. This primary dashi may be stored for up to three days in the refrigerator or frozen, though flavor will be lost.

Glaces, or Glazes

Any of the above stocks may be reduced to make a firm, jellylike flavor essence called a glace, or glaze. Glaces may be reconstituted to make stock or used full strength to deepen the flavor of sauces or soups. They are wonderful to have on hand. Glaces take up little refrigerator space and will last unfrozen much longer than stocks stored similarly—up to one month. The only maintenance they require is the occasional scraping off of any surface mold that may form. The mold is perfectly harmless and in no way affects the quality of the glace. Of course, glaces may also be frozen.

To make glace, reduce stock slowly over medium-low heat until it is syrupy. Properly reduced stock will coat a teaspoon lightly. You may use any amount of stock you like, but if you begin with a large quantity you will have to change to a smaller saucepan as the stock reduces to avoid burning. One quart of stock will yield ½ cup of glace. Pour the completed glace into little jars or other heatproof containers and allow to cool before capping. Refrigerate or freeze.

To reconstitute the glace to make stock, melt it in a quantity of water equivalent to its original volume minus the volume of the reduced stock. For example, to retrieve your original quart of stock from the ½ cup of glace derived from it, you would have to melt the glace in 3½ cups of water.

Sauces and Condiments

I call for a number of sauces throughout the book; these should be in your permanent repertoire.

HOMEMADE MAYONNAISE
FOR 1½ CUPS

Homemade mayonnaise is so easy to make and so vastly superior to anything you can buy that I'm surprised more cooks don't keep it on hand.

Raw egg yolks, from which mayonnaise is made, are notoriously vulnerable to bacterial infection, but you need never worry if you use uncracked eggs whose yolks are odorless and without discoloration. Never let yolks or the finished sauce stand unrefrigerated for long periods, especially in hot weather.

Mayonnaise will last four to six days in the refrigerator; it welcomes additional flavorings, as in the variations below.

2 large egg yolks

1 tablespoon Dijon mustard

1 tablespoon Champagne
  vinegar or red wine vinegar

1½ cups vegetable oil

Salt

1. In a medium nonreactive bowl, combine the yolks, mustard, and vinegar. Whisk well.
2. Still whisking vigorously, add the oil slowly in a thin stream. When all the oil has been added and a creamy emulsion has formed, add the salt.

MAYONNAISE WITH FINE HERBS

FOR 1½ CUPS

1 teaspoon chopped fresh chives

2 teaspoons chopped fresh
Italian (flat-leaf) parsley

½ teaspoon chopped fresh
tarragon leaves

½ teaspoon chopped fresh
chervil

1½ cups Homemade
Mayonnaise (page 71)

Spread this intensely herby mayonnaise on a sandwich made with sautéed sole fillets and watercress. It's also great in fish salads. The mayonnaise will keep refrigerated for two to three days.

Combine all the ingredients in a small bowl and mix well.

ORANGE MAYONNAISE

FOR 1½ CUPS

2½ cups fresh orange juice

1½ cups Homemade
Mayonnaise (page 71)

1 teaspoon finely grated
orange zest

This is wonderful with fried fish or cold seafood of all kinds. Use it also as a dressing for cold lobster salad. Orange Mayonnaise will keep refrigerated two to three days.

1. In a medium nonreactive saucepan over high heat, reduce the orange juice to ¼ cup. Allow it to cool to room temperature.

2. Combine the juice with the mayonnaise in a small bowl. Add the orange zest and mix well.

TOMATO MAYONNAISE

FOR 1 ½ CUPS

Tomato Mayonnaise makes a good case for following the European custom of serving mayonnaise with it French fries. Try it as a dip for Belgian Fries (page 297) or with cold shrimp. It will keep refrigerated for two to three days.

1. In a small nonreactive saucepan, heat the oil until hot over medium heat. Add the shallots, garlic, and tomatoes and cook until the tomatoes soften, 6 to 7 minutes.

2. Add the tomato paste and the basil and cook 5 minutes more. Remove the pan from the heat, allow the mixture to come to room temperature, then refrigerate until cool. (This ensures that the mixture will not curdle the mayonnaise when it is added.)

3. Add the mixture to the mayonnaise and blend well. Using a plastic spatula, put the mayonnaise through a fine strainer. Add drops of Tabasco, if you wish.

1 teaspoon olive oil

2 medium shallots, finely sliced

2 garlic cloves, minced

2 medium tomatoes, cored, seeded, and coarsely chopped

1 teaspoon tomato paste

6 large basil leaves, coarsely torn

1 ½ cups Homemade Mayonnaise (page 71)

Tabasco Sauce (optional)

BLACK BEAN MAYONNAISE

FOR 1 ½ CUPS

Luscious in Poached Salmon Salad with Radicchio and Black Bean Mayonnaise (page 119), this Asian-inspired accompaniment is also great served with cold cooked shellfish like lobster or crab. It will keep refrigerated two to three days.

In a medium nonreactive saucepan combine all the ingredients except the mayonnaise and the chives. Reduce the mixture until almost dry, 8 to 10 minutes. Cool. Add the mayonnaise and chives and blend.

1 medium shallot, minced

1 small garlic clove, minced

¼ cup sake

1 tablespoon rinsed and coarsely chopped canned black beans

1 teaspoon soy sauce

½ cup Homemade Mayonnaise (page 71), or best-quality store-bought

1 tablespoon chopped fresh chives

PICKLED PLUM MAYONNAISE

FOR 1 CUP

1 cup Homemade Mayonnaise
(page 71), or best-quality
store-bought

2 tablespoons pitted, mashed
pickled plums (umeboshi)

1 teaspoon soy sauce

2 teaspoons chopped fresh
chives

4 dashes of Tabasco Sauce

$1/2$ teaspoon fresh lemon juice

This tart-sweet, mayonnaise-based sauce gets its fruity excitement from umeboshi, Japanese pickled plums. It's another sauce that's great not only for fried food but as a sandwich spread. Umeboshi are available at Japanese and other Asian food stores. The sauce keeps refrigerated for one week.

Combine all the ingredients in a medium bowl and mix well.

CURRY APPLE MAYONNAISE

FOR ABOUT 1 CUP

1 teaspoon olive oil

1 medium shallot, minced

1 small green apple, peeled,
cored, and finely diced

1 heaping tablespoon best-quality
curry powder

2 tablespoons dry white wine

1 tablespoon minced fresh
cilantro (coriander)

1 cup Homemade Mayonnaise
(page 71), or best-quality
store-bought

Salt and freshly ground black pepper

The warmth of curry and the aromatic tartness of green apple blend beautifully in this sauce. Serve it with cold shrimp or as a dressing for fish salads.

1. In a medium skillet, heat the oil over medium heat. Add the shallot and apple and sauté until softened without coloring, about 3 minutes.
2. Add the curry powder, reduce the heat, and cook, stirring constantly, until the curry is fragrant, about 1 minute. Add the wine and allow it to evaporate until the mixture is almost dry, about 2 minutes. Transfer the mixture to a nonreactive bowl, cool, and refrigerate until chilled.
3. Add the cilantro and mayonnaise and mix well. Season with the salt and pepper.

ROASTED RED PEPPER AÏOLI

MAKES ABOUT 1½ CUPS

Aïoli is the classic French sauce that takes its name from *ail*, which means garlic, and *oli*, oil in the Provençal dialect. It's the traditional mayonnaiselike accompaniment to the dish of boiled seafood, meats, and vegetables also called aïoli.

My own savory version contains roasted red bell peppers; you'll find yourself using it not only as a seafood accompaniment but also as a tongue-tingling fillip added to the soup just before serving.

Roasted Red Pepper Aïoli lasts four to six days in the refrigerator.

1. Put the yolks, garlic, peppers, and lemon juice in the bowl of a food processor. Pulse and then process until the mixture is smooth, about 2 minutes.

2. With the machine running, slowly pour the oil through the feed tube until a creamy emulsion has formed. Season to taste with the Tabasco, salt, and pepper, being particularly generous with the pepper.

2 egg yolks

1½ tablespoons garlic, minced

2 red bell peppers, roasted,
   peeled and seeded

Juice of ½ lemon

1⅓ cups olive oil,
   approximately

Tabasco Sauce

Salt and freshly ground black
   pepper

BEURRE BLANC

FOR ABOUT 2¼ CUPS

½ pound cold unsalted butter,
   cut into tablespoons

2 medium shallots, thinly sliced

1 teaspoon Champagne vinegar
   or other white wine vinegar

2 cups dry white wine

2 fresh thyme sprigs

2 tablespoons heavy (whipping)
   cream

Salt and freshly ground
   black pepper

Delicately creamy and flavored with a touch of thyme, this Beurre Blanc is the perfect accompaniment to many seafood dishes. There is no magic involved in its successful preparation. Just remember to keep the heat under the reduced ingredients very low as you add the cold butter gradually. The butter must not melt, but remain in creamy suspension.

1. In a heavy, medium saucepan, melt 1 tablespoon of the butter over medium heat. Add the shallots and sauté without browning until soft, about 2 minutes.

2. Add the vinegar, wine, and thyme and reduce by two-thirds, 6 to 8 minutes.

3. Add the cream and reduce the mixture until thick, about 3 minutes. Turn the heat to very low and whisk in the remaining butter, adding first 1 tablespoon and then 2 tablespoons at a time to form a light emulsion. If the butter gives any indication of melting, remove the pan from the stove.

4. Season the warm sauce with the salt and pepper and strain.

TRUE ORANGE SABAYON

FOR ABOUT 1 CUP

2 large egg yolks

1 large egg

1 teaspoon grated orange zest

2 tablespoons fresh orange juice

2 tablespoons dry white wine

6 dashes of Tabasco Sauce

½ teaspoon salt

I think of this sauce as the Hollandaise of modern seafood cookery. Especially good with poached or grilled fish, this sabayon, with its sunny orange flavor and illusion of richness, is a sauce every cook should know.

1. Combine all the ingredients in a medium nonreactive bowl. Set up a double boiler, adding 3 inches of water to the bottom pot. Bring to the boil.

2. Whisk the ingredients until frothy. Pour into the double boiler and continue to whisk until the sauce is lightly thickened, about 7 minutes. If the sauce seems to be thickening too rapidly, lift the top pot off the heat, whisking continuously to disperse heat. Return the pan to the double boiler and continue whisking until done.

Dipping Sauces

Whether piquant or cooling, suave or down-to-earth, these savory sauces add color, dash, and dimension to the foods they accompany. They may be made in advance and stored as indicated.

ORANGE-LEMON HOT SAUCE

FOR 3 CUPS

A perfect blend of tangy citrus with the heat of sambal oelek and the burnished sweetness of honey, great with fried foods. The sauce keeps refrigerated up to two weeks.

Combine all the ingredients in the bowl of a food processor and process until roughly pureed, about 2 minutes. Do not overblend; the sauce should be somewhat chunky.

2 oranges, cut into 8 equal pieces

1 lemon, peeled and cut in half horizontally

1 cup orange marmalade

1 heaping tablespoon honey

2 teaspoons dry sherry

1 tablespoon Champagne vinegar or other white wine vinegar

2 tablespoons orange juice

1 tablespoon sambal oelek, or 2 teaspoons Chinese chili paste

1 teaspoon salt

PICKAPEPPA COCKTAIL SAUCE

FOR 2 CUPS

1 cup ketchup

4 tablespoons coarsely chopped
    fresh horseradish

1/4 cup tomato juice

2 tablespoons fresh lime juice

1/2 cup Pickapeppa Sauce

3 whole cloves, ground

3 allspice berries, ground

1 quarter-size slice peeled
    fresh ginger

1/2 teaspoon lemongrass powder,
    or 1 lemongrass stalk

Salt

This tomato-based sauce is made with the bottled Jamaican chili pepper sauce called Pickapeppa. It has a rich, sweet-sour kick—save some for hamburgers. The sauce, unstrained, will keep in the refrigerator for up to two weeks.

Add all the ingredients except the salt to the bowl of a food processor and process until well blended, about 3 minutes. Just before serving, strain the sauce by working it through the strainer mesh with a wooden spatula. Season with the salt.

SPICY HONEY MUSTARD

FOR 1 1/4 CUPS

1/2 cup Dijon mustard

1/4 cup honey

3/4 teaspoon Tabasco Sauce

1 teaspoon salt

1/3 cup vegetable oil

This sweet-hot sauce is especially good with tempura vegetables. It's lighter than a mayonnaise, creamier than a vinaigrette, and absolutely addictive. It keeps, refrigerated, for at least two weeks.

1. In a medium nonreactive bowl, whisk together the mustard, honey, Tabasco, and salt.

2. Slowly whisk in the oil in a thin stream to form a light emulsion. Adjust the sauce with more honey if too tart, or with additional salt if too sweet.

BEST TARTAR SAUCE

FOR 1¾ CUPS

I've always been a tartar sauce fan, even when the sauce at hand was far from perfect. My interpretation, made with chives, chervil, and crunchy cornichons, will dispel any doubts you may have about the sauce. It's excellent as a dip (see Grouper Beignets with Beet Chips, page 214, or Golden Tuna Cornmeal Dumplings, page 255), and also makes a wonderful sandwich spread (it's super in the Corn-Fried Oyster Po'Boy, page 300). Try mixing the sauce with leftover cooked fish for a delicious salad. It keeps refrigerated for three to four days.

Combine all the ingredients except the salt in a medium bowl. Season with the salt to taste.

2 teaspoons chopped fresh chives

1 teaspoon chopped fresh chervil
   or parsley

2 teaspoons mashed capers

1 teaspoon chopped cornichons

1 teaspoon Worcestershire sauce

¼ teaspoon cayenne

½ teaspoon grated lemon zest

½ teaspoon fresh lime juice

1½ cups Homemade Mayonnaise
   (page 71), or best-quality
   store-bought

Salt

PONZU

FOR 1½ CUPS

Ponzu, the savory Japanese dipping sauce associated with sashimi, is great with all kinds of fried seafood. It keeps for one week.

1. In a small nonreactive saucepan, bring the soy sauce, vinegar, and stock to the boil. Add the cornstarch mixture and cook until the sauce is lightly thickened, about 2 minutes.
2. Add the lemon and lime juices. Transfer to a bowl to cool, then refrigerate. Serve at room temperature.

⅓ cup soy sauce

⅓ cup rice vinegar

½ cup Chicken Stock (page 66)

1 teaspoon cornstarch, dissolved
   in 2 tablespoons soy sauce

Juice of ½ lemon

Juice of ½ lime

PREPARATION STRATEGIES

It seems obvious, but most cooks don't realize the time they can save by thinking beforehand about what they intend to prepare. I don't mean in the morning for the evening meal ahead; what is needed is some strategic planning that takes into account the cook's schedule, and that of family members, for the upcoming week or longer. Here's the blueprint for cooking great food with maximum kitchen efficiency:

• *Budget your cooking time.* What does the week look like? Begin to think more globally about meal planning. I don't mean that you should draw up calendars of menus, which can't begin to take into account daily appetites or what will be freshest in the marketplace. Rather, have some sense of what an upcoming week will hold. Once you look at the larger picture you can begin to match meals to schedules, and tasks to meals. You'll know what you'll want to have on hand so you can budget your cooking time.

• *Make the dish in your head.* Do what we do in the restaurant kitchen: think a dish or a dinner 100 percent through before preparing it. This means reading a recipe thoroughly before starting to cook it and noting what can be done hours, or even days, in advance.

• *Do prep.* For example, peeled garlic cloves, onions, and shallots can all be stored, moistened with vegetable oil and well covered, in the refrigerator for one week.

Blanch carrots, broccoli, and red peppers and store them in resealable plastic bags. Julienne or dice hard soup vegetables and store them the same way.

Marinades can be made in advance—the flavored oils on pages 60 to 61 make spectacular marinades—as can fish rubs (pages 64 to 65). Keep marinades and flavored oils on hand as a permanent bath for fish or shellfish you'll grill or broil.

Let me reiterate the importance of having your own best-quality stocks made and frozen in 1-quart containers for use in so many of the recipes in this book and your own day-to-day cooking.

• *Assemble ingredients first.* Invest in a number of small bowls (or use paper bathroom cups—no washup). Put your prepped ingredients in the bowls or cups and arrange them on a small tray, one for each dish. Then cook away. You'll be amazed at the immediate dip in stress that results from working with the bowls. If you have sufficient refrigerator space, store prepped ingredients in the bowls. That way you've really created the shortest distance between cooking and serving. Planning is what a working seafood kitchen is all about

4. A NOTE ON UNDERCOOKING AND OVERCOOKING

Of all the culinary worries that trouble both would-be and experienced seafood cooks, those of over- or undercooking probably rank first. It's understandable—seafood protein is delicate, and sweet, toothsome flesh can become dry in an instant. On the other hand, undercooking is hardly desirable.

Opinions have varied over time as to what constitutes properly cooked fish and shellfish. Anyone who has dipped into cookbooks written as recently as ten years ago may smile over their frequent instruction to "cook the fish until it flakes." To me fish that flakes apart is fish that's been overcooked. So at what point is fish properly cooked?

Like many cooks today, both at home and in restaurant kitchens, I believe that most fish and many shellfish are best when not completely cooked through, so that flesh is medium rare. Flavor and texture are better, truer, and there's no fishy smell or taste that develops inevitably when flesh has cooked too long. By medium-rare I mean that the fish is cooked about 75 percent through; the interior 25 percent is allowed to become warm, but just that. If this degree of doneness makes you uneasy, you are of course free to cook your fish any way you choose—cooking must be about making people happy. But let me tell you a story.

I had a man come into the restaurant who swore he hated fish. He had tried it again and again, but had never managed to down more than a forkful. This was not my first tough case, so I was prepared. I told the man that I would make something delicious for him, but I sneakily neglected to say that it wouldn't be fish. I sent out some seared tuna that I serve almost rare, cooked about 30 percent through. My guest was obliging and dug into the fish. I think you know the rest. Soon he was asking for more, telling me the tuna was "the best filet mignon" he had ever eaten.

The point isn't that I had fooled him into thinking he was eating something he had not; rather, he was responding to the tuna's unexpected freshness and purity of flavor. I've followed my penchant for less cooking with the recipes in this book. What I call done in most cases is on the rare side of just done. The exceptions include cod as well as tile and grouper, which need to be cooked about 95 percent through to become tender and palatable. Of course, you may—and should—adjust cooking times to please yourself. And you should be aware that any fish that is not cooked through should be considered raw—that is, you must observe all the rules concerning freshness and safety that apply to eating raw fish (see Chapter 7, "Sushi, Sashimi, and Other Raw Specialties"). Let me add immediately that the risks are few while the rewards of medium-rare or barely cooked-through fish are great.

Though I wish I could, I can't make *specific* rules for cooking fish and shellfish. (I don't hold with the Canadian rule for doneness determined by measuring the thickest part of a fish and cooking it for 10 minutes per inch because you'll end up with partly overcooked flesh—and, in any case, every piece of fish has its own cooking requirements.) I wish things worked the way they do for determining when your steak is done, but I can't say, as others have, that your fish is properly cooked when it feels like the tip of your nose or the thick of your thumb. Nonetheless, there are some general recommendations about doneness I *can* offer.

When in doubt, err on the side of undercooking. Cut into the fish you're preparing and have a look. Overcooked flesh is hard to the touch and without any differentiation in color or translucency; the flesh will flake when touched with the tip of your knife. Stop cooking the fish while it is still resistant to the touch, when (as I often direct) it is on the soft side of resilient, or when cod, grouper, or tile have reached the yielding stage. The center of a fillet or steak, or the flesh along the center bone of a whole fish, should be slightly translucent, or just opaque to slightly milky if you like your fish cooked longer than I do. Swordfish, tuna, shark, and marlin—game fish—must not be allowed to cook through because they lack fat. These fish are really best when cooked medium-rare, or rare for purists.

For shellfish, "just done" is the rule of thumb. This means that cooked shrimp should have a slightly translucent center rather than being firm and chalky-colored throughout. The same goes for lobster. Hard-shell crab needs to be cooked to flaking, but soft-shells should cook until just done.

We've all been taught that bivalves need to be cooked until their shells open, but mussels can still be underdone at that point. Check to make sure that they've lost all trace of sliminess, then remove them from the heat. Because clams are thick-shelled, they *are* done when their shells open. Oysters need only the briefest of cooking—enough to warm them through and curl their edges.

Scallops require the same treatment as tuna. They should remain slightly translucent at their centers. Unlike other kinds of seafood, however, properly cooked scallops feel firm. Cut into one to check for doneness; its center should be warm to the touch.

Baby squid can go rubbery very quickly if the cook is not attentive. There are two ways around this problem. One is to be vigilant and make sure the squid doesn't cook beyond the just-warm stage, about 2 minutes; the other is to cook through the toughness until the squid is tender again, about 1 hour. When dealing with mature squid, long cooking is necessary for enjoyable eating.

Because of the density of its flesh, all octopus needs long cooking. If possible, buy baby octopus that's been precooked—it's easier to handle.

Like everything else in cooking, practice makes perfect. Once you begin to prepare seafood attentively you'll learn just what you and your stove need to do to achieve the degree of doneness you prefer. There's no mystery to it—just keep on cooking and tasting; poke your fish, cut into it, get to know it as it cooks. The signs that guide you to success reveal themselves from the first.

The Recipes

5. SOUPS, STEWS, AND CHOWDERS

I grew up eating homemade soups. There wasn't a cough, sneeze, or holiday that didn't prompt my mother to make her rich, soothing chicken soup. I love making soup because I can harmonize many flavors to create a single dominant taste, the objective when preparing a soup. Mom's soup, for example, was absolutely about the flavor of chicken. What's your soup supposed to be about? When you can answer that question you're on your way to assuring yourself soup with real character.

What I like especially about seafood soups, stews, and chowders is that they take very little time to prepare. (Even fish stock is quickly made—fish bones, unlike their animal equivalents, give their all within minutes.) Seafood soups are made by preparing a savory flavor base, adding liquid, then putting in the fish or shellfish. You cook the seafood through—a matter of minutes—and soup's on. Absolutely Simple Oyster Stew can be put together in a half-hour. The Scallop Vegetable Soup with Shiitake Mushrooms, a blend of root vegetables and plump sea scallops, is just as quick to fix. The other soups, including a light, Asian-inspired Miso Soup with Shrimp, an unconventional lobster bisque made without stock or pureed rice, and a fiery crab, lobster, and shrimp Cajun gumbo are also done without fuss.

Soups are very forgiving and adapt to whatever ingredients are in the refrigerator. (Which doesn't mean that you can just empty the fridge into a pot; soups must be thought through.) The mild, sweet taste of seafood combines easily with a wide variety of flavors. For example, suppose you want to make the scallop soup with shiitake mushrooms. You haven't got the scallops, but you do have shrimp in the freezer. Use them instead. No shiitakes? Try another mushroom of comparable "strength." If you've got an abundant store of celery in the vegetable bin, slice some into the soup. You can even play with your soup medium. If you substitute dashi for fish stock the next time you prepare a clear soup, you'll enjoy a subtle new seafood dish. Just remember to let proportion, balance, and harmony guide your hand. In soup making this means that all your ingredients must support the soup's "idea"; if you're preparing a fresh tomato soup, for example, you wouldn't want to compromise the taste of the fruit with a too-insistent herb presence or with too much heat from Tabasco Sauce or cayenne.

Good soups require good stock. Stocks take very little supervised time to prepare. They simmer obediently on the back of the stove while you're doing other things. A few hours spent making and freezing them will reward you with delicious, quickly prepared soups, stews, and chowders whenever you feel like them (see Chapter 3, "The Working Seafood Kitchen," for the information you need to create your own stock pantry).

Many of my soup recipes use a combination of fish and chicken stock. What's chicken stock doing in soup recipes based on seafood? Providing silken body and mitigating the tendency of fish stock to overwhelm the soup it appears in. My Spicy Conch Chowder with Okra, Chayote, and Tomatoes owes its rich texture and well-calibrated piquancy to this two-stock technique. I never use starch thickeners when animal protein will do the trick.

It's best not to prepare any soup in an aluminum or tin-lined copper pot. The aluminum can discolor the food and the tin can leach into it. I often use a well-seasoned cast-iron cauldron that can go directly from the stove to the table—it's a treasure; lacking that, you can use enameled iron or stainless steel.

Finish soups and chowders with flavorful oils. Olive oil, sesame oil, or dragon oil (also known as chili oil) add depth and variety of flavor (or spiciness) when added to soups at the last minute. Olive oil, for example, makes a great addition to a soup like the Pumpkin Soup with Bay Scallops and Mushrooms. Check out pages 60 to 61 for flavored-oil recipes.

I like to have *warm* bread when I eat soup; it's one of the few occasions on which I heat bread. But I don't butter it—butter coats the palate unpleasantly and interferes with my soup sense. Keep a pepper grinder and coarse sea salt on the table. I don't think sea salt is a food affectation—it really does taste more lively than other salts. If you're serving soup as a main course—and most of the soups in this chapter are meant to be eaten that way—give each diner two ladlefuls from the pot at a time—no more—and tell everyone there are seconds. That way, more good soup stays hot for additional helpings.

ABSOLUTELY SIMPLE OYSTER STEW

FOR 4

3 cups half-and-half

1 tablespoon Worcestershire sauce

1 teaspoon Tabasco Sauce, or to taste

1/2 teaspoon fresh lemon juice

20 oysters, shucked, with their liquor

Salt and freshly ground black pepper

3 large fresh artichoke bottoms, cooked, or 1 cup flash-frozen, defrosted, or canned, thoroughly rinsed under cold water (optional)

COOK'S OPTION

You can use 32 shucked cherrystone clams in place of the oysters.

I promise you—this oyster stew is not only the best you'll ever eat but the easiest to prepare. Creamy, soothing, and brimming with plump oysters, it surpasses the great Bourbon Street stews I savored as an apprentice in New Orleans. And it's ready in just fifteen minutes.

Remember that oyster stews must never actually "stew." The oysters *simmer* until just done, which takes no time at all. And use only the best oysters. Clean, coppery-tasting malpeques from Prince Edward Island, Canada, are the most wonderful oyster, in my opinion, but any absolutely fresh variety will do beautifully. I've added artichoke bottoms for a toothsome garnish; their pleasing texture and subtle nuttiness underline the stew's pure, rich goodness.

1. In a small saucepan, bring the half-and-half to the boil.
2. Stir in the Worcestershire, Tabasco, and lemon juice. Add the oysters with their liquor, reduce the heat, and simmer just until the edges of the oysters curl, 3 to 4 minutes. Be careful not to overcook the oysters.
3. Season the stew with the salt and pepper. Cut the artichoke bottoms in eighths, if using, add, and serve. Accompany the stew with Pilot or oyster crackers.

MATELOTE OF MONKFISH

FOR 4

I made my first matelote, the great French fisherman's stew, at a friend's restaurant in Dijon. I was really excited about cooking fish in red wine—the idea was new to me then. Now I'm a major fan of red wine with fish, a traditional pairing I wish everyone would try at least once. Red wine has more depth and complexity than white, and when not too tannic, it marries perfectly with all but the lightest, mildest seafood dishes. If I never had white wine again, with or without seafood, I really wouldn't miss it.

Matelotes typically use eel, but monkfish, with its sweet lobsterlike flesh, makes a marvelous stew and is certainly easier to prepare. Serve this fine heady dish with homemade croutons or freshly boiled new potatoes. Mash the potatoes into the matelote as you eat it—and drink more red wine!

1. In a heavy-bottomed soup pot, heat 1 tablespoon of the oil over medium heat until hot. Sear the monkfish in 2 batches until well colored on both sides. Remove to a plate and set aside.

2. Add the vegetables to the pot and sauté for 2 minutes. Add the stock, wine, and herbs and bring to the boil. Reduce the heat and simmer until the carrots are tender, 8 to 10 minutes.

3. Return the fish to the pot and simmer gently for 10 minutes.

4. Dissolve the cornstarch or arrowroot in 1½ teaspoons water or red wine. Bring the matelote to the boil, stir in the starch mixture, and cook until lightly thickened, about 1 minute. Remove the bay leaves. Season with the salt and pepper and serve in bowls with croutons or potatoes.

2 tablespoons vegetable oil

1½ pounds monkfish fillet, cut into 2-inch pieces

5 well-washed leeks, white parts only, cut into 1-inch pieces

2 small carrots, peeled and sliced diagonally ¼ inch thick

2 celery stalks, sliced diagonally ¼ inch thick

2 garlic cloves, crushed with the flat of a knife and peeled

20 small mushrooms, wiped with a damp paper towel

½ cup Fish Stock (page 67)

2¼ cups dry red wine (preferably Burgundy)

2 bay leaves

8 fresh thyme sprigs, or 1 teaspoon dried

1½ teaspoons cornstarch or arrowroot

Salt and freshly ground black pepper

Croutons or 4 boiled potatoes, for garnish

CARIBBEAN BOUILLABAISSE WITH LONG CROÛTES

FOR 4

CROÛTES

1 ficelle or baguette

Basil Oil (page 60) or olive oil

1 garlic clove, crushed with the
flat of a knife and peeled

BOUILLABAISSE

4 tablespoons olive oil

1 small onion, diced

1 small red bell pepper, cored,
seeded, and diced

1 small green bell pepper,
cored, seeded, and diced

1 medium tomato, cored,
seeded, and diced

2 garlic cloves, mashed

1/2 teaspoon hot red pepper
flakes

Two 1-pound live lobsters

8 ounces andouille sausage, cut
into 1/2-inch slices

16 littleneck clams

1/4 cup dry white wine

8 bay leaves

2 1/2 cups Fish Stock (page 67)

4 medium sea scallops

4 medium shrimp (21 to 30
count), peeled and deveined

12 mussels (preferably culti-

Don't laugh. I feel a oneness with bouillabaisse. It's a dish that reminds me of my own impromptu dockside inventions based on the day's catch. Like sailors before me who improvised tomato-based stews using the fish they couldn't sell, my own bouillabaisses are made from sweet white-fleshed fish and shellfish, pungent herbs, ripe tomatoes, and just enough garlic.

I've taken poetic license here, but I haven't changed the poem. Like many Caribbean seafood stews, this luscious island-inspired bouillabaisse incorporates meat—rich, spicy andouille sausage—sweet, firm lobster, a squeeze of lime juice, and cilantro. To finish it off, I've added long croûtes fragrant with garlic and Basil Oil.

1. Preheat the oven to 400° F. To prepare the croûtes, cut the bread diagonally into 1/8-inch-thick pieces approximately 4 inches long. Brush with the oil and rub with garlic. Bake until crispy, 6 to 8 minutes. Set aside.

2. In a medium saucepan, heat 2 tablespoons of the olive oil over medium-high heat. Add the onion and peppers and cook, stirring occasionally, until softened, 10 to 12 minutes. Add the tomato, garlic, and hot pepper flakes. Simmer until most of the liquid has evaporated, 12 to 15 minutes. The mixture should resemble a thick marinara sauce. Scrape into a bowl and reserve.

3. Cut each lobster in half lengthwise (see page 43). Remove the claws and crack the sides of each with the back of a heavy knife. Separate the body and tail sections. You will have 12 pieces in all.

4. In a large, heavy-bottomed soup pot over high heat, bring the remaining oil to the smoking point. Add the sausage and all the lobster parts except the tail sections. Cook, stirring, until the lobster turns red, 2 to 3 minutes.

5. Add the clams, the onion-pepper mixture, wine, and bay leaves. Cook 2 minutes longer. Add the stock, allow it to boil, then reduce the heat to medium. Add the scallops, shrimp, mussels, and lobster tail sections and simmer just until the mussels open, about 2 minutes.

6. Remove the bay leaves. Add the lime juice, cilantro, and Pickapeppa Sauce, if using. Arrange 2 croûtes at opposing angles in each soup bowl, add the bouillabaisse, and serve immediately.

vated), cleaned and bearded

3 tablespoons fresh lime juice

$1/2$ cup coarsely chopped fresh
   cilantro (coriander)

2 tablespoons Pickapeppa Sauce
   (optional)

MISO SOUP WITH SHRIMP

FOR 6

Soup just doesn't get any better than miso, the fragrant Japanese broth. When I sip it slowly I feel like I'm drinking the sea and earth.

Miso is simple. It's composed of dashi (the Japanese stock made from water, sea kelp, and dried bonito flakes), the savory fermented bean paste which gives it its name, soy, and a garnish. (The "special" ingredients called for are readily available at Asian groceries and many supermarkets, see pages 56 to 59.) I've used fresh shiitakes and baby shjrimp for the garnish, but you could use slivered lemon rind, a nice contrast to the soup's delicately hearty taste.

I like to have miso for breakfast, as do the Japanese, but whatever hour it comes to the table, it makes a deeply satisfying beginning.

1. In a soup pot, bring the water and konbu to a boil. Strain. (Reserve the konbu for future use; allow it to dry on cake racks, then wrap it lightly in foil. It may be used up to 3 times.)

2. Return the soup to the pot and add the bonito flakes. Cook over the lowest possible heat for 5 minutes. Strain. Add the sake, mirin, miso, and soy sauce.

3. Divide the soup among bowls. Garnish with the shrimp and mushrooms and serve.

6 cups water

6 inches konbu (dried kelp)

$1/2$ cup dried bonito flakes

$1/2$ cup sake

$1/4$ cup mirin

6 level tablespoons white miso

3 tablespoons soy sauce

$3/4$ pound tiny ocean shrimp
   (50 to 70 count), sold
   shelled and cooked,
   for garnish

$1/2$ cup fresh shiitake mushrooms, or $1/4$ cup dried
   and reconstituted, cut in fine
   julienne, for garnish

CRAB AND CORN SOUP WITH RED PEPPER CORNBREAD

FOR 6

SOUP

1 tablespoon olive oil

5 pounds live blue crabs, each cut
　　into 4 pieces

1 medium onion, coarsely
　　chopped

2 celery stalks, coarsely chopped

1/4 cup dry white wine

5 cups half-and-half

2 teaspoons chopped fresh thyme,
　　or 1 teaspoon dried

3 bay leaves

1 garlic clove, crushed with the
　　flat of a knife and peeled

GARNISH

1 tablespoon unsalted butter

1 cup corn kernels, fresh or frozen

1 large red bell pepper, roasted,
　　peeled, seeded, and cut into
　　medium dice

1/2 teaspoon cayenne pepper

Salt and freshly ground pepper

Juice of 1 lemon

1/2 pound crabmeat, fresh or
　　canned (preferably lump),
　　shell and cartilage removed

I love dishes that combine the sweet with the sweet—as long as each element shakes hands with the other. This feast for crab and corn lovers works for just that reason. The milder sweetness of the crab makes the statement and the corn and peppers support it deliciously. The jalapeño-spiced cornbread accompaniment reiterates the theme while providing a tingling counterpoint.

Do be generous with the salt. (Only 15 percent of us need to be concerned about salt intake.) It takes a fair amount to bring out the full, sweet flavor of the crab. Salt makes its sweetness blossom.

1. In a heavy-bottomed soup pot, heat the oil over high heat until hot. Add the crabs and sear on all sides until the shells turn a reddish brown, about 4 minutes.

2. Reduce the heat to medium-high, add the onion and celery, and cook, stirring occasionally, until the onion starts to brown, about 5 minutes.

3. Add the wine and deglaze. Add the remaining ingredients and bring the soup to the boil. Reduce the heat and simmer for 10 minutes.

4. Strain the soup and keep it warm. Pick the meat from the crab shells and reserve it for the garnish.

5. To make the garnish, melt the butter in a medium saucepan over medium heat. Add the corn and cook for 5 minutes if fresh, 1 minute if frozen. Add the red pepper and cayenne and season with the salt, pepper, and lemon juice. Fold in all the crabmeat and remove from the heat.

6. Divide the garnish among the soup bowls. Ladle the soup on top and serve immediately with the Red Pepper Cornbread.

VARIATION

Use 6 soft-shell crabs in place of the blue. Proceed as above, but do not remove the crabs from the prepared soup. Place a whole crab in each diner's bowl, pour in the soup, and serve.

RED PEPPER CORNBREAD

FOR 6

1. Preheat the oven to 425°F. Lightly grease a 9 by 9 by 2-inch baking pan.

2. In a medium bowl, combine the cornmeal, flour, sugar, baking powder, and salt. Cut in the shortening.

3. In a separate bowl, mix the egg and milk and add to the dry ingredients, using a few rapid strokes. Fold in the red peppers, jalapeño, if using, and chili powder. Bake for 20 to 25 minutes. The cornbread is done when a toothpick inserted into the center comes out clean.

1 cup yellow cornmeal

1 cup sifted all-purpose flour

$1/4$ cup sugar

3 teaspoons baking powder

1 teaspoon salt

$1/4$ cup solid vegetable shortening

1 large egg, beaten

1 cup milk

2 teaspoons chopped roasted red pepper

$1/2$ teaspoon finely chopped jalapeño pepper (optional)

$1/4$ teaspoon best-quality chili powder

SPICY CONCH CHOWDER WITH OKRA, CHAYOTE, AND TOMATOES

FOR 4 TO 6

1/2 pound conch meat

1 medium onion, diced

1 medium green bell pepper, cut
 into 1/2-inch dice

1 medium red bell pepper, cut into
 1/2-inch dice

8 small fresh okra, cut into
 1/2-inch dice

1 medium chayote, cut into
 1/2-inch dice

3 tablespoons olive oil

1 teaspoon finely chopped garlic

1 1/4 teaspoons finely chopped
 fresh ginger

2 tablespoons sweet paprika

3 tablespoons tomato paste

7 plum tomatoes, coarsely chopped

1/2 cup dry white wine

2 1/2 cups Fish Stock (page 67)

2 1/2 cups Chicken Stock (page 66)

2 teaspoons soy sauce

3 tablespoons ketjap manis
 (page 56)

Tabasco Sauce, to taste

Juice of 1 lime

2 heaping tablespoons chopped
 fresh cilantro (coriander)

Conch chowder is a classic dish—for me, as venerable as bouillabaisse. Unfortunately, conch chowders often neglect the conch. I've created this delicious dish to celebrate its smoky-sweet flesh—and the tropical chayote. This pear-shaped member of the gourd family has a unique character reminiscent of both zucchini and cucumber. Along with okra, a versatile American staple, chayote adds a lovely vegetable note to this savory, seasoned-to-make-your-tongue-dance chowder.

1. Trim the conch meat of all dark tissue, if necessary. Place in the bowl of a food processor and pulse until coarsely ground.

2. In a heavy-bottomed soup pot over medium-high heat, cook the onion, peppers, okra, and chayote in the olive oil until the onions are translucent, about 5 minutes. Add the garlic, ginger, paprika, and tomato paste and cook for 5 minutes, stirring occasionally. Add the tomatoes and wine and cook for 2 minutes.

3. Put the stocks in a large bowl and stir in the conch meat, separating it. Add it to the soup pot, bring to the boil, then reduce the heat and simmer gently, uncovered, for 45 minutes.

4. Just before serving, add the soy sauce, ketjap manis, Tabasco, lime juice, and cilantro and ladle into soup dishes.

NOTE: You may substitute additional chicken stock for the fish stock; use 5 cups of chicken stock in all.

CHILLED TOMATO SOUP WITH BASIL AND CRABMEAT

FOR 6

I'm a purist when it comes to cold soups. They must represent a *single* dominant flavor. And since everything that goes into the pot should be garden-fresh, save making cold soups for the spring and summer.

This delicious soup, made with ripe tomatoes, pungent basil, and sweet crabmeat, subtly balances the tart, spicy, and creamy. It's really a lesson in how flavors combine—with the rich taste of tomato carrying the day. Use the wine vinegar to season the soup as you would salt and pepper. It heightens flavor and gives the dish backbone. If you grow tomatoes, choose fruit that's a little overripe; as in other areas of life, mature is better.

1. One day to 3 hours in advance, if possible, combine the tomatoes, half the basil, mint, garlic, tomato paste, stock, and vinegar in the bowl of a food processor. Process until pureed, about 3 minutes. Refrigerate the soup and remaining basil if preparing the soup for the next day.

2. When ready to serve, add the cream, salt and pepper, and Tabasco and process for 1 minute more. If the soup seems too thick, add a bit more stock. Season with additional vinegar, if necessary.

3. Pour the soup into chilled bowls. Garnish with the crabmeat and remaining basil and serve.

2 pounds absolutely ripe tomatoes (beefsteak preferred), cored and cut into wedges

1/2 cup coarsely chopped fresh basil

2 tablespoons coarsely chopped fresh mint

2 garlic cloves

1 tablespoon tomato paste

1 cup Chicken Stock (page 66), or more as needed

1/4 cup Champagne vinegar or other mild white wine vinegar

1 1/4 cups heavy (whipping) cream

Salt and freshly ground black pepper

1 teaspoon Tabasco Sauce, or to taste

1/2 pound crabmeat (preferably jumbo lump), any shell or cartilage removed

COOK'S OPTION

You can substitute an equal quantity of cooked medium shrimp or cooked mussels for the crabmeat.

FISHERMAN'S CHOWDER

FOR 6

STOCK

2 tablespoons unsalted butter

1 large leek, white part only, cut in
half lengthwise and well washed

3 to 4 pounds fish bones (preferably
from white flatfish; may include
skeletons from the fish used for
the chowder)

4 cups water

CHOWDER

2 tablespoons olive oil

1 medium onion, chopped

1 small bouquet garni

2 medium red-skinned potatoes, cut
into 1-inch dice

5 ounces each shrimp and scallops,
or 10 ounces skinless fish (such
as grouper, snapper, or sole), cut
into $\frac{1}{2}$-inch strips; or any combination shrimp, scallops, or fish
equaling 10 ounces

2 cups milk

Salt and freshly ground black pepper

3 tablespoons coarsely chopped
fresh Italian (flat-leaf) parsley

Most of the classic dishes of fish cookery were first made by and for fishermen, and this is *the* prime example. Actually, it's less a specific recipe than a wonderful category of recipes that can adapt to the catch and what suits your fancy.

My version is very simple, and because it's based on a rich, leek-enhanced stock prepared with the skeletons of the fish you'll use, it is also economical. When I lived in Paris as a student chef and had little money I sometimes made this chowder with a salmon tail, two shrimp, and an eighth-pound of scallops—and it was magic. What counts is freshness and the method, which keeps all the pure sea flavors "in one place."

1. Make the stock. In a heavy-bottomed soup pot, melt the butter over medium heat. Add the leek and bones and sauté for 3 minutes.

2. Add the water. Bring to the boil, reduce the heat, and simmer 45 minutes. Strain and set aside.

3. In the soup pot, heat the olive oil over medium-high heat. Add the onion and sauté until translucent, 2 to 3 minutes. Add $2\frac{1}{2}$ cups of the stock (store any remaining) and the bouquet garni. Bring to a simmer and add the potatoes. Cook until almost tender, 8 to 10 minutes.

4. If using shellfish, add it and the milk to the pot, bring to a simmer, and cook for $1\frac{1}{2}$ minutes. Add fish, if using, and cook for 1 minute more. If using fish only, add it and the milk and simmer 1 minute only.

5. Remove the bouquet garni and season with the salt and pepper. Ladle into deep bowls, sprinkle with parsley, and serve with plenty of oyster crackers.

VARIATION

Serve the chowder with 3 pounds boiled small new or fingerling potatoes tossed with 3 tablespoons melted butter and coarsely chopped parsley. Diners should mash the potatoes into the chowder with a fork before eating.

CUCUMBER YOGURT SOUP WITH LOBSTER

FOR 6

This cold soup is for people who don't usually enjoy cold soup. Suave, tart, and satisfying, it's also a great example of the way acids enliven flavors.

Cucumbers need a lot of doing-to, and the two vinegars called for in this recipe wake them up. Besides providing its own tang, the yogurt contributes a creaminess that belies its low calorie content. Yogurt is a wonderful way to have richness without guilt.

When I was devising this soup I auditioned a number of shellfish before deciding on lobster. Its plush texture is just right for the tart, creamy background.

1. Place 4 of the dill sprigs, the cucumbers, thyme, yogurt, chicken stock, vinegars, Tabasco, and salt in the bowl of a food processor and process until the mixture is smooth, about 1 minute. Allow to rest 1 hour to blend the flavors, then strain through a large-mesh strainer. Correct the seasonings, adding additional salt and/or Tabasco, if needed.

2. Pour the soup into bowls, garnish with the remaining dill sprigs and lobster meat, and serve.

10 dill sprigs

8 Kirby cucumbers, split, seeded, and cut into eighths

4 fresh thyme sprigs

16 ounces low-fat yogurt

$\frac{1}{2}$ cup Chicken Stock (page 66)

3 tablespoons Champagne vinegar or other white wine vinegar

2 teaspoons sherry vinegar

$\frac{3}{4}$ teaspoon Tabasco Sauce

Salt

$\frac{3}{4}$ pound cooked lobster meat, diced, for garnish

LOBSTER BISQUE

FOR 6

Two 1½-pound lobsters, or 2
   pounds lobster shells
2 tablespoons olive oil
1 medium onion, cut into eighths
2 small carrots, peeled and cut into
   ½-inch lengths
2 celery stalks, cut into ½-inch
   lengths
3 tablespoons tomato paste
1 medium tomato, cut into eighths
2 garlic cloves, crushed with the
   flat of a knife and peeled
6 fresh thyme sprigs, or ¼ teaspoon dried
2 fresh tarragon sprigs, or ¼ teaspoon dried
3 tablespoons brandy
¾ cup dry white wine
4 cups heavy (whipping) cream
Juice of ½ lemon
1 tablespoon soy sauce
Salt
⅛ teaspoon cayenne pepper, or
   to taste

I cannot tell a lie: my lobster bisque is the most decadent, wonderfully luxurious version of the dish you'll ever taste, if I do say so myself. That's because it's just lobster, seasonings, and cream—no stock is called for nor is rice used for thickening. The secret of this lobster bisque is a concentrated flavor base called a *fond*. To make a fond means caramelizing—almost burning—the ingredients, then deglazing them with liquid to achieve an extraordinary depth of flavor.

Here is a fine opportunity to use those stored cooked or uncooked lobster shells you have. If you do use stored shells, the bisque becomes an economical delicacy that can be prepared at the last minute.

1. Dispatch the live lobsters (page 43), if using, and section, reserving the tails. If using shells only, section if necessary. Place lobster bodies and claws or the shells in a kitchen towel and, using a mallet, break up as much as possible. Place in the bowl of a food processor and pulse until the lobsters or shells are coarsely chopped.

2. In a heavy-bottomed soup pot, heat the oil over high heat until smoking. Add the lobster, if using, with the reserved tails. Distribute the pieces evenly and cook without stirring until the shells color, about 4 minutes. Turn the lobster and cook 4 minutes more. If using shells only, cook until the shells color, stirring occasionally.

3. Add the onion, carrots, and celery and cook, stirring occasionally, until the onion is golden, about 10 minutes; allow the onion to color fully. Add the tomato paste and cook, stirring constantly, until the bottom of the pot develops a coating, or *fond*. Add the tomato, garlic, and herbs and cook 3 minutes more.

4. Add 2 tablespoons of the brandy to the pot. Pour the remaining brandy into the bowl of a ladle and warm it over medium heat. Avert your face and flame. Add the ignited brandy to the pot to flame its contents. Extinguish the flame with the white wine. (Extinguishing with the wine saves some of the alcohol in the brandy.) Deglaze the fond by scraping the pot well with a wooden spatula or spoon. Mix all the ingredients thoroughly.

5. Add the cream and bring to the boil. Reduce the heat and simmer 20 minutes, or until the cream has thickened slightly. Add the lemon juice, soy sauce, salt, and cayenne.

6. Strain the bisque, using a fine strainer. If using whole lobster, remove the meat from the tails and chop coarsely. Pour the bisque into large soup plates and garnish with the reserved meat, about 2 tablespoons per person.

COOK'S OPTION

Use 4 pounds blue crabs in place of the lobster. Do not attempt to remove their meat for garnishing the bisque.

POT AU FEU DU PECHEUR

FOR 4

BOUILLON

1³/₄ quarts Fish Stock
(page 67)

³/₄ cup dry vermouth

3 medium carrots, diced

4 celery stalks, sliced ¹/₄ inch
thick

4 small new potatoes, washed

2 bay leaves

4 fresh thyme sprigs, or ¹/₂ teaspoon dried

1 star anise

2 garlic cloves, crushed with the
flat of a knife and peeled

MENU 1 (TOTAL COOKING
TIME: 13 TO 14 MINUTES)

One 2¹/₂-pound whole snapper,
cleaned, head removed, and
cut into 6 equal pieces

One 1-pound whole porgy,
cleaned, head removed, and
cut into 6 equal pieces

4 large shrimp (21 to 30 count),
peeled and deveined

2 small soft-shell crabs, halved

Here's my favorite family-style feast for friends who love to eat. It's a dream of a dish, actually—a one-pot fisherman's stew cooked at the table in minutes and dished up with lots of crusty bread, a crock of Roasted Red Pepper Aïoli (page 75) and a big bowl of coarse salt.

You prepare a heady seafood bouillon, transfer it to a tabletop burner, then add a variety of fish and shellfish. I love to watch the expression on my friends' faces when I prepare this dish. The fun of participating in the cooking creates a wonderful party atmosphere.

I offer two possible seafood combinations as guides, but you can create your own to suit your palate and market availability. If using fish filets, be sure to personally inspect the fish for freshness before filleting. The only rules are to use a wide, relatively shallow pot and to add the seafood progressively—from longest to the shortest cooking. If you're uncertain about cooking times for your own choices, check the chart at the back of the book, or see page 316, "A Note on Undercooking and Overcooking." The bouillon and aïoli may, of course, be prepared beforehand.

Serve the seafood with the bouillon as well as the aïoli, and don't forget to pass the sea salt!

The tabletop burner: To make this dish at the table, you will need a portable burner that provides sufficient heat for cooking while safely supporting the pot. Use any of the following:

• A chafing dish or fondue heater with a spirit heat source such as Sterno

• A self-contained butane gas burner

• An easily improvised heater made by surrounding a can of Sterno with three bricks placed on a protective surface, such as a cutting board.

Cooking equipment: You will need the following:

- A cooking pot about 14 inches wide and 8 inches deep; a *rondeau* is ideal, but a soup pot of comparable diameter will do nicely

- A tray or cookie sheet sufficiently large to bring ready-to-be-cooked seafood to the table

- A strainer with a long handle or a slotted spoon for removing seafood from the cooking broth

- Plates for seafood and for shells

1. Combine the ingredients for the bouillon in the pot. Bring to the boil, then simmer for 15 minutes. Transfer the pot to the tabletop burner.

2. Bring the bouillon to the simmer at the table. Add the fish and shellfish from menu 1 or 2 in the order in which they appear. For menu 1, cook the snapper for 6 minutes; add the porgy and cook for 4 minutes; add the shrimp and crab and cook 3 to 4 minutes. For menu 2, cook the lobster for 5 minutes; add the monkfish and cook 3 minutes; add the grouper and cook 4 minutes; add the scallops and cod and cook 2½ minutes (see Note). When the last addition is cooked, the dish is ready to serve.

Note: If any seafood appears insufficiently cooked, simmer for 2 to 3 minutes longer.

MENU 2 (TOTAL COOKING TIME: 14½ MINUTES)

Claws and tail of one 1½-pound live lobster (reserve the body for future use), halved

6 ounces monkfish fillet, cut into 6 equal pieces

4 ounces grouper fillet, cut into 6 equal pieces

4 medium sea scallops

3 ounces cod fillet

BEST CAJUN GUMBO

FOR 6 TO 8

1/2 cup (1 stick) unsalted butter

1 cup all-purpose flour

3 tablespoons olive oil

2 blue crabs, each cut into 4 pieces (page 47)

One 1-pound lobster, cut into 6 pieces (page 44)

1 medium red bell pepper, cut into 1/2-inch dice

1 medium green bell pepper, cut into 1/2-inch dice

1 medium yellow pepper, cut into 1/2-inch dice

3 celery stalks, cut diagonally into 1/2-inch pieces

16 small okra, cut diagonally into 1/2-inch pieces

1 large onion, coarsely chopped

1/2 pound andouille sausage, cut into 1/4-inch slices

2 large tomatoes, cored, seeded, and coarsely chopped

3 garlic cloves, finely minced

3 cups Fish Stock (page 67)

3 cups Chicken Stock (page 66)

16 chicken wings (approximately 1 pound)

1 pound small shrimp (16 to 20 count), peeled

I've tried many a gumbo, seafood and otherwise. These spicy Louisiana soup-stews, which reflect the culinary ingenuity of Spanish, French, African, and Choctaw cooks, can be delicious or a big disappointment. When a gumbo is good, every ingredient brings its special virtues to the whole to create a blend of the earthy, sweet, and savory.

I have definite specifications for a great seafood gumbo. It must contain crab, peppers, green onions, sausage, Tabasco Sauce, Worcestershire, okra, and gumbo filé and it must be made with a nutty-brown roux. Take one element away, and all you've got is a stew. I *like* to add chicken, crustaceans, and/or mollusks—they add extra dimension to the dish—but they're not essential.

To assure yourself of a really superior gumbo, make and refrigerate the dish a day before you intend to serve it. The flavors have a chance to blend and the result is fantastic. My gumbo is a great dish for a gathering—just break out the Dixie Longrock or Falstaff beer and enjoy!

1. Make the roux. In a heavy, medium saucepan, melt the butter over medium-low heat. Add the flour and stir to blend. Cook slowly, stirring, until the flour becomes a deep caramel color, about 7 minutes. Pay close attention: after the flour begins to brown it can burn very quickly, so remove the pan from the heat a moment before the roux reaches the desired shade. Reserve. (The roux may be made beforehand and kept at room temperature.)

2. In a large, heavy soup pot over high heat, bring 2 tablespoons of the olive oil to the smoking point. Add the crab and lobster and cook, stirring occasionally, until the shells redden, about 4 minutes. Remove and reserve.

3. Add the remaining olive oil to the pot, reduce the heat to medium, and add the peppers, celery, okra, onion, and sausage. Cook, stirring, until the vegetables are tender, about 6 minutes.

4. Add the tomatoes and garlic and cook 4 minutes more. Add the stocks and bring to the boil. Thicken by adding the roux tablespoon by tablespoon until the gumbo has the consistency of a thick pea soup. Allow the gumbo to thicken after each addition before adding the next. Reduce the heat and simmer for 25 minutes.

5. Add the chicken wings and cook for 10 minutes. Add the shrimp, scallops, and reserved crab and lobster. Cook for 3 minutes, then add the dissolved filé powder mixture. Simmer for 2 minutes longer and remove the gumbo from the heat. Season liberally with the salt, pepper, Tabasco, and Worcestershire. Serve the gumbo in crocks or bowls with about ½ cup of the rice spooned on top of each portion. Garnish with the chopped scallions.

4 sea scallops, halved

1 tablespoon filé powder, dissolved in 2 tablespoons water

Salt and freshly ground black pepper

Tabasco Sauce

Worcestershire sauce

4 to 5 cups cooked rice

½ cup chopped scallions

PUMPKIN SOUP WITH BAY SCALLOPS AND MUSHROOMS

FOR 6 TO 8

3 bacon strips, quartered

1 small onion, diced

2 garlic cloves, crushed with the
flat of a knife and peeled

1 medium carrot, peeled and
coarsely chopped

1 medium sweet potato, peeled
and cut into medium dice

1½ pounds peeled pumpkin
flesh, cut into medium dice
(see Note)

7 cups Chicken Stock (page 66)

1 tablespoon unsalted butter

½ pound fresh wild mushrooms,
such as porcini, chanterelles,
portobello, or shiitake,
cleaned

Salt and freshly ground black
pepper

1 teaspoon chopped fresh thyme

1 teaspoon chopped fresh
rosemary

1 teaspoon chopped fresh chives

1 pound bay scallops, well
drained

COOK'S OPTION

*Substitute 1 pound tiny
shrimp for the scallops.*

I first made this delicious pumpkin soup for an appearance on the "Today" show. It was Thanksgiving and I was asked to do something with pumpkin and seafood that didn't involve molasses, nutmeg, or mace—the very flavorings we think of as the taste of pumpkin. Actually, pumpkin has a delicate sweet flavor—wonderfully bolstered in this dish by the briny sweetness of fresh scallops and the earthiness of wild mushrooms.

Each mouthful of this soup presents the yielding consistency of the pumpkin, the smokiness of the bacon, and the sweetness of the scallops. I cook every day and I'm constantly amazed how the simplest ingredients can produce dishes of great refinement. This is one.

1. In a large soup pot over medium heat, sauté the bacon until its fat is rendered, about 1 minute. Add the onion and cook gently until translucent, 3 to 4 minutes. Add the garlic and cook until its aroma is released, about 1 minute.

2. Add the carrot, sweet potato, pumpkin, and stock and bring to the boil. Reduce the heat and simmer until the vegetables are tender, about 35 minutes.

3. Meanwhile, in a medium sauté pan over high heat, melt the butter. When it sizzles, add the mushrooms and cook until they soften, about 3 minutes. Season with the salt and pepper. Add the herbs, stir, and remove the mushrooms to a plate.

4. Season the soup with salt and pepper. Add the mushrooms and scallops and remove the soup from the heat. Stir the soup for about 30 seconds; the scallops need only be warmed through to be cooked. Serve immediately.

Note: Pumpkin quality is notoriously inconsistent. Choose medium pumpkins (those from a farmstand are, of course, best) that yield slightly to pressure. Alternatively, you can use butternut squash in the same quantity as the pumpkin.

SCALLOP VEGETABLE SOUP WITH SHIITAKE MUSHROOMS

FOR 4

Root vegetables are among my favorite soup ingredients. Their homely appearance conceals the subtlety of their earthy flavors, which soup celebrates. For this richly satisfying dish I've paired parsnip and potato with plump sea scallops. Shiitakes add a woodsy depth of taste and lemon provides zing. Try this for lunch on a cool fall day with thickly sliced black bread.

1. In a medium pot, cook the potato in boiling salted water until tender, 8 to 10 minutes. Drain and set aside.

2. In a soup pot, melt the butter over medium heat. Add the leeks, mushrooms, and parsnip. Cover and stew them, not allowing the vegetables to color, 6 to 8 minutes.

3. Add the scallops, bay leaves, thyme sprigs, red pepper flakes, and lemon rind and cook for 2 minutes. Add the stocks, bring to a boil, and immediately remove the scallops with a slotted spoon. Reserve.

4. Simmer the soup for 15 minutes. Remove the bay leaves. Return the scallops to the pot and add the potato. Season with the salt and pepper.

5. Stir in the parsley, chopped thyme, and lemon juice. Ladle into soup bowls and serve immediately.

1 medium potato, peeled and cut into 1/4-inch dice

1 tablespoon unsalted butter

2 leeks, white parts only, split in half lengthwise, well washed, and cut diagonally into medium slices

1/4 pound shiitake mushrooms, stems removed, cut into strips about 1 inch wide

1 medium parsnip, peeled and cut into 1/2-inch dice

1/4 pound large sea scallops, cut in half horizontally

2 bay leaves

2 fresh thyme sprigs, or 1/4 teaspoon dried

1/4 teaspoon red pepper flakes

1 large strip lemon rind (approximately 1 by 2 inches)

3 1/4 cups Fish Stock (page 67)

1 cup Chicken Stock (page 66)

Salt and freshly ground black pepper

1/2 cup fresh Italian (flat-leaf) parsley leaves, loosely packed

8 fresh thyme sprigs, chopped

1 teaspoon fresh lemon juice

CURRIED MUSSEL SOUP

FOR 4

SOUP

2 tablespoons unsalted butter

4 medium shallots, thinly sliced

1 garlic clove, coarsely chopped

2 very ripe medium tomatoes,
   coarsely chopped

1 heaping tablespoon unsweetened
   shredded coconut

2 tablespoons best-quality curry
   powder

2½ pounds mussels (preferably cultivated), cleaned and bearded

1½ cups unsweetened coconut milk

3 cups half-and-half

Salt and freshly ground black pepper

¾ teaspoon fresh lemon juice

GARNISH (OPTIONAL)

1 tablespoon unsalted butter

½ cup cooked wild rice

1 medium tomato, cored, peeled,
   seeded, and diced

3 tablespoons corn kernels, fresh or
   frozen

2 tablespoons coarsely chopped
   fresh cilantro (coriander)

Salt and freshly ground black pepper

This creamy soup, fragrant with curry, is comfort itself. Use the best curry powder you can find. I like cultivated mussels here and elsewhere because they have a high meat-to-shell ratio and require only a quick rinsing. If you like, try the green-lipped New Zealand mussels in place of the domestic variety. To assure that the mussels stew evenly, prepare them in your biggest soup pot.

The wild rice, corn, and cilantro garnish is optional, but it's really too good to miss. You can make and refrigerate it beforehand if you like, bringing it to room temperature while you prepare the soup.

1. In a large, heavy-bottomed soup pot, melt the butter over medium heat. Add the shallots and garlic and cook until softened, about 2 minutes.

2. Add the tomatoes and shredded coconut and cook for 2 minutes more.

3. Add the curry powder, mussels, coconut milk, and half-and-half. Bring to the boil and cook just until the mussels open, about 5 minutes. Strain the soup; remove the mussels from their shells and reserve.

4. Return the soup to the pot. Simmer to reduce slightly, about 10 minutes. Season with the salt, pepper, and lemon juice.

5. Make the garnish, if using: in a small pan, melt the butter over medium heat. Add the rice and sauté until hot. Add the tomato, corn, and cilantro and cook 1 minute. Season with the salt and pepper.

6. Divide the garnish among soup bowls, if using. Remove the soup from the heat, add the mussels, and pour into bowls. Serve immediately.

6. SALADS, SMALL AND SUBSTANTIAL

When I was growing up a salad meant cold iceberg lettuce with Russian dressing. My first encounter with arugula just about knocked me out. Here was a delicious lettuce at last, far removed from the chilled-water taste of the appropriately named iceberg heads. I became fanatical about searching out and combining different greens—hard going then because there was little lettuce variety.

Happily, times and markets have changed. My salads revel in an abundance of lettuces with sparkling flavors and crisp, tempting vegetables. They're what the French call *salades composées,* a flowering of multiple ingredients in tantalizing and often new combinations. For the seafood lover, these salads promise a real treat: luscious fish and shellfish harmonize perfectly with other fresh ingredients in salads that work beautifully as first courses or light meals.

I don't know which I love more—devising salads from scratch or reworking old favorites. Poached Salmon Salad with Radicchio and Black Bean Mayonnaise, Oriental Shrimp and Cabbage Salad, and Squid Salad with Jicama and Orange Vinaigrette will introduce you to wonderful new flavor marriages while helping perfect your seafood cooking skills. The Ultimate Salad Niçoise, made with fresh tuna, and Warm Potato Salad with Mussels and Pesto Mayonnaise are classics enticingly updated. Monkfish Salad with Roasted Red and Yellow Peppers and Sunday Night Fish Salad prove, respectively, that great salads needn't contain greens and can be delicious even when made with leftover fish.

My ultimate wish is to help you create your own good salads. That means devising a "dimensional" dish of well-balanced tastes and textures. Each green has a dominant flavor—spicy, peppery, flowery, mustardy, or bitter (bitter tastes should never dominate a dish, but add a subtle counter note). Try using unexpected seafood in a salad. Squid, for example, makes a great salad ingredient; its chewiness invites the use of greens or vegetables with contrasting textures.

The salads that follow are easy to do, but as with most simple dishes, they require attention to their ingredients and composition. It goes without saying that everything must be fresh. Greens must be well dried and salads dressed lightly to avoid limp or waterlogged lettuce. Whenever possible, try *not* to refrigerate cooked ingredients. All salads should be served at room temperature; fruits, vegetables, and seafood are actually flavorless when they are served very cold.

Think of dressings as sauces for salads. You can achieve great complexity in their composition. Citrus and spice, sweet and salty—the flavor permutations are endless. The Baby Shrimp Salad with Zesty Papaya-Mint Dressing began with a magazine's request for a sprightly salad. I knew the dressing should contain fruit, which is refreshing, and mint for its invigorating greenness. Lime juice and Tabasco Sauce did the rest. With just a little experimentation I had a salad that was deliciously spirited, a garden on a plate made subtle and savory with the taste of the sea. These's no magic to making great salad—the recipes here will get you started triumphantly.

CRABMEAT SALAD WITH PICKLED FENNEL AND CARROTS

FOR 4

With their crisp textures and pleasing sourness, pickled vegetables make perfect accompaniments to mild fish and shellfish. Here, pickled fennel and carrot are a fine foil for the luxurious sweetness of fresh lump crabmeat.

You may pickle the vegetables up to eight hours in advance, but if you need to prepare the dish quickly, one hour of pickling will do the trick.

1. In a medium nonreactive bowl, combine the fennel, carrot, vinegar, sugar, salt, and garlic. Allow the vegetables to pickle in the refrigerator for 1 to 8 hours. (If you want to pickle the vegetables 12 or more hours in advance, cut them thicker, up to $\frac{1}{4}$ inch.)

2. About 1 hour before serving, toss the crabmeat with the dill, lemon juice, and cayenne. Drain the pickled vegetables well. (Reserve the liquid for future pickling in a sealed jar; refrigerated, it will keep for up to ten days.)

3. Divide the pickled vegetables among 4 plates, arrange the crab on top, and serve.

1 small fennel bulb, cut into lengthwise slices approximately $\frac{1}{8}$ inch thick

1 medium carrot, peeled and cut into thin rounds

2 cups rice vinegar

$\frac{1}{2}$ cup sugar

2 teaspoons salt

1 large garlic clove, crushed with the flat of a knife and peeled

1 pound lump crabmeat, any shell and cartilage removed

1 tablespoon chopped fresh dill

1 teaspoon fresh lemon juice

$\frac{1}{8}$ teaspoon cayenne pepper

COOK'S OPTION

Sixteen large shrimp
(21 to 30 count) can be
substituted for the crab.
Boil the shrimp (see page
187) and toss with the dill,
lemon juice, and cayenne.

ORIENTAL SHRIMP AND CABBAGE SALAD

FOR 4

SHRIMP

4 quarter-size slices peeled fresh
    ginger, chopped
1 tablespoon Asian sesame oil
1 garlic clove, mashed
1 teaspoon honey
1 pound medium shrimp (31 to 35
    count), shelled and deveined
1 tablespoon vegetable oil

DRESSING

2 teaspoons olive oil
2 tablespoons Asian sesame oil
1 tablespoon soy sauce
2 quarter-size pieces peeled fresh
    ginger, smashed
1½ tablespoons rice vinegar
1 teaspoon honey

SALAD

Vegetable oil, for deep-frying
2 ounces harusame (Japanese bean
    starch noodles) or see Note
¾ cup shredded green cabbage
¾ cup shredded red cabbage
1 medium carrot, peeled and grated
1 bunch scallions, trimmed and cut
    into ½-inch lengths
¼ cup alfalfa sprouts
2 tablespoons roasted peanuts

As a young chef working in France, I learned that any French dish *à l'orientale* contained ingredients associated with Turkey and the Balkans. Not exactly what we think of as "East meets West." This deliciously intriguing salad, full of the flavors of ginger, garlic, soy sauce, and sesame, comes closer to the mark. Cabbage, peanuts, and alfalfa sprouts provide satisfying crunch, as does the delicate Japanese noodle called harusame.

1. One hour before serving, combine the ginger, sesame oil, garlic, and honey in a mixing bowl. Add the shrimp, combine well, and set aside to marinate.

2. Dry the shrimp well. In a large, heavy skillet, heat the tablespoon of vegetable oil until smoking. Add the shrimp and sauté until just pink, about 3 minutes. Transfer to a clean mixing bowl.

3. Mix all the dressing ingredients well.

4. Heat the additional vegetable oil in a fryer with basket, deep heavy skillet, or wok. (If you are using a wok, make sure it is balanced securely with a wok ring or overturned burner grid.) Heat the oil until very hot, 375°F. on a frying thermometer. Plunge the harusame noodles into the oil and cook them until they are crispy and white, 20 to 30 seconds. Drain on paper toweling.

5. Chop the peanuts coarsely. Add with the shredded cabbages, carrot, scallions, and sprouts to the shrimp and mix well. Toss with the dressing and divide among plates. Sprinkle with the harasume or soup noodles and serve.

Note: Crispy soup noodles left over from Chinese takeout can substitute for the harusame thus eliminating the need for deep-frying them (step 4).

CURRIED FISH SALAD WITH PAPPADUM

FOR 4

I love curry salads if the dressing is light and the curry fragrant. This curried fish salad more than fills the bill. It combines fish with a delicate, aromatic dressing, which is served on the irresistible Indian cracker-bread called pappadum. Toasted coconut, a traditional curry condiment, finishes the salad with its rich yet subtle sweetness.

Make this salad with equal success using fresh or leftover fish and shellfish or a combination of the two.

1. Make the dressing. In a small sauté pan over medium heat, warm the oil until it is moderately hot. Add the shallot, garlic, and apple and sauté until softened, about 4 minutes.

2. Add the curry powder, reduce the heat to low, and cook, stirring, until fragrant, about 4 minutes. Remove the pan contents to a bowl. When the mixture has come to room temperature, add the mayonnaise and mix well.

3. Meanwhile, preheat the oven to 425°F. Place the pappadum on a cookie sheet and bake until fragrant and very brittle, about 3 minutes. Allow to cool. Reduce the oven to 325°F.

4. Toast the coconut. Place it on the cookie sheet and bake, stirring frequently and watching carefully, until golden, about 20 minutes. Allow to cool.

5. Toss the celery, tomato, and parsley with the dressing. Add the fish and/or seafood and combine very gently. Fold in the coconut and season with the lemon juice.

6. Place a pappadum on each plate. Mound the salad on top and serve.

Note: Pappadum are sold in most Indian markets and many Asian groceries; avoid, if possible, those sold in tins. Commercial flatbread, plain or flavored with pepper or garlic, can take the place of the pappadum.

DRESSING

1 tablespoon olive oil

1 medium shallot, minced

1 garlic clove, minced

$\frac{1}{2}$ small green apple, peeled and finely diced

2 tablespoons best-quality curry powder

$3\frac{1}{2}$ tablespoons Homemade Mayonnaise (page 71), or best-quality store-bought

SALAD

4 pappadum (see Note)

2 tablespoons unsweetened shredded coconut

2 celery stalks, finely chopped

$\frac{1}{4}$ cup diced tomato

$\frac{1}{4}$ cup loosely packed fresh Italian (flat-leaf) parsley

1 pound cooked skinless fish (such as grouper, tile, flounder, or bass), broken into large pieces; or cooked seafood (such as shrimp, scallops, or mussels); or any combination

Fresh lemon juice, to taste

SQUID SALAD WITH JICAMA AND ORANGE VINAIGRETTE

FOR 4

SQUID

4 cups Court Bouillon (page 69)

1 pound cleaned squid, the
bodies cut into 2-inch lengths

VINAIGRETTE

2 cups fresh orange juice

1 teaspoon chopped fresh thyme,
or ¼ teaspoon dried

1 tablespoon fresh lime juice

¼ cup olive oil

2 tablespoons vegetable oil

Salt and freshly ground black
pepper

SALAD

1 small jicama, peeled and cut
into strips ⅛ inch wide and
1½ inches long

2 oranges, peeled and separated
into segments without pith

2 bunches arugula, stems
trimmed and well washed

Salt and freshly ground black
pepper

I devised this salad for a squid-loving customer. He asked me to create a light dish that would let him enjoy his favorite seafood au naturel. I poached some squid gently, then combined it with arugula, crunchy jicama, and the sharp citrus tang of fresh orange. My friend was delighted by the finished dish, as was everyone else who tried it. It became a great restaurant favorite—thank you, John Colbert.

1. In a medium saucepan, bring the court bouillon to the boil. Add the squid, reduce the heat, and simmer gently for 2 minutes. Allow the squid to come to room temperature.

2. Make the vinaigrette. In a small saucepan, reduce the orange juice over high heat until you have ½ cup, about 5 minutes. Allow the juice to cool.

3. In a blender or the bowl of a food processor, combine the orange juice with the remaining vinaigrette ingredients. Blend or process for 1 minute.

4. Toss the squid with the jicama, oranges, arugula, and vinaigrette. Season with additional salt and pepper. Divide among plates and serve.

LOBSTER AND CAVIAR SALAD

FOR 4

This sumptuous salad, perfect for an intimate supper, uses two caviars: the small-grained gray sevruga and salmon roe, the Chinese-red eggs sometimes called keta. The caviars are combined with lobster, scallion, and just enough sour cream to lightly bind them, then served on buttery Bibb lettuce leaves.

Though this dish seems elaborate, it's utterly simple to prepare. Champagne would, of course, be a lovely accompaniment here, but any dry, not-too-fruity white wine will do very nicely, indeed.

1. Gently mix all the ingredients except the sevruga caviar, if using, and the greens.
2. Arrange the greens on individual plates and top with an equal portion of the lobster mixture. Crown each serving with ½ teaspoon of the sevruga caviar, if using, and serve with melba toast.

One 2-pound lobster, cooked, meat removed and cut into ½-inch dice

2 tablespoons sour cream

2 tablespoons chopped scallions

1 tablespoon salmon roe (keta) or flying fish roe (tobiko)

½ teaspoon fresh lemon juice

3 dashes of Tabasco Sauce

¼ teaspoon freshly ground black pepper

2 teaspoons (1-ounce jar) sevruga caviar (optional)

1 head Boston or Bibb lettuce, leaves torn into bite-size pieces

COOK'S OPTIONS

1. *Serve the lobster mixture atop a potato pancake. Sprinkle the sevruga over all.*

2. *Cut the lobster into a small dice. Prepare the lobster mixture as above and spoon it onto individual leaves of endive. Top with the sevruga and serve as an hors d'oeuvre.*

WARM POTATO SALAD WITH MUSSELS AND PESTO MAYONNAISE

FOR 4

SALAD

½ cup dry white wine

2 fresh thyme sprigs, or ¼ teaspoon dried

3 pounds mussels (preferably cultivated), bearded

6 small Creamer, Yukon Gold, or
Red Bliss potatoes

1 teaspoon olive oil

3 medium shallots, thinly sliced

1 tablespoon sherry vinegar

1 bunch chives, cut into ¾-inch
lengths

Salt and freshly ground black
pepper

PESTO MAYONNAISE

1 large egg yolk

1 large egg

1 tablespoon pine nuts

1 cup fresh basil leaves

3 mint leaves

1 tablespoon fresh cilantro
(coriander) leaves

1 tablespoon Dijon mustard

2 tablespoons olive oil

¼ cup vegetable oil

2 teaspoons fresh lemon juice

I'm a real fan of potato salads made with seafood, which are at their best served warm or at room temperature. This one, which features a pesto mayonnaise made with mint and cilantro, uses potatoes steeped in a sherry vinegar dressing flavored with shallots and chives. The potatoes are surrounded by mussels finished with the herby mayonnaise.

I like to make this with Creamer or Yukon Gold potatoes, which add a sense of richness without extra calories, but Red Bliss or any other boiling potato will do perfectly.

1. Prepare the mussels. In a nonreactive pot, bring the wine and thyme to a boil. Add the mussels, cover, and cook until they open, about 3 minutes. Remove the mussels, reserving the cooking liquid.

2. When cool enough to handle, remove the mussel top shells and arrange mussels on a cookie sheet. Saturate a kitchen towel with the cooking liquid and cover the mussels to keep them moist and flavorful.

3. Fill a medium pot with water, salt well, and add the potatoes. Simmer the potatoes until fork-tender, about 35 minutes. Drain and cut into ½-inch slices.

4. In a small pan, heat the olive oil over medium heat and add the shallots. Sauté until soft, about 4 minutes. Add to the warm potatoes and toss. Add the vinegar and chives and season with the salt and plenty of pepper.

5. To make the mayonnaise, combine all the ingredients except the oils and lemon juice in the bowl of a food processor and process for 2 minutes. Combine the oils in a measuring cup and drizzle through the feed tube slowly until an emulsion is achieved. Season with the salt and pepper and lemon juice.

6. Divide the potatoes among 4 plates. Surround them with the mussels. Dollop the mussels lightly with the mayonnaise and serve.

SCALLOP AND FRISÉE SALAD WITH TOMATO SHALLOT DRESSING

FOR 4

If we think of salad dressings as sauces, we begin to appreciate their potential as palate pleasers. I remember my growing enthusiasm as I first put together the vinaigrette for this salad of poached scallops and pungent frisée. I had made an oniony oil, vinegar, and tomato emulsion and thought, Well, what next? Next turned out to be the licoricelike warmth of fresh tarragon and toasted coriander seeds—a perfect complement to the frisée and scallops. The coriander adds crunch and a hint of citrus to this excitingly flavored dish. You really *have* to try this.

1. Prepare the scallops. In a medium saucepan, bring the stock, shallots, and thyme to the boil. Add the scallops, cover, and turn off the heat. Allow the scallops to steep for 3 minutes, then remove them with a slotted spoon. Reserve the liquid.

2. To make the dressing, combine all the ingredients except the tarragon in the bowl of a food processor. Process for 1 minute. Pour the dressing into a small bowl and add the tarragon leaves.

3. Wrap the coriander seeds in a kitchen towel and crack with a kitchen mallet or other heavy object. In a small, heavy pan over medium heat, toast the coriander seeds until golden, about 2 minutes. Shake the pan often to prevent burning.

4. Toss the frisée with three-fourths of the dressing. Divide the greens among 4 plates and place a portion of the scallops on top of each. Drizzle the reserved scallop cooking liquid and dressing over the scallops, sprinkle with the toasted coriander seeds, and serve.

SCALLOPS

3/4 cup Fish Stock (page 67)

1 medium shallot, minced

1 teaspoon chopped fresh thyme leaves, or 1/4 teaspoon dried

1 pound bay scallops

DRESSING

4 tablespoons olive oil

1 teaspoon Champagne vinegar

2 medium shallots, coarsely chopped

1/2 teaspoon salt

1/2 teaspoon freshly ground black pepper

2 medium beefsteak tomatoes, cored, seeded, and coarsely chopped

4 drops of Tabasco Sauce

3 tablespoons water

2 tablespoons fresh tarragon leaves

SALAD

1 tablespoon coriander seeds

2 heads frisée, torn into bite-size pieces

ULTIMATE SALAD NIÇOISE

FOR 4

DRESSING

1 large egg yolk

3 tablespoons Dijon mustard

2 tablespoons olive oil

1 teaspoon sherry vinegar

1 teaspoon Champagne vinegar,
    or more as needed

Salt and freshly ground black
    pepper

SALAD

½ pound haricots verts or thin
    regular string beans, ends
    trimmed

4 small new potatoes, cut into
    quarters

¾ pound fresh tuna

1 Belgian endive, root end
    trimmed, cut lengthwise into
    1½-inch segments

1 large tomato, halved, seeded,
    and cut into ½-inch slices

2 hard-cooked eggs (optional)

1 large handful arugula, torn into
    large pieces

2 tablespoons capers, rinsed

8 anchovy fillets (optional)

Salad Niçoise is something of a culinary cliché, but it can be utterly special if its ingredients are carefully cooked and combined with care.

This version *is* the best. In addition to the traditional ingredients, there are endive, a sherry-mustard vinaigrette, and freshly cooked tuna. It's the fresh tuna that makes all the difference. You can broil, steam, sauté, or poach the fish, as you like—each method produces a subtly different and utterly delicious salad.

1. To make the dressing, combine the egg yolk and mustard in a stainless-steel or ceramic bowl. Whisk until well blended. Add the oil slowly, whisking until you achieve a mayonnaiselike consistency. Gradually add the vinegars and season with the salt and pepper. Set aside.

2. For the salad, blanch the haricots verts or string beans until tender-crisp, about 4 minutes. In the same water, boil the potatoes until a fork just pierces them easily, 10 to 12 minutes. Cut each into 4 pieces.

3. Up to 30 minutes in advance, cook the tuna by one of the following methods: (1) steam for 5 to 8 minutes; (2) sauté in 1 tablespoon of olive oil for 7 to 8 minutes; (3) broil 4 to 5 inches from the heat source, turning once, for about 6 minutes; or (4) poach in Court Bouillon (page 69) for 3 to 5 minutes. The tuna should feel resilient to the touch; the interior will be medium-rare. (If you prefer it cooked through, cook until the tuna feels firm.) Allow the fish to come to room temperature.

4. To assemble the salad, toss together gently the endive, tomato, eggs, arugula, capers, anchovies, and beans. Add the dressing a tablespoon at a time until everything is well coated. Add additional Champagne vinegar by droplets if you think it is needed.

5. Divide the salad among 4 large plates. Break or cut the tuna into bite-size pieces and place around the other salad ingredients. Drizzle additional dressing over the tuna and serve.

MONKFISH SALAD WITH ROASTED RED AND YELLOW PEPPERS

FOR 4

A salad needn't include lettuce or dressing. This savory salad of sautéed monkfish, set off with ribbons of roasted red and yellow peppers, illustrates the point deliciously. Garlic, freshly torn basil leaves, and a bit of hot red pepper add dimension to the dish, which is cooked in minutes and served at room temperature. This is both delicate and satisfying—my idea of a perfect light supper.

1. In a small, heavy skillet, toast the pine nuts over medium heat, stirring constantly, until golden, 3 to 4 minutes.

2. In a medium sauté pan, heat the oil over medium heat until smoking. Add the monkfish and sauté on both sides until golden, about 4 minutes in all. Add the peppers, garlic, tomato juice, and red pepper flakes. Cook, stirring constantly, until the flavors are just blended and the tomato juice has reduced, about 1 minute.

3. Remove the pepper mixture to a bowl and allow to come to room temperature. Season with the salt, pepper, and lemon juice. Fold in the basil and serve.

Note: Dishes like this, which are to be eaten at room temperature, should not receive their final seasoning until just before they are served.

3 tablespoons pine nuts

1½ tablespoons olive oil

1¼ pounds monkfish fillet, cut into bite-size cubes

1 red bell pepper, roasted, peeled, and cut into strips 2 inches long and 1 inch wide

1 yellow bell pepper, roasted, peeled, and cut into strips 2 inches long and 1 inch wide

2 teaspoons minced garlic

¾ cup tomato juice

¼ teaspoon hot red pepper flakes

½ cup loosely packed fresh basil leaves, torn into large pieces

Salt and freshly ground black pepper

Fresh lemon juice

SUNDAY NIGHT FISH SALAD

FOR 4

4 cups Court Bouillon (page 69), if using raw fish

1 pound cooked fish (moderately firm fish such as halibut, grouper, tile, or swordfish preferred; do not use cod), broken into bite-size pieces; or uncooked fish (such as previously trimmed pieces from fillets), cut into bite-size pieces; or a combination

3 medium tomatoes, halved, seeded, and cut into strips

3 tablespoons coarsely chopped fresh cilantro (coriander)

1 medium shallot, minced

1 small avocado, peeled and diced

$1/2$ cup frozen corn kernels, defrosted by running under warm water, or fresh corn kernels (see Note)

2 tablespoons olive oil

1 tablespoon sherry wine vinegar

Juice of $1/2$ lime

$1/4$ teaspoon ground cumin

$1/2$ teaspoon best-quality chili powder

When I was a kid, Sunday night dinner was usually potluck. I always looked forward to these suppers because of the great way my mother had with leftovers. In the spirit of those wonderful homey meals I devised this salad, which allows you to use cooked leftover fish, uncooked trimmings, or both. The fish is dressed with a tomato-cilantro vinaigrette seasoned with cumin and chili powder. The sweet corn and rich avocado help to make this simple salad a good-enough-for-company treat.

1. If using trimmings or other raw fish, bring the court bouillon to the boil in a medium nonreactive saucepan. Reduce the heat until the liquid simmers and add the fish by type until each is just cooked. (Firmer or darker fish such as swordfish will take about 4 minutes; lighter or flakier fish such as snapper or fluke will take about 2 minutes. Check for doneness by removing a piece of fish and breaking it open. The flesh should be slightly translucent at its center.) Allow cooked or leftover fish, if using, to come to room temperature.

2. In a medium bowl, combine the remaining ingredients and toss gently. Add the fish and toss once, being careful to keep the fish as intact as possible. Divide among plates and serve.

Note: If using fresh corn kernels, cook by poaching gently in salted water until tender, 6 to 8 minutes.

POACHED SALMON SALAD WITH RADICCHIO AND BLACK BEAN MAYONNAISE

FOR 4

The *sauce salade* used here is deliciously different: a sake-warmed mayonnaise containing the New World staple black beans. It accompanies salmon, radicchio, which are dressed with a tart-sweet balsamic vinaigrette. It's always a pleasure finding ways to bring the flavors of diverse cultures together and making the combinations seem inevitable.

1. Prepare the salmon. In a medium saucepan, bring the wine, stock, shallots, thyme, and lemon to the boil. Add the fish and barely simmer, covered, until the salmon is pale-colored, about 4 minutes. Let the salmon cool in the liquid. Reserve.

2. Make the balsamic vinaigrette. In a small bowl, combine the oil and vinegar. Season with the salt and pepper to taste.

3. Toss the radicchio and endive with 2 tablespoons of the vinaigrette. Divide the salad among 4 plates, mounding it in the center of each. Place 1 salmon portion on top of each mound. Dollop about 1 teaspoon of the mayonnaise mixture on top of the salmon. Add garnish, if using, and serve.

SALMON

1/2 cup dry white wine

1 cup Fish Stock (page 67)

2 medium shallots, sliced

2 fresh thyme sprigs, or 1/4 teaspoon
   dried

2 lemon slices

1 pound salmon fillet, cut into 4
   equal portions

BALSAMIC VINAIGRETTE

3 tablespoons extra-virgin
   olive oil

2 tablespoons balsamic vinegar

Salt and freshly ground black pepper

SALAD

1 head radicchio, torn into large
   pieces

2 Belgian endive, split lengthwise,
   cores removed, and cut crosswise into 1-inch lengths

1/2 cup Black Bean Mayonnaise
   (page 73)

GARNISH (OPTIONAL)

1 red bell pepper, cored, seeded,
   and minced; or 1 bunch chives,
   cut into 2-inch lengths

MOROCCAN LOBSTER SALAD

FOR 6

One 1- to 2-pound lobster

2 cups cooked instant couscous,
prepared according to package directions

¼ medium unwaxed cucumber,
diced

1 small tomato, halved, seeded,
and diced

1 tablespoon chopped fresh mint
leaves

2 tablespoons olive oil

2 teaspoons chopped fresh
cilantro (coriander)

½ teaspoon harissa, or 8 drops of
Tabasco Sauce

½ teaspoon fresh lime juice

Salt

COOK'S OPTION

*You can use ¾ pound small
peeled shrimp or bay scallops in place of the lobster.
Sauté shrimp or scallops in
olive oil until just cooked,
about 2 minutes.*

I was wondering how I could use couscous in a salad one morning when I found myself thinking about Morocco. I began to make a list of some of its zesty ingredients—lime, cilantro, mint, and the incendiary red chili paste called harissa. It wasn't long before I'd devised this salad, which combines those piquant ingredients with lobster, cucumber, and nutty-tasting couscous. The resulting salad, which makes a great summer supper, is both tongue-tingling and suave.

1. Dispatch the lobster (page 43). Place in a steamer or steaming apparatus and steam over high heat until the shell is consistently red. (If you are uncertain about doneness, split the tail and check to see if the meat is cooked through.) When cool enough to handle, remove all the meat and cut it into bite-size pieces.

2. At least 30 minutes before serving, combine the lobster with the remaining ingredients. Let stand at room temperature to blend flavors. Divide among 4 plates and serve.

SQUID WITH BASIL, MINT, AND BUCKWHEAT NOODLES

FOR 6

The Japanese buckwheat noodles called soba have a wonderful wheaty chewiness and are a perfect complement to fresh squid sautéed in olive oil with garlic, mint, and basil.

I think of this savory, quickly done dish as a salad, but please feel free to call it a pasta and to serve it as such.

1. In a medium skillet, heat the oil and garlic over medium heat until the garlic colors lightly, about 2 minutes.

2. Add the squid and sauté until the flesh becomes opaque, about 3 minutes. Transfer the squid to a large bowl; discard the garlic.

3. Cook the buckwheat noodles in abundant boiling water until al dente, about 3 minutes. Drain and bring to room temperature.

4. Add the remaining ingredients to the bowl with the squid and combine. Add the pasta, toss well, and serve.

Note: You can substitute capellini or rice noodles for the buckwheat pasta. Cook the capellini until al dente or soak the rice noodles. Drain well.

4 tablespoons olive oil

3 garlic cloves

1 pound cleaned squid, the body cut into 1-inch lengths

4 ounces buckwheat pasta (soba)

$1/2$ cup julienned fresh basil leaves

$2^1/2$ tablespoons soy sauce

2 teaspoons julienned fresh mint leaves

$1/2$ teaspoon red pepper flakes

BABY SHRIMP SALAD WITH ZESTY PAPAYA-MINT DRESSING

FOR 6

DRESSING

½ papaya, peeled, seeded, and
   coarsely chopped
3 fresh mint leaves
½ cup water
3 drops of Tabasco Sauce
3 teaspoons fresh lime juice
3 teaspoons rice vinegar
Salt and freshly ground black
   pepper

SALAD

4 cups Court Bouillon (page 69)
1¼ pounds small shrimp (35 to
   45 count), peeled
6 handfuls mizuna lettuce or
   mâche (lamb's lettuce)
½ jicama, cut into thin strips
½ papaya, peeled, seeded,
   and diced

COOK'S OPTION

*Use 1 small peeled very ripe
mango, coarsely chopped,
in place of the papaya.*

As a chef, I'm often asked how I come up with a particular dish. I don't mean to dodge the question, but inspiration comes from everywhere. I'm happiest when just a few well-chosen ingredients produce a flavor as deliciously complex as that of this refreshing salad. The sweetly floral taste of ripe papaya combined with lime, mint, and Tabasco Sauce make a really amazing dressing. Prepared in minutes, this is a wonderful indoor-outdoor dish that would be perfect for summer lunch.

1. Combine all the dressing ingredients in the bowl of a food processor. Process for 2 minutes.

2. In a medium nonreactive saucepan, bring the court bouillon to the boil. Add the shrimp and cook just until the bouillon returns to the boil. Drain the shrimp, reserving the bouillon for reuse if you like, and allow the shrimp to come to room temperature. (To save the bouillon for reuse, cool and store it refrigerated, as you would a stock.)

3. In a mixing bowl, toss the cooled shrimp with the greens, jicama, and diced papaya. Add sufficient dressing to coat well. Divide the salad among 6 plates and serve.

7. SUSHI, SASHIMI, AND OTHER RAW SPECIALTIES

It's easy to understand why sushi and sashimi have become so popular. Discovering the direct pleasures of these superbly simple Japanese treats is like encountering seafood for the very first time. Eating fish and shellfish in their purest form is not only an addictive delight but a way to learn about the essential nature of seafood itself.

Nigiri sushi ("hand-shaped" sushi) is the primary sushi variety. Like all sushi, it melds the pure flavor of raw fish or shellfish with rice that has been seasoned with a tart vinegar dressing. The rice is first molded into "fingers" that are seasoned with piquant wasabi, then covered with a slice of the freshest seafood. You pick up a piece of sushi, dip it into a dish of pungent soy sauce (fish side down!), and enjoy fresh seafood as never before. The other sushi we are most familiar with is maki sushi ("rolled" sushi). To make it, a sheet of toasted seaweed called nori is first spread with the vinegared rice, then rolled around strips of seafood, vegetables, or pickle. The maki are then cut into sections, as delicious to eat as they are wonderful to look at.

Sashimi is simpler still. Five or six slices of succulent raw fish are served aside a mound of the shredded giant white radish called daikon. Arranged alongside are enticing condiments like pale green wasabi and freshly grated ginger. Everyone receives a little dish of soy sauce for dipping. Each diner mixes a bit of wasabi into the soy sauce, then dips a piece of the glistening sashimi into it. The taste, at once vivid and pristine, is a revelation.

Sushi and sashimi can be served as a first course or as a whole meal. They can be served alone, as an hors d'oeuvre, or in combination plates. When other food is to be served with them, however, sushi or sashimi should always be eaten first. Their subtle flavors really demand a fresh palate.

Though neither sushi and sashimi are difficult to prepare once basic techniques are understood, each has its traditional methods, which reflect the Japanese passion for the freshest materials, in their seasonal prime, and presenting them as beautifully as possible. But don't worry about exacting requirements. My aim here is to make authentic sushi and sashimi absolutely accessible, so I've clarified procedures, included detailed drawings, and simplified matters wherever possible. I don't pretend to be a sushi expert, of course, but I've enjoyed mastering many sushi and sashimi techniques, and you can too. I think you'll find making sushi and sashimi a practical at-home activity, and one that is great fun. I've also included recipes for other raw seafood specialties I know you'll find delicious.

FRESHNESS AND SAFETY

If freshness is essential to all seafood cookery it is of peerless importance when preparing sushi and sashimi. I have a Japanese friend living in Tokyo who wouldn't dream of eating his sashimi any later than lunchtime. He assumes that he will be eating fish caught and prepared early in the day; by nightfall it wouldn't be worth a chopstick's touch. This is an extreme position, of course, but it underlines the necessity of scrupulous attention to quality when buying seafood to be eaten raw. The search for freshness merges with concerns about risk. The problems attendant to eating improperly handled raw fish—bacterial and parasitic infection—can be easily avoided. Here are guidelines for buying fish to be served raw:

1. *Choose an appropriate fish.* Avoid freshwater fish, which have a higher potential for parasites. The best fish for sushi and sashimi are tuna, Spanish mackerel, tilefish, fluke, striped bass, yellowtail, sea bass, sea bream, and cuttlefish. These fish swim in deeper waters where their food is generally free of parasites. Avoid salmon, herring, rockfish, mackerel, cod, and halibut, all of whose diets make them potentially prone to parasitic infection. (I used to be an advocate of using fish from cold waters for sushi and sashimi, which I believed were less likely to harbor parasites. No more. Cold-water fish may not be any safer. The lesson is that water temperature in itself is no indication of fish safety.)

2. *Tell your fish merchant that you intend to make sushi or sashimi.* A reputable seller should be willing to help you make a selection or, if necessary, to discourage the project entirely. Your fish merchant may not be liable for any ill effects that result from eating his stock, but he certainly doesn't want to endanger his reputation. It should go without saying that sushi and sashimi cannot be made from fish bought in supermarkets (though I am aware that certain West Coast markets have special sushi "chefs" on hand who will prepare sushi and sashimi on the spot; ask if they can provide you with the raw ingredients to assemble yourself at home).

3. *Reread all the rules concerning freshness in Chapter 1.* Ideally you would buy live fish, which are most often found in Chinatowns or other Asian markets. Failing that, choose whole fish, whose freshness is more easily verifiable by checking gill color, surface appearance, and so on. It is preferable to buy ungutted whole fish, if possible. Viscera—

and the liver in particular—may carry toxins that can spread to the flesh if the evisceration process is sloppily handled—that is, if punctured organs come in contact with flesh. Most retailers know what they are doing; still, it's wisest to observe the evisceration process, or to do the work yourself (page 27).

4. *If you use fillets, select only those with the skin still on.* Skinless fillets, no matter how acceptable for cooking, have undergone too much handling to be suitable for sushi. Furthermore, skin itself is a good indicator of freshness. Look for glistening, unwrinkled surfaces and traces of bright blood along the center of the flesh. There is a bonus to buying fillets for sushi with the skin, which is retained for certain preparations.

5. *If you are still uncomfortable, avoid all risk by freezing fish first.* Fish frozen in home freezers for a week at -10° F. will be absolutely safe to eat raw, as any lurking bacteria or parasites will have been killed. (See the section on freezing and defrosting fresh fish in Chapter 2.) But doesn't frozen fish negate the spirit, not to mention the character, of fish to be eaten raw? Yes, frozen fish is invariably a compromise; there's bound to be some degradation of flavor and texture. But people crave sushi and sashimi for a number of reasons—the total lack of added fat, the healthfulness of the seafood, the enjoyment of a yielding consistency as it plays against the tartness of vinegared rice or the heat of wasabi. My feeling is this kind of sushi or sashimi is better than none at all. If you do freeze, go for the less delicate species such as yellowtail tuna or salmon. (I recommend salmon for sushi or sashimi *only* when it has first been frozen or cured.)

If none of these precautionary steps totally allays your fears, consider making vegetable sushi, pages 142 to 147.

6. *Always use the fish the day you buy it.* Make sure there are no long waits between buying and preparing the raw seafood. If you anticipate a delay, have the fish packed in ice. Always slice fish for sushi and sashimi just before serving.

HANDLING AND EQUIPMENT

If you follow all these rules, you'll be on your way to delicious, healthful sushi and sashimi. A successful *result* depends upon proper handling and the appropriate equipment:

• *Cutting Boards.* Always use a nonporous cutting surface. Most of the chefs I know have switched from wood to plastic cutting boards, which are easily washed and do not retain bacteria. Look for one that is large (10 by 14 inches) and thick. If you have a lightweight board, it can be steadied by placing a damp cloth beneath it before cutting.

- *Knives.* Japanese knives are marvelous instruments, forged so that only one side of the blade holds the cutting edge. Unless you are familiar with their use, however, it is wisest and completely acceptable to cut with Western knives. Use a flexible 10-inch slicing knife, the kind made for slicing beef or poultry. Keep the knife sharp through repeated use of a steel or other sharpener.

- *The Slicing Solution.* When slicing, your knife, hands, and work surface should be constantly wiped with a clean dishcloth that has been soaked in a solution of *3 tablespoons of rice vinegar to 2 cups of ice water.* This solution, which you'll easily get into the habit of using, helps prevent tender fish flesh from sticking to your knife and hands and also acts as a disinfectant.

- *Bamboo Mats.* Called *maki-su* in Japanese, these ingenious devices are made from bamboo strips woven together with cotton cord. They are used to help roll nori into neat cylinders for maki sushi. Bamboo mats are widely available in Japanese provisions stores.

SLICING FISH FOR SUSHI AND SASHIMI

The beautiful plates of sushi and sashimi that trained sushi chefs produce convince many home cooks that mysterious or complicated knifework is required. Not so. Although you can't expect to achieve immediately what Japanese chefs accomplish after much practice, you *can* learn how to slice raw fish with enough skill for fine results.

Start by trimming the fish. Sushi and sashimi are cut from fillets or loin pieces. When using fillets, trim away the sides to obtain a rectangular shape of even thickness. (Save the trimmings; julienne-cut, they make a delightful haystacklike sashimi.) When preparing large fish like tuna, buy a piece of the loin sufficiently thick to yield a block roughly 1¼ inches wide by ¾ inch high by 5 inches long. Your objective is to produce a bar of fish from which you can cut uniform slices. Remember to use the slicing solution for cleaning your knife and fingers during slicing.

For home purposes, you will use five cuts—the rectangular, the diagonal, the rosette, the strip, and the julienne.

THE RECTANGULAR CUT (FOR SASHIMI; ALL FISH)

With a continuous smooth stroke, make uniform slices ¼-inch thick of a trimmed fillet or loin piece, as shown. Avoid force or pressure. On a garnished serving plate, immediately overlap the slices in the order in which they were cut.

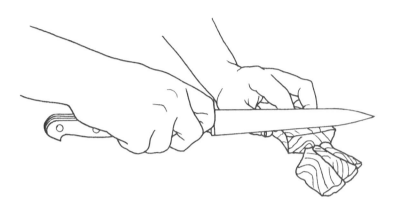

THE DIAGONAL CUT (FOR NIGIRI SUSHI; ALL FISH)

Place the block of fish lengthwise on your board. Holding the knife almost parallel to the fish—at a 35° angle—cut diagonal slices about ¼ inch thick. Make confident, drawing strokes.

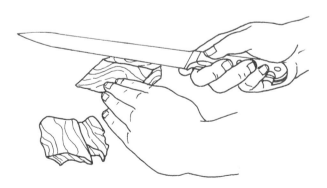

THE ROSETTE CUT (FOR SASHIMI; FOR FIRMER-FLESHED FISH LIKE FLUKE, TILEFISH, AND WHITEFISH)

Follow the instructions for making the diagonal cut, but slice the fish about ⅛ inch thick. Overlap three slices of fish and roll the overlapped slices loosely. Stand the rolled fish on end and gently open the layers to create a rosette. Arrange on a shiso leaf on a serving plate.

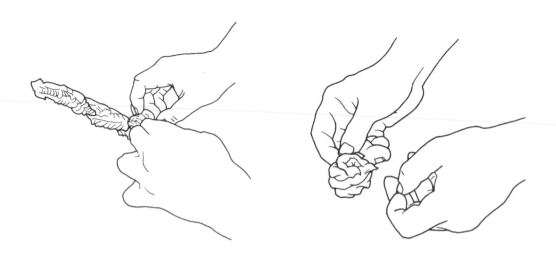

THE STRIP CUT (FOR MAKI SUSHI; ALL FISH)

Cut strips from trimmed fillet about ¼ inch thick and between 2 to 5 inches long.

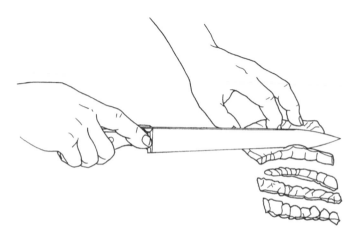

THE JULIENNE CUT (FOR SASHIMI; ALL FISH)

Julienne the fillet trimmings. Start by making an X of two overlapping strips. Continue building until you have a haystacklike mound. Compress gently with your fingers and arrange on a plate.

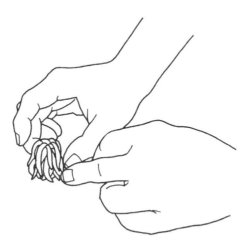

GARNISHES AND CONDIMENTS

A fascinating array of garnishes and condiments is integral to the presentation and taste of sushi and sashimi. A serving of sashimi will, for example, invariably include shredded daikon, a knob of wasabi paste, and a dish of soy sauce for dipping. Garnishes other than daikon range from thinly sliced lemon to such wonderfully intriguing items as hanatsuke kyuri, a yellow-petaled flowering cucumber, and benetade, deep red sprouts with a subtly tangy aftertaste. Of course, not all garnishes are readily available, even in Japan. The list below includes the items you're most likely to find in gourmet shops, supermarkets, Japanese and Asian groceries, and natural food stores. You can always substitute Western items; shredded carrot or icicle radish make good (though obviously different) stand-ins for daikon and parsley or cress can enhance sushi and sashimi plates beautifully.

DAIKON

These giant white radishes, now widely available at supermarkets, look like oversize parsnips. Their flesh is simultaneously sweet and sharp, with a characteristic metallic note. When buying daikon, choose firm specimens with bright creamy skins (which must be peeled) and dark green tops, if sprouting. Daikon can be thinly julienned with a mandoline or thin-bladed knife. To julienne daikon by hand, slice it lengthwise into the thinnest possible sheets. Roll each sheet and cut it crosswise into fine strips. Store whole daikon in the vegetable bin of your refrigerator.

KAIWARE

These daikon sprouts are sometimes labeled radish sprouts. In addition to their role as a garnish, they are chopped and used to season maki sushi like the Spicy Tuna Roll, page 141. They are purchased in 4-ounce hinged plastic containers, in their growing medium. Store them in the refrigerator.

SHISO (OBA LEAF)

There are red and green varieties of this aromatic member of the mint family. The green is most widely available and the most fragrant. This lovely garnish leaf is sold stacked in packages. Wrapped in damp paper towels and stored in the vegetable bin of your refrigerator, shiso will last about a week. Its aroma diminishes as it ages, so use the leaves as soon as possible.

AKA TOASAKA AND OGA NORI

These are salt-preserved decorative seaweeds. Both are feathery; aka toasaka is magenta and oga nori is a bright green. Both should be rinsed several times in cold water before using. They are sold in packages or 1-cup plastic containers. Return unused seaweed to its original container or wrap in film and store in the refrigerator.

WASABI

The roots of this plant, which is unique to Japan, yield a potent, horseradishlike condiment. In this country fresh wasabi is almost impossible to find; instead buy fresh frozen grated wasabi root or canned wasabi powder. As a last resort, prepared wasabi can be bought in tubes. Defrost the frozen root only when you intend to use it; subsequently, it will last for about one week in the refrigerator. To prepare powdered wasabi (which is actually a derivative of our own horseradish), pour a tablespoon of the powder into a small bowl. Add water gradually while mixing until the wasabi has the consistency of putty. Wasabi is best made fresh, but may be stored in the refrigerator for about one week.

PICKLED GINGER

An indispensable accompaniment to the sushi course, pickled ginger is readily available. Like many bottled pickles, however, it is really best when made fresh, which you can do easily at home. You will find yourself craving this tart-sweet condiment, which is likely to become part of many non-Japanese meals (the pickling juice makes a great addition to salad dressings). The following recipe yields enough pickled ginger to garnish 8 plates.

1 tablespoon plus 1 teaspoon salt

3 tablespoons rice vinegar

2 tablespoons water

1 teaspoon sugar

5 inches (about 4 ounces) fresh ginger

Drops of grenadine, for color (optional)

1. Make the pickling solution. In a nonreactive bowl, combine ½ teaspoon of the salt with the vinegar, water, and sugar.

2. Peel the ginger and, using a thin slicing knife, mandoline, or sturdy peeler, cut it diagonally along the grain into paper-thin slices. Soak the slices in cold water for 5 minutes; drain.

3. Place the ginger in a nonreactive saucepan with enough water to cover. Add 1 tablespoon salt and bring to the boil. As soon as the water begins to boil, drain the ginger and add it to the pickling solution. Add the grenadine if you wish the pickled ginger to have a rosy color.

4. Allow the ginger to steep at least until it comes to room temperature. The pickled ginger may be stored indefinitely refrigerated in the pickling solution, but it begins to lose its punch after a week.

SOY SAUCE

The preeminent seasoning for all Asian cooking, this pungent brown sauce was orig-inally used to preserve foods. Made from fermented soybeans, wheat, and salt, Japanese soy sauce is particularly bright in taste and aroma and less salty than its Chinese cousins. It is also lighter than many Chinese soy sauces, which can be dark and somewhat viscous, and are labeled black, mushroom soy, or Soy Superior Sauce. Check labels carefully to make sure soy sauce is "naturally brewed." Never buy synthetic soy—made from hydrolyzed vegetable protein, caramel, and corn syrup. I have found that low-sodium soy sauce tastes better with sushi because sushi rice already contains sufficient salt. Try to get high-quality Japanese brands like Yamasa or San-J.

NORI

Sometimes called laver, nori are thin toasted sheets of iridescent dark green or pur-plish seaweed, used as the wrapper for maki sushi. Nori is sold flat or folded in packages or cans; the sheets measure 7 to 8 inches square. Rewrap unused nori in plastic film and store out of direct sunlight.

PICKLED SQUASH

Called kampyo in Japanese, these pickled strips of hubbard squash are used in maki sushi. Kampyo are sold in jars.

KATSUO-BUSHI

Rose-colored flakes of dried bonito, a fish that has been an important part of the Japanese diet from earliest times, katsuo-bushi is used in the preparation of dashi, the Japanese cooking stock, and makes a welcome sashimi and sushi seasoning. Buy it in bags or boxes in stores with a rapid turnover, as the flakes lose their flavor if held too long. Store in airtight containers.

RICE

Short-grained rice is required for sushi. It has sufficient firmness to provide "bite" while cohering perfectly for making nigiri or maki sushi. Choose such widely available Japanese brands as Cal-Rose and Botan. Make sure the grains are transparent, without milkiness or striping.

SESAME SEEDS

White and black sesame seeds (shiro gomma and kuro gomma, respectively) are used to coat and season sushi. They are available in small packets and should be toasted just before using. Toast sesame seeds in a small, dry, heavy skillet just until fragrant and beginning to color. They keep indefinitely in the refrigerator or freezer, but can become rancid quickly if left at room temperature.

MIRIN

Sometimes called sweet sake, mirin is a sweet, syrupy rice wine used only for cooking. It is a readily available seasoning. Store it away from heat in a cupboard, where it will last for several months, or refrigerate it indefinitely.

TOBIKO

Flying fish roe, available at Japanese markets, is salty with a definite crunch. Tobiko is used as a decorative seasoning in maki and rice rolls (rolled maki without a nori "wrapper"). It is colored a bright orange-yellow and adds vivid contrast to a sushi platter. You can substitute cod or smelt roe (magaro). Both tobiko and magaro can be purchased frozen.

SASHIMI

Sashimi isn't hard to do, but like many seemingly simple things, its excellence depends on a few careful considerations.

The fish must be absolutely fresh and wholesome. I can't repeat this too often. Cutting should be clean and attractive. Don't be discouraged if early attempts produce less than desirable results; try again. Once cut, the fish should be pleasingly presented, as unadorned fresh raw fish requires a proper setting. Nothing elaborate is required, but time-honored rules governing the creation and composition of a sashimi plate should be observed:

• All slices from a given piece of fish should be arranged touching one another, in the order in which they were cut. You can serve one or more kinds of fish together. Use three to five pieces of *rectangular-cut* slices per variety of fish, depending on the number of people to be served and the role the sashimi plus in the meal (first course, whole meal, or part of a platter also containing sushi).

• For individual servings, arrange the slices on small plates. Square or rectangular plates, available at Japanese shops, are particularly nice.

• The sliced fish is invariably placed on or aside a mound of shredded daikon, which is accompanied by a knob of wasabi or any of the additional garnishes discussed earlier. Small dishes of soy sauce are offered for dipping. Chopsticks are required.

INDIVIDUAL AND COMBINATION SASHIMI PLATES

We begin with a simple sashimi plate for one, then proceed to a combination plate containing several varieties of fish and cuts.

The basic plate above makes a satisfying bite for one person and is so simple to fix that a "recipe" seems inappropriate. To compose it, place three slices of rectangular-cut fresh tuna on a small mound of julienned daikon. Add a knob of wasabi and serve with soy sauce for dipping.

To prepare an "intermediate" sashimi plate, build on the basic plate. To the tuna, daikon, and wasabi plate add a bed of aka toasaka. Place a fluke rosette against it and decorate the rosette with kaiware. Add a small pillow of oga nori and lay three slices of rectangular-cut bass atop it. Serve with soy sauce for dipping.

This third combination plate builds upon the intermediate plate. Lay rectangular-cut Spanish mackerel atop the aka toasaka. Add a shiso leaf and a lemon fan (thin half-slices of lemon arranged as shown). Serve with soy sauce for dipping.

SUSHI RICE

MAKES 4 CUPS

VINEGAR DRESSING

7 tablespoons rice vinegar

2 scant tablespoons sugar

2 teaspoons salt

RICE

2 cups short-grain Japanese rice

2½ cups water

Sushi rice is made from a medium-sticky short-grain rice native to Japan. Because sushi rice is cooked with less water than the usual boiled rice, it is deliciously chewy. Japanese chefs fan the cooked rice to cool it quickly; fanning encourages the proper consistency and ensures a lovely gloss. I urge you to try this method using a simple hand fan or folded newspaper (with or without a partner), or cool the rice more simply by spreading and turning it on a sheet pan. To avoid mashing the warm rice, combine it and the vinegar dressing lightly, as you would fold egg whites into a batter. Always cook the rice just before assembling your sushi and allow it to come to room temperature.

1. Mix the dressing ingredients until the salt and sugar have dissolved completely. Reserve.

2. Pour the rice into a colander and rinse under cold running water until the water runs clear.

3. In a heavy saucepan, combine the rice and water. Cover and bring to the boil. Reduce the heat to low and simmer, covered, for 10 minutes. Remove the rice from the heat and allow to stand, covered, for 10 minutes more.

4. Turn the rice into a wooden or other nonreactive bowl. (Wood is traditional and allows the rice to cool more quickly.) Pour the vinegar dressing over the rice and, using a wooden or plastic spatula, blend with light, cutting motions. Fan the rice while folding, if you wish. (If this seems too acrobatic to you, get a helper to do the fanning.) Alternatively, spread the rice on a sheet pan and, using a wooden spoon or rubber spatula, fold in the vinegar dressing, blending across the surface of the rice. The rice is ready to use when it reaches room temperature.

NIGIRI SUSHI (MASTER RECIPE)

MAKES 20 PIECES

Nigiri, or hand-shaped, sushi consist of diagonal-cut slices of the freshest fillet seasoned with a smear of wasabi, then draped over fingers of sushi rice. The completed nigiri are quickly arranged with appropriate garnishes and served with wasabi, pickled ginger, and a dish of soy sauce for dipping.

Nigiri sushi may be served alone or in combination with maki sushi and/or sashimi. Nigiri make a splendid hors d'oeuvre or a perfect first course. Until you have found your "hand" in making them, it's probably best not to attempt to prepare more than two different kinds of fish nigiri at a time. A sushi zen, or master chef, would take about seven steps to mold the rice fingers and drape the fish over them; I've simplified the procedure without sacrificing the integrity of the dish.

Don't forget to use plenty of slicing solution to facilitate forming the nigiri.

4 cups slicing solution (see page 126)

4 cups Sushi Rice (page 136)

2 teaspoons fresh frozen grated wasabi, or 1 tablespoon prepared powdered

1 pound diagonal-cut fish bars, from 2 pounds skinless fillet(s) of fluke, yellowtail, Spanish mackerel, sea bream, tilefish, or bass; or from 1¼ pounds tuna, alone or in combination

Pickled Ginger (page 131), for serving

Soy sauce, for dipping

1. To prepare the rice-finger base, first dip your working hand into the slicing solution—this prevents sticking. Take a small handful of the rice (about 1½ tablespoons) and squeeze it gently to form an oval finger no longer than 1½ inches. Squeeze hard enough so that the rice coheres, but not so hard that you end up with a gummy mass. Make as many fingers as you want nigiri and lay them on a plate. Keep the rice covered with a damp towel as you work.

2. Smear a slice of fish along the middle with a line of wasabi. Pick up a rice finger and drape the fish slice over it. Gently but firmly mold the fish slice to conform to the mound of rice. Make sure the fish has adhered. Repeat with remaining fish and rice fingers.

3. Arrange the nigiri touching one another (to prevent drying out) on plates. Serve with the pickled ginger and the soy sauce.

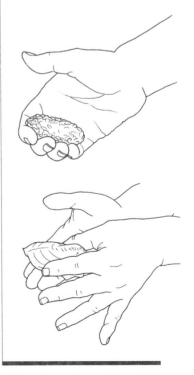

SEARED SPANISH MACKEREL NIGIRI

MAKES 20 PIECES

2 cups slicing solution
(page 126)

4 cups Sushi Rice (page 136)

2 Spanish mackerel fillets (10 to
12 ounces each), taken
preferably from a whole fish
personally inspected for
freshness

2 teaspoons fresh frozen grated
wasabi, or 1 tablespoon prepared powdered

1/4 cup kaiware (radish sprouts),
for garnish

Pickled Ginger (page 131), for
serving

Soy sauce, for dipping

Sushi is synonymous with raw skinless fish, but this variation uses seared Spanish unskinned mackerel fillet. The result is remarkable—each slice of fish contains the cool briny taste of raw fish *and* the seared, smoky flavor of its crisped skin.

1. Prepare the rice fingers as described in step 1 of the Nigiri Sushi recipe, page 137.

2. Heat a heavy skillet large enough to contain a single fillet until very hot. (A drop of water thrown into the pan will bounce and dry immediately.) Place a fillet skin side down in the dry pan and sear it for 10 seconds, pressing down on the fillet to prevent it from "cupping." With a pair of tongs, flip the fillet, and sear for 5 seconds more. (The second side will not require holding.) Remove the fillet to your cutting board. Sear the second fillet.

3. Using the diagonal cut, slice the fillets. Form the nigiri using the wasabi. (See step 2 of the Nigiri Sushi recipe, page 137.) Arrange the nigiri, touching one another, on plates. Garnish with kaiware, placing sprouts between the nigiri. Serve with the pickled ginger, additional wasabi if you like, and the soy sauce.

CURED SALMON-BELLY NIGIRI

MAKES 20 PIECES

Salmon belly consists of strips of flesh taken from the thin bottom sides of whole fish. Each piece is approximately 1¾ inches wide. Ask your fish seller to cut (or save) the belly strips for you—often as not, you'll get them for free. The at-home curing gives the salmon a tart, satisfying saltiness that plays beautifully against the sushi rice. (You can slice the cured fish more thinly than this recipe directs to make rosette sashimi, page 128.) Because the salmon has been cured, there's no need to be concerned about consuming it raw.

1. Spread half the salt on a large platter spread in an even layer. Place the belly strips on the salt and sprinkle with the remaining salt. Allow the strips to cure for about 1½ hours. Wash them thoroughly and pat dry.
2. In a shallow nonreactive pan large enough to hold all the fish, combine the ingredients for the brine. Add the cured bellies and allow them to steep for 20 minutes. Remove, dry, and trim off any white membrane. Using the diagonal cut, slice the bellies for nigiri. Form the rice fingers and make the nigiri. (See steps 1 and 2 of Nigiri Sushi recipe, page 137.) Arrange on plates touching one another and garnish with the pickled ginger. Serve with the pickled ginger, additional wasabi if you like, and the soy sauce.

FISH

1 pound kosher salt

4 salmon belly strips, washed
    and dried (see headnote)

BRINE

3 cups rice vinegar

½ cup mirin

½ cup water

2 teaspoons soy sauce

2 quarter-size slices fresh ginger

2 cups slicing solution
    (page 126)

4 cups Sushi Rice (page 136)

2 teaspoons fresh frozen grated
    wasabi, or 1 tablespoon
    prepared powdered

Pickled Ginger (page 131),
    for serving

Soy sauce, for dipping

MAKI SUSHI (MASTER RECIPE)

MAKES 2 ROLLS, ABOUT 6 BY 2½ INCHES

2 sheets nori seaweed

2 cups slicing solution
(page 126)

4 cups Sushi Rice (page 136)

2 teaspoons fresh frozen grated
wasabi, or 1 tablespoon prepared powdered

¼ pound strip-cut fluke, Spanish
mackerel, tilefish, snapper,
tuna, or striped bass

Pickled Ginger (page 131), for
serving

Soy sauce, for dipping

Maki are nori-wrapped rolls of sushi rice with raw fish and/or vegetable centers. They are made with the bamboo rolling mat called a *maki-su*, which compresses the core ingredients into a neat cylinder. If you cannot find a *maki-su*, you can improvise one by cutting an undyed flexible place mat into a 10-inch square. Or double-fold a large sheet of aluminum foil, cut it into a 10-inch square, and cover it with a sheet of plastic film cut to the same size.

Maki require only a little practice to do and look particularly wonderful when they are cut into segments (straight across or on the bias) that are then stood on end to display their mosaiclike fillings. They can be made relatively large in circumference (about 2 inches) or smaller (1¼ inches). Maki can be made with sushi rice and nori only in which case they are called rice rolls. Rice-roll segments look and taste marvelous with a dab of caviar placed in a depression made in one end. Maki are served alone or in combination with other kinds of sushi and/or sashimi.

1. Place 1 sheet of the nori, shiny side down, on the bamboo mat.

2. Moisten your hands with the slicing solution and take a large handful

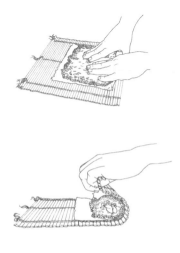

of the sushi rice (about 1¼ cups). Pat the rice in an even ¼-inch layer to the sides of the nori, leaving a margin of 1½ inches on the top. Dot 1 teaspoon of fresh grated wasabi or ½ teaspoon prepared powdered wasabi in the center of the rice rectangle and spread it to form a band. Align the strips of fillet along the wasabi. To roll, bring the bottom of the nori up and roll toward the far end of the rice, as shown. The ends should just meet, overlapping slightly. Gently but firmly press the bamboo mat to seal the roll. Look at the side of the roll to check the position of the fillet strip; it should be at its very center. If it is not, you'll need a bit of practice. Repeat the procedure for the second roll.

3. Cut the completed maki into quarters, straight across, or cut the first and third slices on the bias. Stand the maki segments on a plate touching one another and serve with the pickled ginger, additional wasabi if you like, and the soy sauce.

SPICY TUNA ROLL

MAKES 2 ROLLS, ABOUT 6 BY 2½ INCHES

This maki variation blends East and West with tantalizing results. Once the sushi rice is made, the tuna is chopped and blended with a mayonnaise-based "filling" containing chopped scallion, sesame oil, and chili paste. This is a fine opportunity to use fish scraps that might not qualify for other raw fish preparations.

1. In a mixing bowl, combine the tuna, mayonnaise, scallions, chili paste, sesame seeds, and oil. Following steps 1 and 2 in the recipe for Maki Sushi, pat half of the sushi rice onto one sheet of the nori.

2. Spread half the filling in a line across the middle of the rice. Roll the maki and repeat the procedure for the remaining roll. Cut the maki as you wish. Garnish with the kaiware and serve with the pickled ginger and the soy sauce.

2 ounces tuna, minced

1 teaspoon Homemade Mayonnaise (page 71)

1 teaspoon minced scallions

½ teaspoon Chinese chili paste

1 teaspoon white sesame seeds, toasted

2 drops Asian sesame oil

2 sheets nori seaweed

2 cups slicing solution (page 126)

4 cups Sushi Rice (page 136)

¼ cup kaiware for garnish

Pickled Ginger (page 131), for serving

Soy sauce, for dipping

CRAB AND AVOCADO ROLL

MAKES 2 ROLLS, ABOUT 6 BY 2½ INCHES

2 ounces jumbo lump crabmeat, shell and cartilage removed

2 teaspoons Homemade Mayonnaise (page 71), or best-quality store-bought

¼ teaspoon Chinese chili paste

2 sheets nori seaweed

2 cups slicing solution (page 126)

4 cups Sushi Rice (page 136)

¼ avocado, sliced lengthwise

Pickled Ginger (page 131), for serving

Soy sauce, for dipping

The addition of avocado to sweet lump crabmeat earned this maki the nickname of California Roll. Whatever you call it, the crab and avocado combination is inspired.

1. Combine the crab, mayonnaise, and chili paste. Following steps 1 and 2 in the recipe for Maki Sushi (page 141), pat half the sushi rice onto one sheet of the nori.

2. Spread half the crabmeat mixture in a line across the middle of the rice and lay 2 strips of avocado over the filling. Roll the maki and repeat the procedure for the second roll. Cut the maki as you wish and serve with the pickled ginger and the soy sauce.

VEGETABLE ROLL WITH CUCUMBER, DAIKON, AND PICKLED PLUM MAYONNAISE

MAKES 1 ROLL, 6 BY 2½ INCHES

The cool acidity of the cucumber combines beautifully with the sharpness of the daikon and the creamy tang of the Pickled Plum Mayonnaise in this vegetarian roll.

1. Blanch the lettuce leaves quickly in boiling water and pat them dry. Roll the leaves and cut them crosswise into strips about ½ inch wide. You should have about ⅛ cup.

2. Following steps 1 and 2 of the recipe for Maki Sushi (page 141), pat the sushi rice onto the nori. Spread the mayonnaise in a line across the center of the rice and lay the cucumber and daikon strips across it. Sprinkle the vegetables with the shredded lettuce and roll the maki. Cut as you wish and serve with the pickled ginger and the soy sauce.

Large outer leaves from 1 small head Boston lettuce

1 sheet nori seaweed

2 cups slicing solution (page 126)

2 cups Sushi Rice (page 136)

1½ tablespoons Pickled Plum Mayonnaise (page 74)

2 strips peeled and seeded cucumber, ¼ by ¼ by 2 inches

2 strips daikon, ⅛ by ⅛ by 2 inches

Pickled Ginger (page 131), for serving

Soy sauce, for dipping

VEGETABLE ROLL WITH SCALLIONS, PICKLED SQUASH, AND SESAME SEEDS

MAKES 1 ROLL, 6 BY 2½ INCHES

4 scallions, green parts only

1 sheet nori seaweed

2 cups slicing solution (page 126)

2 cups Sushi Rice (page 136)

½ teaspoon Chinese chili paste

2 strips kampyo (pickled hubbard squash)

1 teaspoon white sesame seeds, toasted

Pickled Ginger (page 131), for serving

Soy sauce, for dipping

Pickled vegetables constitute an important branch of Japanese cooking—traditionally, no meal was complete without them. Eggplant is considered the preeminent pickle, but squash is also favored for its crunchy sweetness. Pickled hubbard squash, called kampyo, is easily found in Asian markets. Combined with scallions and sesame seeds, it makes a sprightly maki filling.

1. Blanch the scallions quickly and pat dry.

2. Following steps 1 and 2 in the recipe for Maki Sushi (page 141), pat the sushi rice onto the nori. Spread the chili paste in a line across the center of the rice. Lay the squash and scallions across it. Sprinkle with the sesame seeds and roll up the maki. Cut as you wish and serve with the pickled ginger and the soy sauce.

VEGETABLE ROLL WITH SPINACH, SWEET POTATO, AND RED PEPPER

MAKES 1 ROLL, ABOUT 6 BY 2½ INCHES

Not only is this all-vegetable maki good to eat but its red, green, and gold interior is ravishing to look at.

Following steps 1 and 2 in the recipe for Maki Sushi (page 141), pat the sushi rice onto the nori. Spread the wasabi in a line across the center of the rice and lay the potato and pepper strips on top. Spread the spinach on top of the strips and roll the maki. Cut as you wish and serve with the pickled ginger, additional wasabi, if you like, and the soy sauce.

1 sheet nori seaweed

2 cups slicing solution (page 126)

2 cups Sushi Rice (page 136)

1 teaspoon fresh frozen grated wasabi, or 1½ teaspoons prepared powdered

2 strips sweet potato, ¼ by 2½ inches, simmered until just cooked through

2 strips red bell pepper, ¼ by 2½ inches

¼ pound spinach, steamed, drained, and squeezed dry

Pickled Ginger (page 131), for serving

Soy sauce, for dipping

OSHI SUSHI (PRESSED SUSHI)

MAKES 4 PIECES

4 slices diagonal-cut fluke, Spanish
  mackerel, sea bream, or tilefish
1 teaspoon fresh frozen grated
  wasabi, or 1½ teaspoons prepared dried
4 tablespoons Sushi Rice
  (page 136)
1 heaping teaspoon katsuo-bushi
  (dried bonito flakes),
  for garnish
Pickled Ginger (page 131), for
  serving

This is a very simple sushi variation. Diagonal-cut fish is placed in a small ramekin, which is then packed with sushi rice. Unmold the rice and serve—that's it. Try this when you crave sushi but don't want to mold the rice for nigiri or prepare maki.

1. Line 4 very small ramekins (1¼ to 1½ inches in circumference and at least ¾ inch deep) with plastic film, allowing it to extend beyond the top of the ramekin.

2. Place 1 strip of fish in each of the ramekins and spread sparingly with wasabi. Press rice very firmly into each ramekin.

3. Turn the ramekins upside down and use the film to help unmold the sushi onto small dishes. Sprinkle with the katsuo-bushi and serve with the pickled ginger and the soy sauce.

BATTERA SUSHI (BOX-MOLDED SUSHI)

MAKES 1 LOAF

Here is another form of pressed sushi that is traditionally made with a special wooden press frame. For this version use any square or rectangular shallow box or tin, such as an empty, well-washed anchovy can. You may want to invest in the traditional press mold, called an *oshiwaku*. It consists of three pieces: a frame, bottom, and lid. To use it, the rice is first packed into the frame with its traylike bottom piece in place. The lid is then pressed into the frame. As you press the lid you lift up and remove the frame, leaving a neat block of molded sushi on the "tray." The block is removed and served.

1. If not using an *oshiwaku*, line the box or tin with plastic wrap, allowing the ends to extend over the top of the container.

2. Place the fish in the center of the film-lined container and coat lightly with the wasabi. Add the rice and pack well.

3. Turn the box over and use the film to help unmold the sushi onto a cutting board. (Or, if using an *oshiwaku*, fill with half the rice, coat with the wasabi, add the remaining rice, and unmold as described in head-note.) Using a wet knife, cut the rice block into 1-inch-wide pieces. Dip some or all of the pieces into the sesame seeds, covering both sides with one color or each side with a different color. Garnish with the kaiware and serve with the pickled ginger, additional wasabi if you like, and the soy sauce.

2 slices diagonal-cut fish, taken from a trimmed, skinless fillet of fluke, Spanish mackerel, sea bream, tuna, or tilefish

About $1/4$ teaspoon fresh frozen grated wasabi or prepared powdered

About $1^1/4$ cups Sushi Rice (page 136)

About 1 tablespoon each black and white sesame seeds

$1/4$ cup kaiware (radish sprouts), for garnish

Pickled Ginger (page 131), for serving

Soy sauce, for dipping.

OTHER RAW SPECIALTIES

Below are a number of non-Japanese dishes prepared with raw fish that I now serve regularly. Again, please observe all the rules concerning raw fish safety (pages 124 to 125) when choosing and handling the fish you'll use.

These are really special. Though they make perfect starters, there's no reason why you couldn't serve them as a light lunch with a bit of bread. (The recipe for the sea scallop ceviche is sufficient for a main course.) They're especially nice in summer with a Sauvignon Blanc or a spicy Gewürztraminer.

STRIPED BASS CARPACCIO
FOR 6, AS A STARTER

MARINADE

2 tablespoons pink peppercorns

4 teaspoons freshly squeezed
    orange juice

3 teaspoons freshly squeezed
    lime juice

3 teaspoons soy sauce

2 teaspoons olive oil

FISH

12 ounces striped bass fillets

3 teaspoons finely julienned
    orange zest

3 teaspoons finely julienned
    lemon zest

This dish of taste-packed bass carpaccio always receives surprised adulation. Surprised because there doesn't seem to be much to it at first, just some pretty sliced fish on a plate. But when people try it, things start to happen. All at once they're aware of the bass, plush and sweet, the heat of red pepper, tangy lemon zest, the crisp savor of sea salt, and musky-fresh cilantro. They're astounded.

At the Sea Grill this makes an elegant, absolutely simple starter and I can't imagine a better first course. The only trick here is slicing the raw bass thin enough. Arm yourself with a very sharp slicing knife and figure you'll need a bit of practice. Save your initial, less-than-perfect slices (dressed first) as a treat for the cook; send your more polished efforts to the table. Then watch your guests' rapturous expressions once they've enjoyed their first bite.

1. Make the marinade. Using a spice mill, clean coffee grinder, or the bottom of a heavy pot, crush the pink peppercorns coarsely. Add them to a small bowl with the orange and lime juices, soy sauce, and olive oil. Blend well with a whisk, cover, and refrigerate until ready to serve the carpaccio.

2. Starting at the thicker end of the bass fillets, cut thin slices as long as possible; keep your knife almost parallel to the surface of the flesh and make smooth, confident strokes. Don't worry if some of your slices aren't absolutely even, but try not to shred the flesh.

3. Place 3 slices on each serving plate without any overlapping. If not serving immediately, cover the portions tightly with plastic wrap and refrigerate.

4. Fill a medium bowl half full of cold water and add ice cubes. Bring salted water to the boil and blanch the julienned orange and lemon zest for about 3 seconds. Remove the zest from the pot and submerge it in the cold water bath. Repeat the blanching and cooling once more, changing the ice water for the second blanching; this will insure that no bitterness remains in the zest. Dry the zest and refrigerate, if not using immediately.

5. When ready to serve, use a pastry brush to dab the fish lightly with the marinade; be sure to cover the entire surface of the fish. Sprinkle each portion evenly with the sea salt, red pepper, and orange and lemon zest. Garnish with the cilantro leaves. Wipe the edge of each serving dish with a clean towel and serve immediately.

1$^1/_2$ teaspoons sea salt
$^3/_4$ teaspoon red pepper flakes
About 30 cilantro leaves, washed and well dried

TUNA TARTARE WITH SALMON CAVIAR
AND WASABI CREAM

FOR 4

TUNA

1½ pounds bigeye or yellowfin tuna

1 teaspoon finely chopped garlic

1 teaspoon finely chopped ginger

1 teaspoon finely chopped chives

1 teaspoon finely chopped fresh mint

¼ teaspoon kosher salt

4 teaspoons soy sauce

1 teaspoon sesame oil

½ teaspoon ketjap manis, plus additional for garnish

½ teaspoon Tabasco Sauce

WASABI CREAM

¼ cup heavy (whipping) cream

2 tablespoons fresh frozen grated wasabi or prepared powdered

¼ teaspoon kosher salt

GARNISH

4 teaspoons salmon caviar

4 sprigs kaiware (radish sprouts)

4 sprigs fennel tops (feathery branches)

I'd gladly shake the hand of the first person to re-create traditional beef tartare using tuna. The idea is inspired. I've eaten and made dozens of tuna tartares in the past couple of years, and this one—the result of much trial and error—is the best. It combines freshly chopped tuna seasoned with mint, chive, garlic, and soy with a pungent cloud of wasabi-flavored whipped cream, and is crowned with salmon caviar (page 14). A small garnish of radish sprouts and fennel tops adds delicacy and distinction.

It's important to prepare the tartare just before you serve it as the soy and ketjap manis it contains quickly break down the fish's flesh.

1. Chill 2 stainless steel bowls, 1 small for whipping the cream, 1 medium for preparing the tartare.

2. Using a spoon, scrape all sinew from the tuna. Chop medium finely; it should have the consistency of coarsely ground meat. Wrap the tuna tightly with plastic wrap and refrigerate until ready to serve.

3. Add the cream to the small chilled bowl and whip. When it starts to thicken, add the wasabi and salt and continue to beat until stiff peaks form. Be careful not to overbeat.

4. In the second chilled bowl combine the tuna, garlic, ginger, chives, and mint. Add the salt, soy sauce, sesame oil, ketjap manis, and Tabasco Sauce. Using a fork, mix all the ingredients well until the mixture is lightly bound.

5. Place a 2½-inch ring mold on each serving plate and pack with the tuna, or form into patties and shape with a fork. If using molds, unmold the tuna onto the plates by pushing it through the rings.

6. Using a teaspoon, form egg-shaped dollops of the wasabi cream and place one on top of each serving of the tartare. Drizzle the plate with additional ketjap manis. Top each portion with about ½ teaspoon of the caviar and sprinkle the plate with additional caviar. Place the radish sprouts and fennel tops in the wasabi cream and serve immediately.

SEA SCALLOP CEVICHE WITH JALAPEÑO AND CUCUMBER

FOR 4

Somewhere, someone crazy must be debating with an equally crazy friend whether ceviche is a cooked or raw dish. I've done it myself. The action of any citrus acid on raw fish appears to "cook" it—the flesh becomes firm and opaque—but the wonderful taste of ceviche, full of bright flavor, evokes the fresh goodness of raw seafood.

In this sparkling version the heat of jalapeño plays against the taste of lime juice and the coolness of cucumber. I serve the ceviche in scallop shells—a lovely presentation—but you may use any pretty little serving plates.

1. In a well-chilled bowl, combine all the ingredients except the cucumber slices. Mix well with a wooden spoon, pressing all the flavor from the cilantro ends. Let the mixture stand unrefrigerated for 15 minutes. Remove the cilantro stems.

2. Place 4 cleaned scallop shells, if using, on a serving dish. Line the bottom of the shells, or small serving plates, with the cucumber slices. Spoon the ceviche over the cucumbers and drizzle with olive oil. Serve at room temperature.

2 medium red onions, sliced about 1/4 inch thick

1/3 bunch cilantro, leaves coarsely chopped; 4 root-end stems, crushed with the back of a knife

4 small jalapeños, minced

1 1/4 cups fresh lime juice

3/4 cup extra-virgin olive oil, plus extra for serving

3 teaspoons kosher salt

1/4 teaspoon freshly ground black pepper, or to taste

2 pounds sea scallops, cut into 1/4-inch slices

2 medium cucumbers, peeled, seeded, and cut into 1/4-inch slices

8. BROILING AND ROASTING

I don't know a cook, myself included, whose first efforts at seafood preparation didn't emerge from the broiler or oven. Many of us may feel a little embarrassed at our continuing dependence on these dry-heat methods, as if we aren't sufficiently accomplished. This is a real shame, as there are times when nothing but simply broiled or oven-roasted seafood will do. What could be better than a moist, mouthwatering fillet flecked with gold from its stay under the broiler, or a whole fish baked to fork-tender perfection? When I want to taste the sweet pure flavor of seafood just as it is, I go right to these quick and easy methods.

Unfortunately, the heat that so deliciously caramelizes fish and shellfish flesh can also rob it of its moisture. One method that virtually eliminates that outcome is moist-broiling—cooking fish under a moisture-producing and -retaining layer of vegetables or herbs. This technique produces matchless results. But there are other ways to ensure the success of your seafood broiling and roasting.

KEYS TO GREAT BROILING

Fish and shellfish protein is delicate and cooks quickly. It sounds obvious, but before broiling seafood take a good look at the thickness of what you're about to prepare. Thin fillets, which cook through rapidly, need fast, nonpenetrating heat and should be broiled close to the heat source. More substantial cuts and whole fish require the heat penetration of slower cooking, so they must be broiled farther from the flame. Finding the proper thickness to distance-from-the-heat ratio is the key to successful broiling. Sea and bay scallops, for example, will require different adjustments of the broiling pan. As you broil, check the progress of seafood, adjusting its height if the flesh seems to be charring too rapidly.

Add moisture when you can. The Best Broiled Lobster Ever is steamed in advance, a good way of getting around the problem of dried-out flesh, but you can also add moisturizing liquid to the pan whenever you broil. Three or 4 tablespoons of water poured into a *preheated* pan when broiling fillets produces the same effect as a similar addition while stir-frying: a burst of moisturizing steam. And leave the broiler open when you cook. A closed broiler traps air, so you're likely to end up baking your seafood; when that happens there goes your lovely broiled taste.

As for timing, trust only yourself. My broiler tells me that 10 minutes is right for a particular piece of fish, but yours may have a different opinion. I know you've heard it before, but recipe times are only guidelines; keep looking as you cook.

. . . AND PERFECT ROASTING

I love to cook whole fish and oven-roasting is a great way to do it. The center bones of the fish conduct heat evenly and the fish's skin acts as a protective glove. Strong external heat creates a mini cooking stock from the juices within that enhances the flavor of the flesh.

The major problem with roasting a whole, large fish is that the outside can get done while the inside remains raw. To avoid this, make sure that the oven temperature isn't too high in relation to the thickness of the seafood. Try roasting fillets following the technique I use for Roasted Monkfish with Balsamic Vinegar and Shallots. Sear the fillets *first* to caramelize their exteriors and color them enticingly, then roast them in an oiled pan at a relatively high temperature (around 425° F.).

To further guard against moisture loss, oil the whole fish, or wrap it with strips of bacon as I do for Roasted Whole Grouper with Garlic, Potatoes, and Bacon. Dishes like these, which are self-basting, will please you because they not only solve the moisture problem but also provide a fast meal-in-a-pan. You can, however, always add water to the pan when roasting whole fish or other seafood, or borrow a method used when cooking outdoors—wrap and protect shellfish with seaweed. Roasted Oysters Buried in Seaweed with Allspice is a good example of this technique, which guards against drying while filling the house with the most wonderful scents of the sea. Properly done, broiling and roasting are not only fast and no fuss but retain the sweet taste of fresh seafood.

BEST BROILED LOBSTER EVER

FOR 1

One 2-pound live lobster
1 tablespoon unsalted butter,
   softened, or olive oil
Salt and freshly ground black
   pepper
Fresh lemon juice

I've never taken sides on the boiled versus broiled lobster issue—both can be great.

The trouble is, broiled lobster can be tricky to cook properly; its sweet, succulent flesh can become dry and chewy in a flash. But you'll never serve overcooked broiled lobster if you follow this easy method. The secret lies in steaming the lobster in advance, which shores up flavor and juiciness. You'll get tender flesh and the great taste that only broiled lobster shell can impart.

I've called for a 2-pound lobster here, an ample meal for one, but feel free to apply this method to lobsters of any size. Cooked by this method, culls—lobsters missing a claw—or chicken lobsters, which weigh about a pound, make marvelous salads. A 3½- to 4-pound lobster is just right for a dinner for two. See the Note below for adjusting cooking times.

1. Preheat the broiler.
2. Pour about 2 inches of water into the bottom of a steamer or pot with a lid into which a colander just fits. Cover and bring to a full boil. When ample steam has collected, place the lobster on the steamer rack or in the colander, cover, and steam without peeking for 8 minutes. The lobster should be consistently red.
3. Split the lobster in half along the back and crack the claws with a heavy knife. Place the halves on a broiling tray, flesh side up, and rub the flesh with the butter or olive oil. Broil about 4 inches from the heat source until the flesh is milky white, about 3 minutes. Remove and discard the stomach sac (located behind the head) and season with the lemon juice.

Note: Steam and broil lobsters of different sizes as follows—chicken lobsters: steam for 4 minutes, broil for 3 minutes; 1- to 1½-pound lobsters: steam for 6 to 7 minutes, broil for 3 minutes; 2-pound lobsters: steam for 10 minutes, broil for 3 minutes; 3½- to 4-pound lobsters: steam for 15 minutes, broil for 5 minutes.

BROILED SCALLOP GRATIN WITH LEEKS AND CRÈME FRAÎCHE

FOR 4

This great seafood gratin, bubbling and golden-crusted, is perfect fare for a winter evening when you don't want to do much cooking but need something really satisfying to eat.

You can prepare the scallops the day before you intend to serve the dish, adding the bread-crumb topping just before you pop the gratin into the oven. The scallops in this dish really shine—their crème fraîche "sauce" is luscious but surprisingly light. Add a crisp green salad and you're all set.

1. Preheat the broiler.

2. Blanch the leeks in salted water for 2 minutes. Drain and shake off excess water.

3. Place the scallops in a shallow ovenproof casserole. Mix the leeks with the crème fraîche and spread over the scallops. (At this point, the dish may be covered and refrigerated 24 hours.) Sprinkle on the bread crumbs and herbs. Drizzle with the oil and salt lightly.

4. Broil approximately 8 inches from the heat source until the crumbs are golden and the casserole is bubbling, 10 to 12 minutes. (If the crumbs brown too quickly, cover the casserole with foil and finish cooking.) Serve immediately.

3 medium leeks, white parts only, split in half lengthwise, well washed, and cut into 1-inch segments

1¼ pounds small bay scallops

¾ cup crème fraîche

3 tablespoons fresh bread crumbs

2 teaspoons each fresh thyme and rosemary leaves

1 tablespoon Garlic Oil (page 61) or olive oil

Salt

COOK'S OPTION

You can substitute 1 pound of jumbo lump crabmeat for the scallops.

BROILED SCALLOPS ON A ROSEMARY SKEWER

FOR 4

4 thick, woody rosemary
    branches, about 5 inches
    long

8 medium mushrooms

8 bacon strips, cut into 2-inch
    lengths

½ pound medium sea scallops

2 medium red bell peppers,
    cored, seeded, and cut into
    1¼-inch pieces

2 tablespoons olive oil

Salt and freshly ground black
    pepper

COOK'S OPTION

*Twelve large shrimp (21 to
30 count) also work well in
this recipe.*

Several years ago, I began to grow rosemary in my apartment window box. The result of my agricultural enthusiasm was a small bush that became increasingly woody as it grew. Snipping a stalk one day, I had an idea. Why not substitute a branch of dried rosemary for the usual wood or metal skewers I'd always used for seafood brochettes?

A woody rosemary branch is sturdy enough to support a savory scallop, mushroom, and bacon kebab while imparting something of its own herby goodness to the scallops and vegetables. These delicious brochettes are done in a minute and make a marvelous first course or light supper.

1. Preheat the broiler.

2. Thread each rosemary branch with the following ingredients in this order: 1 mushroom, 1 bacon segment, 1 scallop, 1 red bell pepper piece, 1 bacon segment, and 1 scallop. If there is more than 1 inch of uncovered branch on either side of the ingredients, trim it to avoid burning.

3. Place the assembled skewers on a broiling rack. Drizzle with the olive oil and season with the salt and pepper. Broil about 5 inches from the heat source, turning once until the bacon is cooked, 5 to 7 minutes. Serve immediately.

QUICK-BROILED JUMBO SHRIMP IN THE SHELL WITH TARRAGON, GARLIC, AND PERNOD

FOR 4

I first encountered Pernod, the anise-flavored liquor, as a fifteen-year-old apprentice at a New Jersey seafood restaurant. I hated it. Years later, living in Paris, I'd sit at the bottom of Montmartre in a little café, very man-of-the-world, sipping glasses of Pernod with pitchers of water. I loved it. I particularly loved Pernod with shrimp, a perfect match.

Here, Pernod and shrimp are joined with fresh tarragon, garlic, and Tabasco. (If you can find fresh shrimp with the heads on, sometimes called sweet-water prawns, enjoy the delicious milky essence contained in the heads.) Once butterflied, the delicious shrimp are ready to serve in about 10 minutes.

1. Preheat the broiler.

2. Place all the ingredients except the shrimp in the bowl of a food processor. Process until well blended, about 1 minute.

3. To butterfly the shrimp, cut through the underside of each and devein. Cut more deeply without severing the "back" shells. Open up the shrimp like a book.

4. Arrange the shrimp, open side up, on a baking sheet. Smear the butter mixture liberally over the shrimp. Broil about 5 inches from the heat source until just opaque, 5 to 7 minutes. Serve immediately.

4 tablespoons (¹⁄₂ stick) unsalted butter

1 large garlic clove

1 tablespoon Pernod, Ricard, or Pastis

1 tablespoon fresh tarragon, or 1 teaspoon dried

1 medium shallot

6 dashes of Tabasco Sauce

1 tablespoon chopped fresh Italian (flat-leaf) parsley

¹⁄₂ teaspoon fresh lemon juice

2 pounds jumbo shrimp in the shell

COOK'S OPTION

Serve the shrimp with a fennel salad. Slice 1 fennel bulb as thinly as possible and dress with a vinaigrette made with 1 tablespoon extra-virgin olive oil, 1 teaspoon fresh lemon juice, and salt, to taste. Allow to stand 15 minutes before serving.

MORT'S PORT BROILED SNAPPER

FOR 4

1¹/₂ tablespoons Dijon mustard

1 medium shallot, minced

1 small garlic clove, minced

¹/₂ cup dry bread crumbs

1 tablespoon unsalted butter, softened

2 teaspoons chopped fresh tarragon, or ³/₄ teaspoon dried

¹/₂ teaspoon freshly ground black pepper

¹/₄ teaspoon finely grated lemon zest

2 tablespoons Homemade Mayonnaise (page 71), or best-quality store-bought

4 portions (7 ounces each) snapper fillet

COOK'S OPTION

This recipe works very well with striped bass or scrod. If using scrod, cook for about 9 minutes.

Mort's Port was the restaurant in Belmar, New Jersey, where I had my first job as a cook. Mort, the chef-owner, was a salty German-born man who had been classically trained. He did everything correctly, by the book. I'm in his debt not only for this great recipe but for a rigorous apprenticeship—we served something like five or six hundred customers a night!

Mort was also ingenious. Why not, he reasoned, use a tarragon and mustard-flavored dressing on the *outside* of a scrod portion to protect its moisture and flavor? The idea works beautifully, as you'll discover when you try my version of Mort's savory recipe.

1. Preheat the broiler.

2. Mix all the ingredients except the mayonnaise and the snapper. Place the fillets on a broiling tray and spread them with the mayonnaise. Pack the stuffing on top of each portion.

3. Broil the fish about 9 inches from the heat source until the dressing is nicely browned and the fish yields very easily to a fork, about 12 minutes. (If the dressing seems to be browning too quickly, move the tray lower.) Serve immediately.

OPEN-FACED BROOK TROUT

FOR 4

Brook trout are wonderful fish, especially delicious when butterflied, brushed with butter, and quickly broiled. You may, of course, substitute other trout species, but aquafarmed brook trout appear with increasing regularity in today's fish stores.

I use this satisfying method with any roundfish up to 2½ pounds (a 1½-pound fish is best). It produces boneless servings with all the freshness and flavor of whole-fish cookery.

Only the simplest of accompaniments for this dish, please—a squeeze of lemon or any of the flavored butters I list at right.

1. Preheat the broiler.
2. Butterfly the trout by splitting each fish through the belly from head to tail. Cut through the bones, but do not sever the fish completely. Open the fish like a book, and using a small sharp knife, trim away the skeleton on both halves. Pull out any pinbones. (This procedure may be done by your fish seller.)
3. Rub the flesh with the butter and season with the salt and pepper.
4. Place as many fish on your broiler tray as it can hold without crowding. Broil 3 to 4 inches from the heat source until the flesh is just cooked through, about 4 minutes. Serve immediately with lemon wedges or the flavored buttter of your choice.

4 brook trout (12 to 14 ounces each), gutted only
4 teaspoons unsalted butter, softened, for broiling
Salt and freshly ground black pepper
1 lemon, quartered; or Red Pepper Butter, Chive Butter, or Hazelnut-Lemon Butter (pages 62 to 64)

BROILED HALIBUT WITH CARAMELIZED LEEKS

FOR 4

4 leeks, white parts only, split
    lengthwise, well washed, and
    cut crosswise into $1/2$-inch
    lengths
$2^1/_2$ tablespoons olive oil
Salt and freshly ground black
    pepper
4 halibut fillets (7 ounces each),
    preferably from a whole fish
    personally inspected for
    freshness

COOK'S OPTION

*You can substitute virtually
any fillets for the halibut;
cod, haddock, and sole
work particularly well. Sole
fillets are done in 12 to 14
minutes.*

This dish uses the moist-broiling technique. I've always loved the simple way it works: when fillets are broiled beneath a layer of vegetables they are protected against moisture loss. Here, halibut is moist-broiled beneath a blanket of leeks, which caramelize and char deliciously, adding a sweet oniony flavor.

This is an excellent dish for dieters—the fish is so moist it requires no sauce. You can, however, serve it with a grainy mustard or a few drops of balsamic vinegar to add punch without calories.

1. Preheat the broiler.
2. Toss the leeks well with the olive oil. Season with the salt and pepper.
3. Brush the fillets with oil and season with salt and pepper. Place the fillets on a broiling tray. Cover each fillet with an equal mound of the leeks.
4. Broil about 8 inches from the heat source until the leeks have wilted and caramelized, 16 to 18 minutes. Don't be concerned if the leeks char here and there, but if they start to blacken, cover them with foil. Check for doneness; the fish should yield easily to a fork.
5. Remove the fillets to plates. Season if you wish (see the headnote) and serve.

BROILED SALMON WITH TOMATOES, BASIL, AND MINT

FOR 4

Nothing could be simpler or better than this dish of broiled salmon with a summery salsa of tomatoes, basil, and mint. Really ripe tomatoes are essential here. I could tell you that plum tomatoes or showy imported specimens will do the trick, but they just won't.

This recipe is another example of moist-broiling. The salmon portions are covered with sliced onions and the onions caramelize deliciously, making a perfect "cooked" contrast to the freshness of the tomato and basil salsa. Steamed spinach, kale, snow peas, or zucchini go beautifully with this dish.

1. Thirty to 40 minutes in advance, mix the salsa ingredients. Cover and reserve.

2. Preheat the broiler. Brush the salmon generously on all sides with the oil and season well with the salt and pepper. Place the onion slices on a sheet of foil, brush with the remaining oil, and season lightly with the salt and pepper.

3. Place the fish in a broiling pan. On each portion, overlap 2 slices of the onion. Broil about 8 inches from the heat source until the onions have wilted and caramelized, 12 to 15 minutes. Don't worry if the onions char here and there, but if they blacken, cover them with foil. Check the fish for doneness: it should look rosy, not deeply salmon-colored.

4. When done, remove the fish to plates. Stir the reserved salsa and spoon it generously over the salmon.

SALSA

2 absolutely ripe beefsteak tomatoes, cored, seeded, and cut into 1-inch dice

5 tablespoons best-quality extra-virgin olive oil

3 tablespoons soy sauce

2 tablespoons fresh lemon juice

$1/2$ teaspoon coarsely cracked black peppercorns

$1 1/2$ cups fresh basil leaves, each leaf torn into 3 pieces

2 teaspoons finely chopped fresh mint

FISH

4 portions salmon fillet (6 to 7 ounces each)

2 tablespoons olive oil

Salt and freshly ground black pepper

Eight $1/8$-inch slices Bermuda onion

COOK'S OPTION

You can substitute snapper or striped bass for the salmon. Broil 10 to 12 minutes.

SAUCE LOVER'S SCROD

FOR 4

1 cup heavy (whipping) cream

3 tablespoons grainy mustard

1 small garlic clove, minced

2 teaspoons Pernod, Ricard, or
Pastis

4 dashes of Tabasco Sauce

Salt and freshly ground black
pepper

1 teaspoon fresh lemon juice

4 scrod fillets (6 to 7 ounces
each), preferably from a
whole fish personally
inspected for freshness

COOK'S OPTION

*Sole or hake work very well
in this recipe.*

This is a dish for those of us who always feel that the sauce is the main attraction. Trace it to my childhood aversion to fish fillets served without a sufficiently luscious accompaniment. No chance of that here—sweet scrod is robed in a creamy, Tabasco-fired sauce made with grainy mustard, Pernod, and garlic.

Make this for times when calories aren't an issue and don't forget to pass a good crusty loaf for plate mopping. Boiled potatoes make an excellent accompaniment.

1. Preheat the broiler.

2. In a small nonreactive saucepan, combine the cream, mustard, and garlic. Bring to the boil, reduce the heat to very low, and simmer for 5 minutes. Add the Pernod and Tabasco and season with the salt, pepper, and lemon juice.

3. Meanwhile, place the fillets on a broiling tray and broil 6 to 8 inches from the heat source until it flakes at the touch of a fork, 4 to 5 minutes.

4. Place the fillets on serving plates and spoon the sauce liberally over each.

LOBSTER WITH VANILLA SAUCE

FOR 4

Lobster with *vanilla* sauce? The truth is that you'll miss one of the best ways ever of doing lobster if you pass this recipe by. Based on the Caribbean technique of cooking seafood over the bark of vanilla trees, the aromatic vanilla pods used here subtly enhance the taste of the lobster. The creamy, vanilla-laced sauce is so good you'll want to bottle it.

Some advice on buying vanilla beans: many vanilla beans are not worth the prices they command. Look for beans labeled "fine vanilla" and make sure they're pliable. White surface crystals are desirable, not a sign of age. Don't keep the beans too long, or they'll dry out and lose the lovely perfume that makes this dish so fabulous.

1 teaspoon butter

1 medium shallot, sliced

2 vanilla beans, split in half

¼ cup dry white wine

½ cup Fish Stock (page 67)

¾ cup heavy (whipping) cream

Salt and freshly ground black pepper

½ teaspoon fresh lemon juice

Two 3½- to 4-pound live lobsters

Olive oil, for coating the lobsters

1. Preheat the oven to 425°F.

2. In a small nonreactive saucepan, melt the butter over low heat. Add the shallot, cover, and cook over low heat for about 2 minutes. Do not allow it to color.

3. Add the vanilla beans, wine, and stock. Bring to the boil, then reduce the heat and simmer until the liquid is reduced by half, about 5 minutes. Add the cream and simmer for 5 minutes more.

4. Strain the sauce and season with the salt, pepper, and lemon juice. Hold in a warm place while you roast the lobsters.

5. Dispatch the lobsters (page 43). Coat each with the olive oil, place on a baking tray, and roast until the lobsters are uniformly red, about 25 minutes. (Note that you need not steam the lobsters in advance to preserve moisture as they are roasted whole in the shell.)

6. Split the lobsters in half and remove the stomach sacs (located behind the lobsters' heads). Place the lobsters on a platter and pass the sauce.

ROASTED OYSTERS BURIED IN SEAWEED WITH ALLSPICE

MAKES 12 HORS D'OEUVRES OR 3 FIRST COURSES

12 medium oysters, any kind,
　　well washed
1/2 pound seaweed
About 20 allspice berries
2 tablespoons unsalted butter

COOK'S OPTION

Use 20 cherrystone clams
in place of the oysters.
Roast until the clams start
to open, 9 to 10 minutes.

I love to pry open fresh oysters and devour them, meat and liquor, in a single gulp. But I love cooked oysters, too—properly cooked, that is, so they retain their delicate texture and sea-infused flavor. Roasting them by this method guarantees great results. The smell of oysters cooked under seaweed and allspice is reason enough to try this tempting dish.

Finding seaweed shouldn't be a problem; most fish sellers will be happy to give it to you for the asking. These oysters make perfect hors d'oeuvres, but may also be served as a first course. They go down *very* easily—be prepared to serve seconds.

1. Preheat the oven to 425° F.
2. Place the oysters on a metal baking sheet. Cover them completely with the seaweed and about 15 of the allspice berries. Grind the remaining allspice using a mortar and pestle, small food processor, or coffee grinder.
3. Roast the oysters until the shells yield to a knife inserted in the hinges, about 12 minutes. Remove the oysters from the oven, and using a small knife, loosen the top shells and discard. (If any oysters refuse to open, return them to the oven for a minute or so longer.)
4. Pour the oyster liquor into a small saucepan and bring to the boil. Remove from the heat and swirl in the butter. Add the ground allspice.
5. Divide the seaweed among individual plates and arrange the oysters in their bottom shells on top. Moisten the oysters with the sauce and serve immediately.

ROASTED MONKFISH WITH BALSAMIC VINEGAR AND SHALLOTS

FOR 4

I've mentioned elsewhere the glories of artisan-made balsamic vinegar from Modena. Dark and syrupy, it tastes like a fine old port and coats a glass similarly. A drop on the tongue tastes woody, then smoky. It's addictive—and, unfortunately, expensive.

Most of the balsamic vinegar available to us is commercially made, but will work perfectly for this dish if it is not overly biting or sweet. I've paired it here with seared monkfish and shallots and added a bit of honey to round out the good flavors of roasting. The honey also "warms" the vinegar—a trick to know when using a balsamic that strikes you as harsh or thin tasting. The monkfish is so good in itself that it doesn't need a big-deal accompaniment; steamed kale would be perfect.

2 teaspoons olive oil

1½-pound monkfish fillet, in 1 piece

4 medium shallots, thinly sliced

½ teaspoon coarsely ground black pepper

⅓ cup balsamic vinegar

1 tablespoon honey

½ cup fresh Italian (flat-leaf) parsley leaves, for garnish

1. Preheat the oven to 425°F.

2. In a heavy, medium skillet, bring the oil to the smoking point over high heat. (The oil must be very hot or the fish will stick.) Add the fillet and brown it quickly on both sides, about 1½ minutes total.

3. Put the fillet into an oiled roasting pan and roast until it is softly resilient to the touch, about 9 minutes. Remove the fillet to a warmed platter.

4. Add the shallots, pepper, vinegar, and honey to the roasting pan. Place the pan over low heat and deglaze it, stirring and simmering until the shallots have softened, 3 to 4 minutes.

5. Slice the fillet into 1-inch pieces. Pour the sauce on top and garnish with the parsley. Serve immediately.

ROASTED WHOLE GROUPER WITH GARLIC, POTATOES, AND BACON

FOR 4

8 bacon strips

Two 3-pound whole groupers,
 cleaned, heads on

6 garlic cloves, sliced thinly

8 fresh thyme sprigs

8 small unpeeled new potatoes,
 washed

12 pearl onions, peeled

½ cup water

COOK'S OPTION

Whole tilefish can be substituted for the grouper.

I'll say it again—a whole roasted fish is one of the great joys of seafood cookery. Whole fish cook evenly and their intact skin acts as a barrier to keep moisture locked in.

Roasted whole grouper, sweet and lean, is perfectly matched with garlic and bacon, which bastes the fish with its smoky goodness. Potatoes and pearl onions, roasted with the fish, complete this hearty dish—good whenever you crave the satisfaction of real "dig-in" food.

1. Preheat the oven to 425°F.

2. Wrap 4 strips of bacon around the fleshiest part of each fish, ½ inch apart.

3. Tuck the garlic and thyme evenly under the bacon slices. If necessary, secure the bacon with wooden toothpicks previously soaked in water (about 30 minutes) to prevent their burning. Place the fish in a baking pan. Surround with the potatoes and onions and add the water.

4. Roast the fish about 28 minutes. Turn, using 2 spatulas, being careful not to tear the skin, and roast for 2 minutes more. The fish is done when a metal skewer inserted into the thickest part of the flesh comes out warm to the touch. If necessary, add more water to the baking pan if it becomes dry before the fish is cooked.

5. Transfer the fish to a serving platter and surround with the vegetables. Spoon the pan juices over all and serve.

ROAST HALIBUT ON THE BONE

FOR 4

Halibut roasted simply "on the bone" makes great eating. Like other forms of bone-in cooking, a roasted halibut section—a three- to four-pound "steak" with an intact center bone—retains its full flavor.

Buy a small section of halibut and while you're at it, stop by the butcher and get some caul fat. This extraordinary membrane, which lines the visceral cavity of the pig, makes a natural moisture-protecting wrapper for seafood. It bastes the food while imparting a wonderful meaty flavor all its own. I use it here to ensure that the halibut remains juicy while cooking, but you may substitute olive oil with equally delicious results.

Serve the halibut with a squeeze of lemon and parslied potatoes—a meal of perfectly simple food that couldn't be more satisfying.

One 3- to 4-pound section of
  halibut
3 to 4 sprigs fresh thyme, or 2
  teaspoons dried
1 bay leaf
3 to 4 ounces caul fat, or 2 to 3
  tablespoons olive oil

1. Preheat the oven to 425°F.
2. Place the fish on a baking sheet and distribute the thyme and bay leaf on top. Wrap the fish with the fat, if using, or brush all over with the olive oil.
3. Roast the fish in the middle of the oven, turning once, 15 to 20 minutes. It is done when the flesh has just separated from the bone.
4. Place the fish on a serving platter, peel away the skin, and serve. Use a large fork and spoon to remove the flesh from the bone.

9. GRILLING — INDOORS AND OUT

Here's what I like about grilled seafood: everything. I wasn't exactly weaned on it. My family's big drum-grill produced one kind of food only—beef—and my mother reserved the indoor "grill," an awesome electric rotisserie called a Roto-Broil, for chicken. But in due time I had my first grilled salmon and char-cooked tuna. The grill marks! The *taste!*

It's difficult to say which kind of grilling I like more—outdoors or in. Dishes like Grilled Mahi-Mahi with Mango and Black Bean Salsa or Sesame-Grilled Baby Squid with Snow Peas make the case for the outdoors. On the other hand, I *prefer* to make my signature Seared Tuna Loin with Chive Butter Sauce indoors, where I can really control the char. But why take sides? All the recipes in this chapter (and especially those for the most delicate cuts of fish) are perfectly suited to indoor grilling by grill pan, heavy skillet, or broiler.

Of course, there's something about cooking over open heat that most people think can't be matched indoors. I'm happy to say that I've devised a method that brings the great taste of outdoor grilling inside—and without expensive equipment. It's called rock-searing and you really should try it. Based on the hot-rock technique of the luau and other forms of pit cookery, it uses slate or a pizza stone for matchless indoor searing. One taste of Rock-Seared Chinese Barbecue Scallops and you'll find it difficult to return to other kinds of indoor grilling.

GRILLING OUTDOORS

Great outdoor grilling means managing the grill properly and that takes no talent at all, just a little practice.

Choose your fuel carefully. I prefer hardwood charcoal to briquettes—the flavor the hardwood coals impart is truer.

Pile the charcoal in your grill to make a layer that's about 6 inches thick over the entire surface. I like to use kindling, but I refuse to get doctrinaire about it. Liquid starters are often accused of affecting food flavor adversely; my experience is that they burn off by the time the coals are ready for cooking. If you're using a liquid starter, you should douse the charcoal thoroughly with it.

Next, mound all the charcoal in the center of the fire bed and douse it again. This charcoal mountain ensures even starting. Now ignite the charcoal carefully from the bottom of the pile. Alternatively, insert kindling beneath the charcoal and fire the kindling.

Allow the charcoal to burn until you've got glowing, ash-covered embers. Then, using a large barbecue spatula, redistribute the embers evenly across the fire bed.

Put the grate on the grill as close to the fire as possible and let it get very hot. This ensures those attractive grill marks and also aids in cooking. When you're ready to cook—and only then—adjust the grill to the proper height. Wipe the grill with an oiled cloth and you're ready to go.

Remember—*never* grill over flames; embers are hotter than flames. If, when you start to cook, the seafood begins burning because it is too close to the fire, remove it from the grill immediately and allow the fire to subside and change the height of the grill using asbestos gloves or other protection. To avoid flare-ups, make sure that any marinated seafood has been well drained before grilling.

Turning fish while they grill can be a problem. Put small fish in a hinged, two-sided grill with a handle; large fish are most easily maneuvered if cooked in a grilling basket. Fillets can be tricky—turn them carefully. Skin-on fillets of firm-fleshed fish do best outdoors.

Shellfish—including lobster, hard-shell crabs, and crawfish—are wonderful on the outdoor grill. Mollusks, such as clams, mussels, and oysters, don't grill successfully but are great when wrapped in foil and steamed in the coals.

Check seafood doneness every 5 minutes or so.

GRILLING INDOORS

For traditional indoor grilling, use a well-seasoned grill pan, stove-top domed grill with a water trough, or heavy skillet. (For rock searing, see page 173.) Make sure the pan is well heated and that your food is either oil-coated or thoroughly dried before grilling; if still moist, your seafood will create steam in the pan, which makes searing difficult, if not impossible. Even well-oiled seafood sometimes sticks to the pan. If it does, don't loosen it right away. Allow the food to cook for a bit—it should loosen itself.

Brochettes, which contain relatively small, irregularly shaped pieces of seafood or other fleshy seafood, are most successfully "grilled" under the broiler. Follow the rules for broiling in Chapter 8, making sure your broiler is very hot and the broiler door is kept open as you cook. Air must circulate freely within the broiler; you don't want the food inside to bake. People sometimes disdain the broiler for grilling, but if sufficiently preheated, it produces excellent results.

SESAME-GRILLED BABY SQUID WITH SNOW PEAS

FOR 4

2 pounds baby squid (about 2
  ounces each), cleaned

3 teaspoons Asian sesame oil

1 teaspoon hoisin sauce

1/2 teaspoon dry sherry

1/4 teaspoon honey

1/2 teaspoon black bean paste
  (available at Asian markets)

1/2 pound snow peas, tipped

2 teaspoons grated fresh ginger

1/2 teaspoon sesame seeds, white
  or black, toasted

Salt and freshly ground black
  pepper

I can't get enough of sesame, in all its forms. Its rich nuttiness is especially delicious with grilled baby squid. Here, sesame oil is part of a black bean and honey-spiked marinade for the squid and the seeds enhance its crispy snow pea accompaniment.

The snow peas are a cinch to prepare and, in themselves, make a great addition to anyone's vegetable repertoire. The finished dish tastes decidedly Chinese and would be perfect served with jasmine rice.

1. Prepare an outdoor grill. Alternatively, preheat the broiler.

2. Cut off the tentacles from the squid bodies; discard or reserve for other dishes, such as salads (they may be frozen). Split open the squid, rinse, and dry well. Score the outside of the flesh in a diamond pattern with a very sharp knife.

3. Thirty minutes in advance, mix the squid with 1 teaspoon of the sesame oil, the hoisin sauce, the sherry, the honey, and the black bean paste. While the squid is marinating or earlier, blanch the snow peas in plenty of boiling salted water until tender-crisp, about 1½ minutes. Drain well.

4. Grill the squid about 7 inches from the heat source until just warmed, about 1 minute per side. If broiling, cook 6 to 8 inches from the heat source for about 1½ minutes per side. (It takes longer for overhead heat to "reach" the thin flesh.) Remove the squid to warmed plates.

5. In a medium skillet over medium heat, sauté the snow peas with the remaining sesame oil, ginger, and sesame seeds until just heated through, about 1 minute. Season with the salt and pepper and serve with the squid.

HERB-GRILLED MAHI-MAHI

FOR 4

Even chefs get the blues; or rather, they haven't the foggiest idea what to make when friends are expected for dinner. This is the dish I prepare for company again and again, for its simplicity and its taste. It's a snap: mahi-mahi fillets are coated with mustard, rolled in chopped herbs, and quickly grilled. The herb blanket becomes aromatic and slightly charred and the fish is wonderfully juicy. The fillets are excellent with grilled red peppers and a cool, fresh red wine.

1. Prepare an outdoor grill. Alternatively, preheat the broiler.
2. On a platter, combine the herbs. Coat the fillets with the mustard. Roll the fillets in the herbs on both sides.
3. Grill the fillets 10 inches from the heat source until they are almost firm to the touch, about 3 to 4 minutes per side. Alternatively, broil the fillets about 10 inches from the heat source, without turning, until firm, 6 to 8 minutes. (Turning would loosen the herb coating.) Place on plates and serve immediately.

2 tablespoons chopped fresh thyme

1 tablespoon chopped fresh chives

2 teaspoons chopped fresh rosemary

4 teaspoons chopped fresh chervil or Italian (flat-leaf) parsley

4 mahi-mahi fillets (about 6 ounces each), preferably from a whole fish personally inspected for freshness

4 tablespoons grainy or Dijon mustard

COOK'S OPTION

Fillets of cobia and corvina (white sea bass) can be substituted for the mahi-mahi.

GRILLED RED SNAPPER WITH SHALLOTS AND CASSIS MARMALADE

FOR 4

MARMALADE

1 teaspoon unsalted butter

15 medium shallots, thinly
  sliced

1¼ cups cassis

½ teaspoon grated lemon rind

2 teaspoons sherry vinegar

Salt and freshly ground black
  pepper

FISH

4 skinless red snapper fillets
  (about 7 ounces each),
  preferably from fish personally inspected for freshness

1 tablespoon olive oil

Salt and freshly ground black
  pepper

COOK'S OPTION

*Striped sea bass works very
well in this recipe. Try
Italian cipolline onions,
thinly sliced, in place of the
shallots.*

I like to serve fruity sauces with seafood, particularly grilled snapper, but they have to be light. The marmalade accompaniment I've created for this dish fits the bill perfectly. It has nothing to do with the familiar orange jam, but is delicate—more of a sauce, really, with only a subtle fruit presence. And it's flavored with cassis, the black currant liqueur used to make a Kir.

The marmalade uses fifteen shallots—a lot, but they cook down, providing a mildly sweet finish that is perfect for the snapper. Serve this beautiful dish with orzo, browned quickly in a dry skillet before boiling, then sauced simply with butter or olive oil.

1. Prepare an outdoor grill. Alternatively, preheat the broiler.

2. Make the marmalade. In a medium skillet, melt the butter over medium heat. Add the shallots and cook until limp, about 3 minutes. Add the cassis and simmer until the mixture is almost dry. Remove from the heat and add the lemon rind and vinegar. Season with the salt and pepper.

3. With a small, sharp knife, score the underskin sides of the fillets, making 3 slashes on each about ¼ inch deep. (This prevents cupping and ensures even cooking.) Coat the fillets with the oil and season with the salt and pepper.

4. Grill the fillets 8 to 10 inches from the heat source, slashed side down first, about 2 minutes. Rotate the fillets about 45° to make an attractive crosshatch pattern and cook 1½ minutes more. Turn the fillets and repeat. The fish is done when the flesh visible through the slashes appears almost white. Alternatively, broil the fillets, slashed side up first, 6 inches from the heat source about 3 minutes per side.

5. Remove the fillets to plates, spoon the marmalade over them, and serve.

ROCK-SEARED CHINESE BARBECUE SCALLOPS

FOR 4

I'm really excited by this technique, which uses oven-heated pieces of slate or pizza stones for matchless indoor searing. This recipe calls for scallops, but once started you'll want to use rock-searing for just about every kind of seafood. Lightly oil-coated shrimp sear beautifully, as do oil-coated fillets of sole or salmon (about ½ inch thick). The fillets cook quickly, about 1½ minutes per side.

You'll need to buy a rectangular piece of slate about 12 by 20 inches and at least ½ inch thick. If your backyard or garage doesn't yield the necessary material, check your local Yellow Pages under "Stone—Natural." Try also large hardware stores or garden supply centers. Scrub your slate thoroughly with a stiff brush under running water and you're in business.

Rock-searing produces a fair amount of smoke, so make sure your range hood fan is on or that the kitchen is well ventilated. The preheated rock or slate may also be taken outdoors and set up on trivets or a concrete surface for the actual cooking. This makes a quick and easy alternative to firing up a grill.

1. Forty-five minutes in advance, preheat the oven to 450°F. Put the slate or pizza stone in the oven and allow it to heat.
2. Thirty minutes in advance, combine the scallops with the remaining ingredients in a mixing bowl. Marinate, covered, in the refrigerator.
3. Using oven mitts or other suitable protection, center the preheated slate or stone on a stove-top burner grid. Outdoors, put the slate on a trivet or concrete surface (if you use a trivet, you may cook at table).
4. Remove the scallops from the marinade and distribute them evenly on the cooking surface. Sear for about 2 minutes, turn, and cook 2 minutes more. The scallops should be well colored and just cooked through.

Note: Allow the slate to cool, then wash with water and the brush.

1½ pounds medium sea scallops
1 teaspoon olive oil
3 teaspoons hoisin sauce
¾ teaspoon minced garlic
¼ teaspoon freshly ground black pepper
¼ teaspoon cracked Szechuan peppercorns
1 tablespoon chopped scallion, white part only

SEARED SWORDFISH WITH BURGUNDY

FOR 4

2 teaspoons unsalted butter

2 medium shallots, thinly sliced

1 bay leaf

³⁄₄ cup Fish Stock (page 67)

2 cups Burgundy wine

1 tablespoon cornstarch, dissolved in ¹⁄₄ cup water

4 swordfish steaks (about 7 ounces each)

2 teaspoons olive oil

Salt and freshly ground black pepper

COOK'S OPTION

Marlin or shark work very well in this recipe.

Everything old is new again—in this case, a sauce based on Burgundy. I enjoy pairing winey sauces with seafood in general and with grilled swordfish in particular. The fish's lean, firm flesh, smoky and charred from grilling, works perfectly with the oniony astringency of this ruby red sauce. This is one-two-three cookery: make the sauce, grill the fish, and sit down to great food.

1. In a medium saucepan, melt the butter over medium heat. Add the shallots and bay leaf and cook until the onions are translucent, about 2 minutes.

2. Add the stock and wine and bring to the boil. Reduce the liquid until about ¹⁄₂ cup remains, 10 to 12 minutes. Whisk the cornstarch mixture into the boiling liquid by tablespoons, allowing the sauce to thicken between additions. The sauce is the proper consistency when it coats a spoon lightly. Remove from the heat and keep warm.

3. Prepare an outdoor grill or preheat a grill pan over high heat for 3 minutes. Coat the steaks with the oil and place on the grill 6 to 8 inches from the heat source or in the pan. (If using a pan, make sure the steaks aren't crowded.) Cook the steaks for 1 minute, rotate them 45° to create an attractive crosshatch pattern, and cook 1 minute more. Turn the steaks and cook on the second side without rotating for 3 minutes only. The steaks are done when they are just resilient to the touch.

4. Remove the steaks to plates, spoon the sauce over them, and serve immediately.

GRILLED MARLIN WITH BACON AND ENDIVE

FOR 4

This is mouthwatering: lean, firm marlin portions are wrapped in smoky bacon, grilled, and served with coal-cooked endive sprinkled with thyme.

Marlin, which can weigh as much as a ton, is one of those fish I've always got an eye out for when I shop for seafood—the loin is cut into portions, which are perfectly suited to grilling when marinated or bacon-basted.

1. At least 30 minutes in advance, soak 4 wooden toothpicks in water. Prepare an outdoor grill.

2. Brush the endive halves with the olive oil and season with the salt and pepper. Grill the endives about 10 inches from the heat source, turning halfway through, until well charred and slightly resilient to the touch, 8 to 10 minutes. Sprinkle with the thyme and keep warm.

3. Adjust the grill so that it is about 7 inches from the heat source. Wrap each marlin steak around the circumference with the bacon and secure with the toothpicks. Season the marlin with salt, pepper, and Worcestershire sauce. Grill until the fish is resilient to the touch and the bacon is golden, about 2½ minutes per side. If the bacon seems to be cooking too quickly, take the fish from the grill, raise the grill, and continue to cook. Remove to plates with the endive and serve.

4 small Belgian endives, split in half and inner cone of leaves removed
1 tablespoon olive oil
Salt and freshly ground black pepper
1 teaspoon chopped fresh thyme
4 marlin steaks (about ½ pound each and 2 inches thick)
4 bacon strips
Worcestershire sauce

COOK'S OPTION

You can substitute swordfish or shark for the marlin.

GRILLED BASS WITH FENNEL, BALSAMIC VINEGAR, AND BASIL OIL

FOR 4

4 small fennel bulbs, tough
  outer layers and feathery
  leaves removed

2 tablespoons Basil Oil
  (page 60) or olive oil

4 sea bass or striped bass fillets
  (about 7 ounces each), taken
  preferably from whole fish
  personally inspected for
  freshness

6 tablespoons balsamic vinegar

1 teaspoon olive oil

Salt and freshly ground black
  pepper

COOK'S OPTION

*Snapper makes a fine sub-
stitute for the bass.*

I devised this dish after a trip to Sicily, where the *sardine al finocchio*—baked sardines with fresh fennel—had me practically leaping with joy. With its aniselike flavor, fennel is a perfect partner for grilled bass. I've added balsamic vinegar as a condiment. It ties the vegetable and fish flavors together and provides its own tart-sweet depth. This is great outdoor cooking that works equally well inside.

1. Prepare an outdoor grill or preheat a grill pan over high heat until very hot, about 3 minutes.

2. Split the fennel bulbs in half lengthwise and brush with the basil oil or olive oil.

3. Place the fennel on the grill about 9 inches from the heat source and cook until just soft, turning several times, about 10 minutes, or add to the grill pan and cook over high heat until soft, about 10 minutes. (If the fennel seems to be charring too quickly, reduce the heat to medium.)

4. Five minutes before the fennel is done, place the fillets on the grill, skin side down, or remove the fennel from the grill pan when done and add the fillets. Cook the fillets for 3 minutes and rotate them about 45° to create an attractive crosshatch pattern. Cook 2 minutes longer, turn, and cook 2 minutes more on the second side.

5. Remove the fennel and fillets to plates. Sprinkle with the balsamic vinegar and olive oil. Season with the salt and pepper and serve.

SEARED SWORDFISH WITH CORIANDER AND BEET JUICE OIL

FOR 4

Tart-sweet, with a note of gingery freshness, beet juice oil makes a perfect seasoning for swordfish grilled with coriander and lemon rind. You can prepare the oil in advance and store it in a cool place for about one week. That way, this dish goes together in minutes.

I like to sear the swordfish using the hot-rock technique (see page 173), but it may be grilled more conventionally as well. While you're at it, make extra oil; it provides a final burst of flavor for a wide range of seared fish, including mahi-mahi and tuna, or may be used to add dash to salads, boiled potatoes, or green beans.

1. If using beets to make the beet juice oil, put them through a vegetable juicer; you'll have approximately 3 cups. In a medium nonreactive saucepan over medium heat, simmer the beet juice with the ginger until it is reduced to a glaze, 15 to 20 minutes. Remove the pan from the heat and let the glaze cool for 5 minutes. Add the oil and whisk vigorously. Add the lime juice and season with the salt and pepper.

2. Prepare an outdoor grill or preheat a grill pan over high heat for 3 minutes. Coat the steaks with the olive oil and sprinkle with the crushed coriander and lemon rind. Season with salt and pepper.

3. Grill outdoors 6 to 7 inches from the heat source about 3 minutes on the first side, 2 minutes on the second. If using a grill pan, sear for 2 minutes per side. The fish is done when it is resilient to the touch.

4. Remove the steaks to a cutting board and slice each diagonally into 4 pieces. Place on plates, drizzle with the beet juice oil, and serve.

BEET JUICE OIL

6 pounds beets, or 3 cups of
  beet juice (available at
  health food stores)
Six ½-inch slices ginger
¼ cup canola oil
1 teaspoon fresh lime juice
Salt and freshly ground
  black pepper

FISH

4 swordfish steaks (6 to 8
  ounces each)
2 teaspoons olive oil
1 tablespoon crushed coriander
  seeds
1 teaspoon finely grated
  lemon rind

COOK'S OPTION

Marlin or shark work very
well with this recipe.

BURIED COAL-COOKED LOBSTERS IN THE SHELL

FOR 6

Six 2½-pound live lobsters

5 pounds damp seaweed (available from your fish seller)

Like most people, I'm crazy about grilled whole lobsters. Their sweet flesh and charred-shell taste are hard to beat.

Unfortunately, even the best chefs can produce dry grilled lobster meat. It's a shame. Follow this technique and you can grill lobsters outdoors, directly in the coals, without any loss of moisture or flavor. The "secret" is a blanket of seaweed that not only protects the lobsters but provides its own fresh flavoring. The lobsters come from the grill sweet and juicy; served with the seaweed, they continue to delight diners with their ocean scent. The only accompaniment you need is melted butter and lots of paper napkins.

1. Prepare an outdoor charcoal grill, filling the fire bed 6 to 8 inches deep. Allow the coals to become ash covered. Shake excess water from the seaweed if necessary and scatter half of it directly over the coals.

2. Dispatch the lobsters (page 43) and place them on top of the steaming seaweed. Cover the lobsters with the remaining seaweed and press down on it to force both lobsters and seaweed into the coals.

3. Cook the lobsters about 45 minutes, sprinkling the seaweed with ¼ cup water every 10 minutes to keep it moist. The lobsters are done when the shells are bright red.

4. Remove the seaweed with tongs to a large platter. Split the lobsters, place them on the seaweed, and serve.

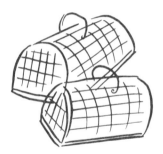

GRILLED POMPANO WITH GARLIC AND ROSEMARY TOMATOES

FOR 4

Grilled fruit has become rather trendy of late, but I'm here to tell you that it all began years ago with my uncle Ken. Ken was one of those men who wouldn't step inside a kitchen, but who did wonderful things with an outdoor grill. His specialty—quite shocking to uninitiated diners—was grilled tomatoes (a fruit, after all) sweetened with a bit of brown sugar and served *for dessert*. Where he got the idea for this superb dish is anyone's guess, but it didn't take long for my family to begin showing off Ken's tomatoes like the treasures they were.

Almost any fruit or vegetable can be grilled with delicious results. Here, tomatoes marinated with fresh rosemary are coal-cooked alongside sweet pompano fillets. I love the idea of grilling several components of a meal at once. Your grill gets a good workout and you produce a complete meal with a minimum of effort.

1. At least 1 hour in advance, mix the 2 tablespoons of olive oil with the vinegar, thyme, and rosemary. Add the tomatoes and marinate at room temperature. Meanwhile, prepare an outdoor grill, allowing the coals to become ash covered.

2. Coat the fillets with the additional olive oil and season with the salt, pepper, and celery salt. Grill 6 to 7 inches from the coals for about $1\frac{1}{2}$ minutes. Rotate the fillets about 45° to make an attractive crosshatch pattern and cook $1\frac{1}{2}$ minutes more.

3. Turn the fillets and place the tomatoes on the grill cut side down. Cook the fillets 2 minutes more and remove with the tomatoes to plates. The tomatoes should be soft to the touch; if not, cook a few minutes longer. Drizzle additional olive oil over the tomatoes and fillets, if you wish.

2 tablespoons plus 1 teaspoon extra-virgin olive oil

1 teaspoon balsamic vinegar

2 fresh thyme sprigs, coarsely chopped

1 teaspoon chopped fresh rosemary

4 absolutely ripe plum tomatoes, cored, cut lengthwise, and seeded

4 pompano fillets (about 6 ounces each), preferably from whole fish personally inspected for freshness

Salt and freshly ground black pepper

$\frac{1}{8}$ teaspoon celery salt

COOK'S OPTION

Mahi-mahi can be substituted for the pompano. Permits, if available, make an economical alternative.

GRILLED MAHI-MAHI WITH MANGO AND BLACK BEAN SALSA

FOR 6

SALSA

1 small, fully ripe mango, peeled,
    pitted, and cut into small dice
3/4 cup cooked black beans (canned
    beans, well rinsed, are fine)
1 small red bell pepper, cored,
    seeded, cut into small dice, and
    blanched
1/2 bunch scallions, green parts
    only, chopped
2 teaspoons rice vinegar
2 tablespoons fresh orange juice
1/2 teaspoon finely grated lime zest
1 very small jalapeño pepper,
    seeded and minced
Salt and freshly ground black
    pepper

FISH

6 mahi-mahi fillets (about
    7 ounces each)
2 teaspoons olive oil
Salt and freshly ground black
    pepper

COOK'S OPTION

This recipe also works well

with swordfish.

Sometimes called dolphinfish but unrelated to the friendly marine mammal, mahi-mahi is a common Hawaiian fish readily available year-round. It's easy to clean and cook, and has a moist, sweet brininess that even reluctant fish eaters take to immediately. Paired here with a fiery salsa made with mango, black beans, and jalapeño, it's a real knockout.

A word on choosing mangos: this lovely fruit, indigenous to Southeast Asia, is often a flavorless disappointment. Buy heavy, firmish fruit with some red or yellow coloration. Stem ends should smell delicately scented; as with most other fruit, no aroma means no flavor. Avoid hot-water treated mangos (labeled "water treated"), which have been pushed into "ripeness" and are usually mealy. Keep mangos at room temperature until they are fragrant and yield easily to pressure.

1. Prepare an outdoor grill. At least 30 minutes in advance, combine the salsa ingredients in a nonreactive bowl. (The salsa may be made and refrigerated up to 2 days in advance.)
2. Coat the fish with the olive oil and season with the salt and pepper. Grill the fillets about 7 to 8 inches from the heat source for 1½ minutes. Rotate the fillets 45° to make an attractive crosshatch pattern and cook 1½ minutes more. Turn and cook for 1½ minutes. Alternatively, heat a grill pan until very hot, about 3 minutes. Sear the fillets following the time schedule above. The fish is done when it is almost firm. Remove the fillets to plates, crosshatched side up. Stir the salsa, spoon it generously over the fish, and serve.

Note: This dish is great accompanied by crispy tortillas. To make them, brush flour or corn tortillas with chili oil and bake them in a preheated 350° F. oven until crispy, about 20 minutes.

SALMON AND SCALLOP BROCHETTES ON ROSEMARY BRANCHES

FOR 4

Multi-ingredient seafood brochettes make quick meals-in-one that are fun to do and great for entertaining. Salmon and scallops work particularly well together, especially when grilled and brushed with a savory "baste."

The rosemary-branch skewers make a pretty presentation and perfume the ingredients delicately, but wooden skewers will do. If you use wooden skewers, soak them first in water for 30 minutes to prevent their burning while the brochettes cook.

1. Prepare an outdoor grill or preheat the broiler.

2. Skewer the brochette ingredients in the following order, per branch: 1 tomato, 1 cube salmon, 1 piece of green pepper, 1 scallop, 1 tomato, 1 cube salmon, 1 piece of green pepper, and 1 scallop.

3. Combine the remaining ingredients in a bowl. Brush the brochettes evenly with the basting mixture.

4. Grill the brochettes about 8 inches from the heat source, covered (use a large overturned pot if your grill does not have a cover), basting once, for 2 minutes. Turn and cook until the scallops are firm, 2 to 3 minutes. (When scallops are firm on the outside, they are medium-rare within.) Alternatively, broil the brochettes about 6 inches from the heat source for 2 minutes, turn, and baste, then finish cooking, 2 to 3 minutes. Remove the brochettes to plates and serve.

4 dried woody rosemary branches, about 7 inches long; or wooden skewers

8 ripe cherry tomatoes

1/2 pound salmon fillet, preferably from a whole fish personally inspected for freshness, cut into 8 equal cubes

1 large green bell pepper, cored, seeded, and cut into scallop-size pieces

12 small sea scallops (about 1 pound)

2 tablespoons olive oil

1 teaspoon sherry vinegar

1 teaspoon finely chopped garlic

1 teaspoon fresh lemon juice

1/4 teaspoon celery salt

1 tablespoon best-quality ketchup

1/2 teaspoon salt

1/4 teaspoon freshly ground black pepper

BARBECUED SHRIMP ON SUGARCANE SKEWERS WITH GINGER-LIME SAUCE

FOR 4

MARINADE

2 teaspoons Szechuan peppercorns, crushed

3 ounces (about 4 inches) fresh ginger, unpeeled, coarsely sliced

½ lime, cut into 6 equal pieces

3 tablespoons honey

2 teaspoons chopped fresh cilantro (coriander)

1 lemongrass stalk, cut into 2-inch lengths and smashed

16 extra-large shrimp (16 to 20 count), peeled except for the tail section and deveined

12 inches of sugarcane, about 3 inches in diameter

SAUCE

2 teaspoons olive oil

2 ounces (2 inches) fresh ginger, peeled and smashed

1 lime, skin and pith removed, cut into 4 equal pieces

2 medium shallots, thinly sliced

¼ cup canned coconut milk

¼ cup Chicken Stock (page 66)

Sugarcane, available at most Latin American or Indian markets, makes a great natural skewer for these spicy-sweet shrimp. Looks aside, the skewers impart a delicate flavor and are delicious to chew on after the shrimp are eaten. (Wooden skewers soaked in water for 30 minutes can be substituted.) The brochettes, with their luscious ginger, lime, and coconut-flavored sauce, go so well with macadamia-laced Hawaiian Rice that I've included the recipe.

1. Two hours in advance, combine the marinade ingredients in a bowl. Add the shrimp, mix well, and reserve in the refrigerator. Prepare an outdoor grill or preheat the broiler.

2. Cut the sugarcane in half lengthwise. With a serrated knife, remove the interior pulp. Quarter the halves lengthwise to produce 8 skewers.

3. Make the sauce. In a nonreactive saucepan, heat the oil over medium heat. Add the ginger, lime, and shallots and sauté until the shallots are translucent, about 2½ minutes. Add the coconut milk and the stock and reduce until the thickness of pea soup, about 3 minutes. Add the cream and cook 3 minutes longer.

4. Strain the sauce into the bowl of a food processor or blender jar and add the butter. Process or blend until creamy, about 1½ minutes. Hold in a warm place.

5. Remove the shrimp from the marinade. Thread 4 pieces of shrimp onto 2 skewers, 1 skewer going through the head end, the other going through the tail. The shrimp should be as straight as possible to prevent their curling while cooking. Repeat with the remaining shrimp and skewers. You will have 4 double skewers, each holding 4 shrimp.

6. Grill the shrimp about 6 inches from the heat source until very charred and just cooked through, about 3 minutes per side. Alternatively, broil the shrimp about 10 inches from the heat source for 3 minutes per side.

7. Remove the shrimp to plates and spoon the sauce liberally over them.

³/₄ cup heavy (whipping) cream

4 tablespoons (¹/₂ stick) unsalted butter, cut into 6 equal pieces

HAWAIIAN RICE

FOR 4

1. Heat the olive oil in a medium skillet over medium heat. Add the nuts, red pepper, and pineapple and sauté until the pineapple is slightly softened, 5 to 6 minutes.

2. Remove the skillet from the heat. Add the chili paste and mix well. Stir in the rice and serve.

1 teaspoon olive oil

¹/₃ cup macadamia nuts, coarsely chopped

1 small red bell pepper, cored, seeded, and diced

¹/₂ cup diced pineapple, fresh or well-drained canned

1¹/₂ teaspoons chili paste

3 cups cooked rice

SEARED TUNA LOIN WITH CHIVE BUTTER SAUCE

FOR 4

MARINADE

$^1/_2$ cup soy sauce

$^1/_4$ cup ketjap manis (page 56)

1 tablespoon chili paste

$^1/_2$ teaspoon lemongrass powder
or 1 lemongrass stalk, cut in
half and smashed

3 teaspoons coarsely chopped
fresh cilantro (coriander)

Four 5-ounce tuna steaks, about
$2^1/_2$ inches in diameter

CHIVE BUTTER SAUCE

2 bunches chives, finely
chopped

$^1/_2$ bunch fresh Italian (flat-leaf)
parsley, coarsely chopped

Juice of $^1/_2$ lemon

2 teaspoons salt

Freshly ground black pepper

$^1/_2$ cup (1 stick) unsalted butter,
cut into 6 equal pieces

2 tablespoons heavy (whipping)
cream

This signature dish, which I first served at the restaurant Tropica, has made the trek with me to every restaurant at which I've been chef. It's my most popular dish—and I think I know why. The tuna is deeply charred on the outside and meltingly rare within. (It's made more converts to lightly cooked fish than any other dish I know.) The chive butter sauce is creamy but light, and works perfectly with the Thai-spiced tuna.

You might want to start the sauce beforehand to finish while the fish is marinating. To do so, refrigerate the chive butter, removing it to room temperature a half-hour before preparing the sauce.

The fish excels when cooked outdoors, but can made in a grill pan with complete success. In fact, I do it that way all the time at home.

1. Prepare an outdoor grill.

2. In a nonreactive bowl, combine the marinade ingredients. Add the tuna and marinate for 20 minutes to 1 hour.

3. Make the sauce. Place all the ingredients except the cream in the bowl of a food processor and pulse until well blended, scraping down the sides of the bowl as necessary. Chill for 15 minutes.

4. In a medium saucepan, warm the cream over medium heat. Remove the pan from the heat and whisk in the chive butter by halves. The butter should not melt, but create a light emulsion. Adjust the seasoning.

5. Grill the tuna 7 to 8 inches from the heat source until the flesh is well charred and lightly resilient to the touch, 1 to 2 minutes per side. The flesh will be rare within. Alternatively, preheat a grill pan until hot, about 3 minutes. Add the tuna and cook about 2 minutes per side. Slice each piece of tuna into 4 pieces and place on plates. Surround with the sauce and serve.

10. BOILING, BRAISING, STEAMING, AND POACHING

When I first began cooking fish and seafood professionally, I avoided the moist-heat methods in favor of flashier techniques like grilling. This culinary shortsightedness astounds me today; I grew up near the shore, where restaurants serving succulent boiled lobsters were plentiful. And I remember clearly a luscious steamed fish with black bean sauce that my family always ordered at our local Chinese restaurant.

Now I know better. Properly done, these "plain" methods produce healthful seafood of astonishingly pure flavor and velvety texture—and they're quickly done.

The pitfalls of moist-heat cooking are insufficiently fresh catch and careless timing. Seafood freshness, particularly important here because you can't depend on the cooking medium to compensate for quality deficiencies. Timing may be more difficult to gauge initially when cooking with liquid or steam, but a little practice should give you your "hand."

Another potential problem is that some traditional methods like poaching can leach away flavor. One way around this is to poach in a highly seasoned broth; shallow poaching is better still. This method uses one-third the customary amount of liquid so all the flavor stays in the fish. After poaching, you reduce the cooking liquid and you've got a great, healthful, ready-to-go sauce. The Shallow-Poached Snapper with Baby Shrimp, Thyme, and Lime and the Shallow-Poached Bluefish in Leek Broth with Mushrooms are two examples of this quick, foolproof technique; you'll come up with your own.

I also enjoy preparing traditionally poached dishes, but with a difference: lighter sauces. Yesterday's poached Dover sole with hollandaise was too often a dish of flavorless fish masked by a killer sauce. The Poached Whole Bass with New Potatoes and Spring Vegetables, served with a splash of lemon juice and shakes of sea salt, is a bouquet of light, fresh flavors—and it's low in fat. If you choose to poach traditionally, use simple accompaniments and delicate sauces, like True Orange Sabayon (page 76).

Among the many pleasures of steaming is the chance it provides to cook luscious whole fish. Whole Flounder Steamed with Soy Sauce, Ginger, and Scallions is basic text in this regard. The recipe (and most others for steamed whole fish) calls for fish up to 2½ pounds, a size most steamers can handle without difficulty. If you lack a steamer of the proper size, here are some easy improvisations:

- Use your biggest soup pot (with a diameter of at least 12 inches). Place empty, labelless tuna cans or ceramic ramekins upside down in the center of the pot and set an ovenproof plate on them. Fill the pot with about 2 inches of water and you're ready to go.

- Use a fish poacher (especially good for steaming larger fish), arranging the perforated interior rack on ramekins so that it clears the steaming water. Cover with foil.

- For smaller fillets or fish portions, fill a soup pot with a closely fitting colander and steam in it, or cover a cake rack with foil, punch steam holes in it, and place it in the bottom of your soup pot. If you still need steamer ideas, call me and we'll figure something out!

Strictly speaking, we never boil fish. We poach, braise, or simmer it. Boiling is traditionally reserved for shellfish, especially lobster, whose tender flesh is well protected from rapidly bubbling liquid. Even so, boiling shellfish can be tricky. Shrimp are usually overboiled, which results in hard, rubbery flesh. To avoid this unpleasant possibility, I've come up with a foolproof method that allows you to cook any size shrimp, fresh or frozen, perfectly, in about fifteen minutes; see opposite. Simple boiled shrimp are great food for dieters and may be served with any number of low-carlorie dips like salsa.

SIZZLE-PLATE POACHING

This terrific restaurant technique is rarely used in home kitchens. The sizzle plate, a concave metal dish with a wide rim, allows you to cook an entire seafood meal in minutes; cleanup is almost nil and you've got a delicious dinner to put on the table.

Sizzle plates are sometimes known as steak plates and can be made of stainless steel or aluminum. Either metal works well, but stainless is preferable. These oval plates are available in a number of sizes—10½ by 7 inches is the most workable. Look for sizzle plates in high-end gourmet equipment shops or in restaurant supply houses. Sizzle plates can also be purchased by mail order from Fantes, a cookware store in Philadelphia (800-878-5557).

Cooking with a sizzle plate is easy. You put fish or shellfish in the center of the plate and add vegetables, seasonings, and stock. Arrange pats of butter along the rim of the plate, cover it with foil, and pop it in the oven. Minutes later, put your perfectly done seafood on a platter. Reduce the accumulated cooking juices and you've got a great sauce for the seafood or a pasta side dish. Sizzle-plate poaching, like the other moist-heat methods, really invites imaginative, healthful cooking.

NO-FAIL BOILED SHRIMP

FOR 4

I eat more shrimp than any other kind of seafood—and so do most other Americans, if seafood consumption statistics are correct. We devour shrimp by the ton—and, sadly, overcook it far too often. How to achieve perfect doneness?

Here's a ridiculously easy method for cooking any size shrimp, fresh or frozen, perfectly, in about twelve minutes. The method works automatically. The proper cooking time is determined by the time it takes the cooking liquid to return to the boil after the shrimp are added—longer for large and/or frozen shrimp, less for small and/or fresh. Once the liquid has returned to the boil the shrimp are simmered for exactly 2 minutes, then drained. That's it. You get perfectly cooked shrimp—toothsome, never tough, with just a bit of softness at the center. They're ready to be eaten as is, with a dip, or to be used in other recipes.

1. In a large saucepan, combine all the ingredients except the shrimp. Bring to the boil, reduce the heat, and simmer for 10 minutes.
2. Strain the liquid and return it to the pan. Add the shrimp. When the liquid returns to the boil, reduce the heat and simmer for 2 minutes exactly. Drain the shrimp and place on a platter. When the shrimp have cooled they're ready to eat or to use in other recipes.

Note: If you wish, prepare the shrimp in plain water.

2$\frac{1}{2}$ quarts water

1 tablespoon salt

2 celery stalks, cut into 2-inch lengths

1 medium onion, cut into eighths

$\frac{1}{2}$ bunch fresh Italian (flat-leaf) parsley

8 black peppercorns

$\frac{1}{2}$ teaspoon cayenne pepper

1 small lemon, quartered

2 bay leaves

2 pounds shrimp, any size, fresh or frozen (preferably unshelled, for best flavor)

BRAISED SALMON IN RED WINE WITH VEAL MARROW

FOR 4

3 ounces veal marrow, taken
    from about 2 bones
1 tablespoon Champagne vine-
    gar or other white wine
    vinegar
2 tablespoons salt
1 teaspoon unsalted butter
3 medium leeks, white parts
    only, split, washed, and
    sliced
4 fresh thyme sprigs, or
    ¼ teaspoon dried
1 bay leaf
2 cups dry red wine (preferably
    a Merlot or Pinot Noir)
1½ pounds salmon fillet, cut
    into 4 equal portions
2 teaspoons cornstarch, dis-
    solved in 1 teaspoon water

COOK'S OPTION

Four monkfish fillets (6 to 7
ounces each) can be used in
place of the salmon. Cook
the monkfish in the butter
over high heat, remove from
the skillet, and proceed.

At the restaurant we call this dish "surf and turf," but let a proud chef elaborate. Here we have delicate, lightly poached salmon portions prepared in red wine and served with marrow, the silken interior of veal shank and other beef bones. The fish is napped by a wine sauce made from the leek-enhanced braising liquid.

Marrow is rich, but it's also irresistibly good; besides, only a small quantity is served per portion. The salmon and its herb sauce are put together in minutes, which makes the dish perfect for times when you've scheduled guests on a workday and yet want something special for dinner.

1. Cut the marrow into nugget-size pieces. One hour in advance, place the marrow in a bowl filled with water. Add the vinegar and the salt.

2. In a large skillet, melt the butter over medium-high heat. Add the leeks, cover, and cook without coloring, about 3 minutes. Add the thyme, bay leaf, and wine and bring to the boil.

3. Add the salmon and allow the wine to return to the boil. Reduce the heat so the liquid barely simmers. Poach the fish until done, 8 to 10 minutes. They will just yield to the touch and be rare at the center.

4. Remove the fish to serving plates. Bring the sauce to the boil, stir in the dissolved cornstarch, and cook, stirring, until lightly thickened, about 1 minute. Add the marrow and cook until it has half melted, about 2 minutes. Pour the sauce over the fillets and serve.

CREAMY HACKED BRAISED LOBSTER

FOR 4

I nearly came to blows—verbal, of course—with a colleague who insisted that the *only* way to really enjoy lobster was to boil it. I enjoy boiled lobster as much as anyone else, but there are times when I want my lobster dressed up with a delicious sauce. When *you* find yourself craving lobster with more than simple drawn butter but don't want to go to the bother of creating elaborate accompaniments, this is for you.

The dish almost makes itself. Roughly cut lobster is sautéed with aromatics, braised in wine, then finished with cream and fresh tarragon. The resulting dish is a luscious, elbows-on-the-table feast that takes less time to make than a dish of pasta.

1. Dispatch the lobsters (page 43). With a heavy knife, remove the claws and cut each body horizontally into 4 equal pieces. Crack the claws with a mallet. You will have 12 pieces in all.

2. In a large, heavy skillet, heat the oil over high heat until smoking. Add the lobster and cook, stirring, until the pieces are bright red, about 5 minutes.

3. Reduce the heat to medium and add the shallots and garlic. Cook for 1 minute, stirring, making sure the aromatics do not brown. And the wine and stock, cover the skillet, and braise until the meat is just cooked, about 3 minutes.

4. Add the cream and tarragon and simmer until the cream has heated through, about 2 minutes.

5. Add the lemon juice and season with the salt and pepper. Serve at once, with lots of crusty bread and a spicy white wine.

Two 2½-pound live lobsters
1 tablespoon olive oil
2 medium shallots, minced
2 garlic cloves, crushed with
    the flat of a knife
½ cup dry white wine
¼ cup Fish Stock (page 67)
1 cup heavy (whipping) cream
1 tablespoon chopped fresh
    tarragon
Juice of ½ lemon
Salt and freshly ground
    black pepper

WHOLE FLOUNDER STEAMED WITH SOY SAUCE, GINGER, AND SCALLIONS

FOR 4

Two 1¾-pound whole flounders,
cleaned, heads and tails on;
or one whole fish up to
2¼ pounds

6 tablespoons soy sauce

1 bunch scallions, white parts cut
into 2-inch lengths, green parts
into 4-inch lengths

2 tablespoons 2-inch-long strands
of very finely julienned
fresh ginger

COOK'S OPTION

Halve the recipe or use any
whole fish up to 2¼
pounds. Sardines and
mackerel are particularly
interesting variations.

My passion for Chinese cooking and whole fish simply prepared merged in the creation of this dish. You've probably had the classic version at a restaurant. My interpretation, which involves steaming a whole flounder, uses no oil of any kind so all the wonderful tastes come across with great purity. The dish is also low in fat.

If your home steamer isn't large enough to accommodate the fish you've chosen, you can cut it up (see the Note below for instructions). Fish freshness is always essential, but it's of utmost importance when the fish is to be treated as simply as it is here.

1. Prepare a steamer. Choose a plate that just fits into it.

2. Make gashes in both sides of the fish about ⅛ inch deep and 2 inches long.

3. When the water in the steamer has come to a boil, place the fish on the plate. Coat with the soy sauce. Tuck the white scallion lengths under the fish and arrange the green lengths evenly on the top. Sprinkle the ginger over the fish.

4. Place the plate in the steamer, cover, and steam until the flesh of the fish is white to the bone and moves easily from it when touched with a fork, 6 to 8 minutes. Serve the fish with the accumulated cooking liquid.

Note: If necessary, remove the head(s) and tail(s) of the fish. The rest of the fish may be further subdivided into 3 pieces of roughly similar size. Make sure the portions do not cover one another when put in the steamer.

STEAMED HALIBUT WITH CLAM BUTTER AND SCALLOPS

FOR 4

Flavored butters have a prominent place in my cooking. I didn't invent them, of course; they've been a staple of French cuisine for centuries, but I love to create new versions. In this recipe I use a flavored butter made with clams, celery, and cayenne—a piquant, clam-infused enrichment for the steamed halibut served with tender scallops. If you like, use the clam butter accompaniment to create a light sauce (see Note)—a great option for those of us watching our caloric intake.

1. In a medium pot, simmer the clams in ¼ cup water until they open, about 3 minutes. Cool.

2. In the bowl of a food processor, combine all the ingredients except the halibut and scallops. Process until well blended, about 30 seconds; do not overprocess. Reserve in a cool place, but do not refrigerate.

3. Prepare a steamer.

4. Season the fillets with salt and pepper. Steam the fillets for 3 minutes. Add the scallops and continue to cook until the halibut is milk-white but still tender to the touch, about 3 minutes more. The scallops should be just cooked through at this point; if they're not, cook for 1 minute longer. Do not overcook them.

5. Remove the fillets to plates and divide the scallops evenly over them. Spoon a tablespoon of the clam butter over each and serve.

Note: To make a sauce of the clam butter, warm 1 tablespoon of water in a medium saucepan over medium heat. Add the clam butter and whisk vigorously. Do not allow the clam butter to melt entirely; what you want is a creamy emulsion. Remove the sauce from the heat and spoon it lightly over the halibut and scallops.

12 littleneck clams, shucked, with their liquor

6 tablespoons (¾ stick) unsalted butter

½ cup yellow celery leaves, taken from the center of the bunch

Juice of ½ lemon

Pinch of cayenne pepper

1 teaspoon best-quality sweet paprika

Salt and freshly ground black pepper

1½ pounds halibut fillet, preferably from a fish personally inspected for freshness, cut into 4 equal portions

½ pound bay scallops

COOK'S OPTION

Sole fillets also work well with this recipe. Roll the fillets before steaming them.

SHALLOW-POACHED SNAPPER WITH BABY SHRIMP, THYME, AND LIME

FOR 4

¼ cup Fish Stock (page 67)

¼ cup dry white wine

1¼ pounds snapper fillet,
preferably from a fish personally inspected for freshness,
with or without skin, cut into
4 equal portions

½ pound small (35 to 45
count) shrimp

8 fresh thyme sprigs

4 lime slices, cut as thinly as
possible

Salt and freshly ground black
pepper

2 tablespoons unsalted butter

COOK'S OPTION

You can use striped or
black sea bass in place of
the snapper.

Shallow-poaching is my favorite poaching method for cooking fish. It's easy and the results are really superior. You use one-third the customary amount of poaching liquid, so the flavor stays in the fish. After cooking the fish, reduce the minimal liquid and you've got a marvelous, ready-to-go sauce.

This dish is full of bright, straightforward flavors—the sea-fresh taste of the shrimp and snapper, pungent thyme, and tangy lime. It's an after-work treat that takes hardly more effort to make than a hamburger, but delivers a royal and considerably less caloric result.

1. In a large nonreactive skillet, preferably with straight sides, bring the stock and wine to the boil.

2. Add the fish and shrimp. Place 2 sprigs of the thyme and 2 slices of the lime on top of each portion of the snapper and season with the salt and pepper. Cover, reduce the heat, and poach gently until the fish is milk-white and the shrimp just cooked through, 4 to 5 minutes. Remove the fish and shrimp to plates and keep warm.

3. Reduce the liquid until it has a saucelike consistency Remove from the heat, swirl in the butter, and pour over the fish and shrimp. Serve immediately.

Note: If you wish, omit the butter and serve the fish with only the reduced poaching liquid.

SHALLOW-POACHED BLUEFISH IN LEEK BROTH WITH MUSHROOMS

FOR 4

Bluefish has a poor reputation—some people find its taste too strong. Too bad. It has rich flavorful flesh when properly cooked, and is wonderful poached and served with mushrooms, leeks, and a simple, brothy sauce.

If you can find mushrooms such as shiitake, chanterelles, pleurottes, or cremini, by all means use them. I've noticed with pleasure the appearance of more and more kinds of cultivated "wild" mushrooms in local supermarkets—try them!

A garnish of diced tomato and chervil leaves makes a colorful accompaniment.

1. In a 12-inch nonreactive skillet with straight sides, bring the stock and leek to the boil. (You can use 2 smaller skillets, if necessary, in which case divide the stock and leek between them.) Reduce the heat and simmer until the leek softens, about 6 minutes.

2. Add the fillets and the mushrooms and shallow-poach until the fillets are resilient to the touch, 5 to 7 minutes. Remove the fillets to a platter and keep warm.

3. Bring the poaching liquid to the boil and reduce by two-thirds. Season with the salt, pepper, and lemon juice.

4. Pour the sauce with the mushrooms over the fish and serve.

1 cup Fish Stock (page 67)

1 large leek, white part only, split lengthwise, well washed, and cut into large dice

4 bluefish fillets (about 7 ounces each), preferably from fish personally inspected for freshness

1/2 pound mushrooms, preferably wild

Salt and freshly ground black pepper

1 teaspoon fresh lemon juice

COOK'S OPTION

Spanish mackerel also works well with this recipe. Shallow-poach the fillets for 4 to 5 minutes.

SHALLOW-POACHED TILEFISH WITH PORT, ONIONS, AND CARROTS

FOR 4

1 teaspoon olive oil

1½ pounds tilefish fillet, cut
   into 4 equal portions

1 cup Fish Stock (page 67)

16 pearl onions, peeled

2 medium carrots, peeled
   and cut diagonally into
   ⅛-inch slices

¼ cup Port

1 teaspoon grated lemon zest

1 tablespoon unsalted butter

Salt and freshly ground
   black pepper

COOK'S OPTION

*Grouper can be substituted
for the tilefish.*

One reason I love to cook fish is that it gives me a chance to create light sauces—which beef, for example, does not. Besides being delicious, these sauces have a real role to play: they heighten the basic character of the fish they accompany.

For example, tilefish has a delicate, mild flesh whose flavor is enhanced by sweet aromatic vegetables like carrots and onions. Port makes a perfect addition to the sauce; its deep, sweet notes further strengthen the fish's flavor.

I always sear tilefish before poaching it—searing really intensifies its flavor. (Keep this trick in mind when poaching other mild fish.) Serve this simple dish with a risotto finished with Reggiano Parmesan cheese, more lemon zest, and plenty of freshly ground black pepper.

1. In a heavy, medium skillet, heat the olive oil over high heat until it is very hot but not smoking. Add the fish and sear quickly on both sides, about 45 seconds per side.

2. Add the stock, onions, and carrots. Bring the liquid to the boil, reduce the heat, and poach gently until the fish is fork-tender, 7 to 8 minutes. Add the wine, lemon, and butter and season with the salt and pepper. Bring to a second boil and remove the skillet from the heat. Divide the fish and vegetables among serving plates and serve.

SHALLOW-POACHED SOLE VÉRONIQUE

FOR 4

A classic of the French repertoire, sole Véronique is made traditionally with a garnish of uncooked grapes. It's a dish I've always loved—or rather, loved the idea of. I set about devising my own version and this is the winning result. In this recipe the fillets are shallow-poached *with* the grapes. The poaching liquid is then made into a light, creamy sauce that naps everything deliciously. Serve the sole with simple boiled rice and you'll enjoy the best of the old and the new.

1. In a medium nonreactive skillet with straight sides, melt the butter over medium heat. Add the shallots and sweat without coloring, about 2 minutes.

2. Add the stock and bring to the boil. Roll up the fillets and add them, seam side down, to the saucepan. The stock should cover the fillets halfway; if not, add more stock. Add the grapes. Reduce the heat and poach the fillets until they are slightly resilient to the touch and milky white to the center of the roll, 7 to 8 minutes.

3. Remove the fish and grapes to a platter and keep warm. Add the cream to the poaching liquid and cook over medium-high heat until reduced by one-third, about 3 minutes. Season the sauce with the lemon juice, salt, and pepper. Pour the sauce over the sole and grapes and serve immediately.

1 teaspoon unsalted butter

2 medium shallots, minced

¾ cup Fish Stock (page 67)

4 fillets of sole (about 6 ounces each), preferably from a whole fish personally inspected for freshness

24 seedless grapes, red or white

¼ cup heavy (whipping) cream

1 teaspoon fresh lemon juice

Salt and freshly ground black pepper

POACHED JOINT OF COD

FOR 4

3 quarts Court Bouillon
  (page 69)
3½-pound joint of cod

COOK'S OPTION

*A joint of haddock can also
be prepared in this fashion.*

This is a satisfying, absolutely simple dish, which may be enjoyed accompanied by a savory side dish like ratatouille or caponata.

The joint is a section taken between the vertebrae of a large whole cod that has been thoroughly cleaned. Ask your fish seller to do the butchering for you. The joint is poached and served. That's it.

A great dish for dieters, this is also perfect for times when you've overindulged on spicy or elaborate dishes and crave something simple. I love to make a picnic of joint of cod—it's perfect for open-air eating.

1. In a medium soup pot, bring the court bouillon to the boil. Add the fish, reduce the heat, and poach gently until the flesh near the bone yields easily when touched with a fork, about 15 minutes.

2. Gently remove the cod from the pot. Peel the skin from the joint and serve.

POACHED WHOLE BASS WITH NEW POTATOES AND SPRING VEGETABLES

FOR 4

I've always enjoyed one-pot meals—they evoke family-style eating prepared with a minimum of fuss. For this seafood version of the boiled dinner, whole bass and new potatoes are poached in a court bouillon with the addition of onions, carrots, asparagus, and mushrooms. Everything is served together on large plates, with only a splash of lemon juice and liberal shakes of sea salt.

This is plain eating at its best, but you may gussy things up a bit by shaving Red Pepper Butter (page 63) or Scallion Butter (page 62) onto the fish and vegetables just before serving.

1. In a large pot, bring the court bouillon to the boil. Add the fish and potatoes, reduce the heat, and simmer for 5 minutes.

2. Add the carrots, onions, asparagus, and mushrooms and cook for 4 minutes more. Continue to cook until the bass are resilient to the touch, and when cut into, reveal a small amount of translucent flesh near the center bones.

3. Remove the fish and vegetables and serve together. Sprinkle with the lemon juice and pass the sea salt.

---

3 quarts Court Bouillon (page 69)

2 whole bass (2½ to 3 pounds each), cleaned, heads and tails left on

8 medium new potatoes, washed

12 baby carrots or 6 small carrots, peeled

8 medium cipolline (small Italian onions) or pearl onions, peeled

16 thin asparagus spears, trimmed to 5-inch lengths

16 small mushrooms

Fresh lemon juice

Sea salt

COOK'S OPTION

Snapper makes a good substitute for the bass.

SIZZLE-PLATE POACHED SOLE WITH LEMON AND PERNOD

FOR 4

4 fillets of sole (6 to 7 ounces each), preferably from a whole fish personally inspected for freshness

1 small onion, very thinly sliced

4 bay leaves

8 fresh thyme sprigs, or 1½ teaspoons dried

12 lemon slices, cut as thin as possible

Salt and freshly ground black pepper

½ cup dry white wine

2 tablespoons Pernod

2 tablespoons unsalted butter, cut into 8 equal pieces

This is really the master recipe for fast and easy sizzle-plate poaching. It calls for fillets of sole, but you can use uniformly sized fillets from virtually any fish except oily ones like mackerel or "steak" fish like tuna, swordfish, and marlin. Adjust the vegetables and seasonings to suit your fancy. I've provided a list of possible variations below and shellfish versions follow. See page 186 for more information on sizzle plates.

1. Preheat the oven to 450°F.

2. Place the fillets on the sizzle plate. Distribute the onion, bay leaves, thyme, and lemon slices evenly over the fish. Season with the salt and pepper and add the wine and Pernod. Arrange the butter evenly around the rim of the plate, cover the plate with foil, and crimp the edges tightly. With a knife or a skewer, puncture a steam vent in the center of the foil.

3. Place the plate over high heat on top of the stove. As soon as you see steam emerging from the vent, put the plate in the oven. Bake 5 minutes, remove the plate, and check the fillets, opening the foil carefully to avoid being burned by the steam. If they are milk-white and fork-tender, remove them and the onion to a serving dish; if not, return them to the oven and cook 1 or 2 minutes longer.

4. After the fillets have been removed, put the sizzle plate on top of the stove over high heat. Reduce the cooking liquids until slightly emulsified, about 1 minute. Pour the sauce over the fish and serve.

VARIATIONS

For snapper, use the ingredients above but substitute the green parts of 1 bunch of scallions, cut on the bias, for the onions, and thin slices of 1 large tomato in place of the lemon. Bake 5 to 7 minutes.

For tilefish, use the ingredients above but substitute 20 small pearl onions for the small sliced onion. Use 2 tablespoons olive oil, drizzled onto the fish, in place of the butter. Bake until milk-white and fork-tender, about 10 minutes.

For cod, use the ingredients above but substitute plum wine for the white wine and 1 thinly sliced lime for the lemon. Add 1 garlic clove, crushed with the flat of a knife before cooking and sprinkle the fish with 1 teaspoon minced fresh ginger. Bake until resilient to the touch, about 9 minutes.

SIZZLE-PLATE POACHED BAY SCALLOPS WITH MUSHROOMS

FOR 4

Bay scallops and mushrooms poached this way emerge with all their goodness intact.

1. Preheat the oven to 400°F.
2. Place the scallops and mushrooms on the plate. Distribute the shallots evenly over the scallops and pour on the stock. Add the lemon juice, sprinkle on the chives, and season with the salt and pepper.
3. Arrange the butter along the rim of the plate. Cover the plate with foil and crimp the edges tightly. With a knife or skewer, puncture a steam vent in the center of the foil.
4. Place the plate over medium-high heat and cook until steam emerges from the vent, about 1½ minutes. Bake for 6 minutes. The scallops should be just heated through.
5. Remove the scallops and the mushrooms to a serving dish. Place the plate over high heat on top of the stove and reduce the accumulated cooking liquids for 1 minute. Pour over the scallops and mushrooms and serve.

1¼ pounds bay scallops
½ pound mushrooms, sliced
6 medium shallots, thinly sliced
⅓ cup Fish Stock (page 67)
1 teaspoon fresh lemon juice
1 tablespoon snipped fresh chives
Salt and freshly ground black pepper
2 tablespoons unsalted butter, cut into 8 equal pieces

COOK'S OPTION

Medium sea scallops also work well with this recipe. Cook for 2 additional minutes.

SIZZLE-PLATE STEAMED MUSSELS

FOR 2

2 pounds mussels (preferably
cultivated), cleaned and
bearded

4 thyme sprigs, or 1 teaspoon
dried

1 bay leaf, crumbled

1 medium shallot, minced

1/3 cup Fish Stock (page 67)

1 tablespoon unsalted butter,
cut into 4 equal pieces

Salt and freshly ground black
pepper

COOK'S OPTION

*Manila clams can be sub-
stituted for the mussels.*

The mussels and the sauce are prepared simultaneously, in about 5 minutes. Serve the mussels accompanied by Belgian Fries (page 297).

1. Preheat the oven to 450°F.

2. Put the mussels on the sizzle plate and add the thyme and bay leaf. Distribute the minced shallot evenly over the mussels and add the stock.

3. Arrange the butter pieces along the rim of the plate. Cover the plate with foil and crimp the edges tightly around the rim. With a knife or skewer, puncture a steam vent in the center of the foil.

4. Place the plate over high heat on the top of the stove. As soon as steam emerges from the vent, place the plate in the oven. Bake for about 3 minutes. Check to see if the mussels have opened, then remove all opened mussels to a serving bowl. Continue to bake unopened mussels until they have opened, about 1 minute longer. At the end of this time, discard any mussels that still have not opened. Discard the bay leaf pieces.

5. Put the sizzle plate on top of the stove over high heat and bring the liquids to a boil. Reduce the liquids for 30 seconds, pour over the mussels, and serve.

STEAMED SALMON WITH A LEEK RAGOUT

FOR 4

I'd always thought of a ragout as a meat- or fish-based dish until I landed in France, in the early 1980s. I soon learned about vegetable ragouts—long part of the French repertoire and newly popular thanks to nouvelle cuisine. These light and delectable compotes are often served as main dishes; in this recipe, a savory leek-based ragout heightens the rich sweetness of freshly steamed salmon.

This dish is garnished with mint. I was put off by that herb at an early age because of those terrible kelly green jellies automatically served with lamb. Fresh mint is another story entirely, and makes a perfect finish for the salmon and leeks.

1. In a medium saucepan, combine the butter, water, and vinegar and bring to the boil. Reduce the heat, add the leeks, and simmer until they are soft and all moisture has evaporated, about 20 minutes. Reserve.

2. Combine the garnish ingredients in a small bowl and reserve.

3. Prepare a steamer. Season the salmon with the salt and pepper and steam until the salmon is resilient to the touch and almost cooked through (the interior will remain a dark pink), 6 to 8 minutes.

4. Divide the leek ragout among the plates and place salmon portions on top of each serving. Sprinkle with the mint garnish and serve.

RAGOUT

1 tablespoon unsalted butter

2 tablespoons water

1 teaspoon Champagne vinegar

6 medium leeks, white parts only, split lengthwise, well washed, and cut crosswise into 2-inch lengths

GARNISH

Zest of 1 lemon, grated

2 tablespoons chopped fresh Italian (flat-leaf) parsley

2 teaspoons chopped fresh mint

1/2 teaspoon crushed pink peppercorns (optional)

1 1/2 pounds salmon fillets, cut into 4 equal portions

Salt and freshly ground black pepper

COOK'S OPTION

Halibut also works well with this recipe. Steam the fillets for 4 to 6 minutes.

11. DEEP-FRYING, SAUTÉING, AND STIR-FRYING

Ever been to a fish fry?

Years ago I had the luck to attend a Wisconsin fry held in a small, very picturesque fishing town. Virtually every one of the town's residents had a role to play in this community feast, benefiting a local hospital. The men fished at night and into the morning, producing a wrigglingly fresh catch; the women did most of the frying. We sat down at long, scrubbed wooden tables, among the noises of crackling fat and the steam produced by frying fish.

Huge piles of golden brown fish arrived on baking sheets covered with newspaper; it was all I could do not to gobble up every one in sight, head to tail. Those I ate were perfectly crisp on the outside, sweetly tender within—and completely greaseless. From that afternoon on, I became seriously passionate about frying seafood. In fact, I got a little crazy on the subject of preparing the cleanest-tasting, most delicate fried seafood ever, as well as mastering the other hot-oil cooking techniques, which include sautéing and stir-frying.

There's no mystery to it. Start by making Popcorn Shrimp, the ultimate munching food, or the Corn-Fried Oysters with Spicy Corn Relish. Besides the wonderful crunch and the great flavors, they'll develop your frying hand. Fried Whitebait with Pastis Aïoli, delicious food for friends who love to eat, provides more good frying practice while introducing one of my favorite dipping sauces. Fried foods seem to call out for this kind of tantalizing sweet-and-spicy accompaniment; many, like Orange-Lemon Hot Sauce and Pickled Plum Mayonnaise, are great to have on hand. I think of them as a paint box for fried seafood. They turn the simplest fried food into dishes of many-hued complexity.

As committed as I am to the pleasures of deep-frying and to helping people deep-fry fearlessly, I rely on the "small-oil" methods of sautéing and stir-frying to produce most of my "foundation dishes"—the cooking that stands for me and what I do. The Sautéed Cod with Sake and Chinese Black Bean Sauce, Stir-Fried Squid with Scallions and Sliced Almonds, or Stir-Fried Monkfish with Chili Paste and Ginger, to name a few, have all the flavor nature put into their ingredients; the oil *makes* that happen. Sautéing and stir-frying are methods that serve the after-work cook especially well; once ingredients are readied, these dishes take only minutes.

Of course, successful deep-frying, sautéing, and stir-frying require attention to a few simple rules. Here are the "grandmother" basics, plus a frying fanatic's pointers for perfect results.

DEEP-FRYING

Rule number 1: Safety first. You'll be working with a quantity of oil heated to a high temperature. Do your prep—make sure all the implements and ingredients you'll need are out and ready. Once the frying process begins you don't want to be searching for a mesh skimmer or putting out paper toweling. You won't burn yourself or set fire to the cat if you're able to concentrate on what you're doing—on the *process* of frying. Prepping also allows you to establish a relaxed cooking rhythm, which facilitates proper timing.

Never fill any fryer more than half-full with oil. This minimizes the possibility of a spill-over if you inadvertently overload the frying vessel with food. Make sure all the food you fry is dry or batter-coated so the oil doesn't spit at you when food is added. (Wet food also discourages the oil from "seizing" the coating, increasing the possibility of its saturating the food within, resulting in greasy fried food.) Allow hot oil to come to room temperature before decanting it for future use or pouring it into a used milk carton for disposal.

Rule number 2: If the oil you fry with isn't hot enough, your seafood won't crisp as it should and coatings will be greasy or come apart. It's important, therefore, to make sure your oil has reached—and stays at—the proper frying temperature. You've un-doubtedly read any number of directions that tell you how to determine when your oil is ready for frying. Watching for light hazes above the oil or throwing in cubes of bread to check for brownness strike me as uncertain—and potentially distracting. Instead, buy a deep-frying thermometer. They allow you to watch the progress of the heating, and you'll be able to see what happens to the oil's temperature when you add food. You can regulate the heat or withhold additional fish or shellfish to keep the temperature high.

Rule number 3: Oil temperature always drops when food is added. The food cools the oil, "absorbing" its heat for cooking. Your objective, therefore, is to maintain the oil at a steady temperature. One way of controlling temperature is to fry in small batches. Just as pasta cooks best when there's plenty of water for it to move around in, food fries most suc-cessfully when it has sufficient oil in which to cook. Never crowd food when you deep-fry it. If necessary, cook a second batch, remembering to allow the oil to return to the proper temperature before you proceed.

Drain your fried food well on paper toweling and always salt it while it's hot—salt won't adhere to warm fried food. If you're going to be frying "small" food, like Popcorn Shrimp, there's no need to keep a first batch warm in the oven while you prepare another, as the whole cooking process goes quickly. Large food, however, should be put on a cookie sheet and held in a 250° F. oven while other batches are being cooked.

SAUTÉING AND STIR-FRYING

The rules that hold for deep-frying apply to sautéing and stir-frying as well. But a word of clarification first. As a student chef I was surprised to learn that what we call sautéing is in France a different procedure from the little-fat cooking we practice here. The verb *sauter* means "to jump," which describes pretty accurately the sautéing procedure in French cooking: food is shaken constantly so that it jumps in a sizzling cooking pan. Shaking food keeps it from sticking and ensures even cooking on all sides. In France the word for our technique of sautéing is *poêlé*, or "panned." In either country the underlying culinary objective is the same: to cook relatively small amounts of food in just enough fat to help caramelize the food's surface deliciously.

For successful sautéing, the food must be dry, the oil must be hot, and the pan must be uncrowded. For stir-frying, temperatures must be as high as you can get them, oil just smoking, and the wok—an ideal "sautéing" medium because of its large surface area—not overfull. The idea, no matter the method, is to sear food, not steam it—unachievable if the food is wet or packed into the pan. When sautéing large batches, I recommend that the cook sauté first, then finish food in the oven to ensure that multiple pieces of seafood finish together. And make sure all your ingredients are prepped beforehand. As with deep-frying, once you start cooking, there's no time for pausing or turning back.

THE WOK

Stir-frying is the Asian version of sautéing, in the French sense of the word. Food is made to jump by stirring and turning it repeatedly in a hot pan to which a small amount of oil has been added. (Actually, stir-frying comprises two methods in one—dry-heat cooking followed, after the addition of liquid, by steaming or boiling.)

The ingenious wok is at the heart of successful stir-frying. Like the wheel, it's one of those designs you'd be hard pressed to improve upon. But you must give a little thought to its selection, preparation, and use.

I'm often asked whether I prefer a thin or thick wok. I'm of the thin school. Though thicker woks hold heat longer, thinner versions are quickly heated and, conversely, cool more easily. This gives you greater cooking control. I like my woks large and suggest you get the biggest size your heating element can handle—at least 14 inches in diameter. Buy woks made of black steel. Woks with round bottoms are best for gas stoves; flat-bottomed woks are excellent for electric ranges. If you cook with gas you'll need a wok ring or inverted burner grid to allow the flames full play on the underside of the wok; the rings or grids are obligatory pan-steadiers if you're using your round-bottomed wok for deep-frying.

Woks need to be seasoned before use to prevent food from sticking. Here's how to do it. Put your new wok over high heat and add 1½ cups of kosher salt. The salt will extract residual moisture from the metal and dry the wok thoroughly. Stir the salt as the pan "cooks." After 10 to 15 minutes the wok will begin to darken, which is desirable. Discard the salt and allow the wok to cool until it is warm to the touch. Dip a clean cloth in vegetable oil and massage the oil into the interior surface of the wok. Now you're in business.

The first couple of times you use the wok the interior may feel slightly sticky and food may tend to cling. By the third or fourth time your wok should have developed a stick-resistant surface. Never scrub the inside of your wok or use abrasive pads on it—you'll remove the "seasoning" you've worked so carefully to develop. Rather, add about 2 cups of water to the wok right after you've finished cooking in it, then discard the water. (You are, in effect, removing oily residue by deglazing the interior.) Tough stick-ons can be removed with salt and a rag. Rinse the wok quickly, wipe it dry thoroughly, then oil the interior lightly using a paper napkin.

What if someone misuses your wok and patches of rust appear? I like to reseason the pan, but you could rinse it out, abrade it with salt, coat it with a little oil, and cook with it as you normally would. You'll never have a problem with rust, however, if you dry your wok thoroughly after each use.

As for wok tools, invest in a wok spatula or shovel *and* a wok spoon—the pair are more efficient for turning ingredients as you stir-fry than two spatulas alone.

I tell people that the secret of great seafood frying is just doing it and paying attention to what you're doing. "Doing it" is a delicious education I hope you'll enjoy, using your own recipes and improvisations.

POPCORN SHRIMP

FOR 4

2 cups plus 3 tablespoons
all-purpose flour

2 teaspoons paprika

2 teaspoons baking powder

3 1/2 teaspoons salt, plus
additional for seasoning
cooked shrimp

1 tablespoon sugar

3 1/2 teaspoons cayenne pepper

One 12-ounce bottle of beer,
any kind

1 large egg white, whipped
until frothy

4 cups vegetable oil, for frying

1 pound large shrimp (21 to 30
count), peeled

COOK'S OPTION

*You can use 1 pound of
squid tentacles in place of
the shrimp. Frying will take
about 2 minutes.*

These puffy, golden shrimp morsels are the ultimate munching food. Bowlsful have been known to disappear with alarming rapidity—and they're easy to make. Besides being an addictive treat, they're a fine place to begin practicing your frying hand. In no time you'll produce delicate fried food that isn't excessively caloric.

Of course, Popcorn Shrimp make an excellent hors d'oeuvre and are particularly great with Orange-Lemon Hot Sauce, page 77.

1. In a medium bowl, combine all but 1 cup of the flour with the paprika, baking powder, 1 tablespoon salt, sugar, and 1½ teaspoons of the cayenne. Add the beer, mixing it in with a fork, then stir in the egg white. Set aside. (This batter may be made ahead of time and refrigerated.)

2. Slowly add the oil to a fryer with a basket, or use a deep, heavy skillet or wok. (If you are using a wok, make sure it is balanced securely with a wok ring or overturned burner grid.) Turn the heat under the oil to high and heat it to 365°F. on a frying thermometer.

3. Have ready a large plate covered with a layer of paper toweling and a mesh skimmer. On a second large plate, mix the remaining flour with the remaining salt and cayenne. Add all the shrimp to the plate and dredge in the seasoned flour. Shake off all excess. Add the shrimp to the bowl of batter.

4. When the oil is ready for frying, remove the shrimp one by one from the batter with your fingers or chopsticks, shake off excess batter, and add to the oil. Each shrimp should be "consumed" by the oil and rise immediately to the surface, surrounded by small, vigorous bubbles. If bubbling doesn't occur or a shrimp sinks to the bottom of the fryer, remove it. This means the oil's heat has been "used up" by the cooking shrimp. Fry this, and other shrimp if any, in a second batch. During cooking use the skimmer to push the shrimp under the surface of the oil so that all sides brown evenly. Fry shrimp until golden, about 3 minutes.

5. Remove the shrimp using the basket or skimmer. Turn the shrimp out onto the paper towel–covered plate to drain. Make sure the shrimp do not cover one another.

6. Sprinkle the shrimp with salt while still hot (salt will not adhere to warm fried food). If you need to cook another batch, allow the oil to return to 365°F. and repeat the frying procedure. Use fresh paper toweling to drain a second batch. Serve immediately to ensure crispiness. Let the oil cool, strain it through a coffee filter, and reserve for another occasion.

FRIED WHITEBAIT WITH PASTIS AÏOLI

FOR 2 AS AN APPETIZER

AÏOLI

1 large egg yolk

1 garlic clove, mashed

1 teaspoon Pastis

2 teaspoons fresh lemon juice

$^1/_2$ cup olive oil

$^1/_4$ cup vegetable oil

Salt and freshly ground black
  pepper

FISH

2 quarts vegetable oil, for frying

$^1/_4$ cup cornstarch

$^1/_4$ cup flour

$^1/_2$ teaspoon salt

$^1/_2$ pound whitebait, rinsed and
  well dried

I had my first taste of whitebait at a country restaurant in France. I was eighteen and traveling with fellow students from the Culinary Institute of America. When the tiny fish arrived at the table, we glanced at each other nervously—could we eat these little *things?* Within minutes of our trying them, the delicious fish were gone—followed by several more plates, all served with a rich mayonnaise the color of fresh butter.

The term whitebait includes five or six species of very small saltwater fish including silverside, herring, and smelt. They're eaten whole, bones and all, and are best fried and served with a dipping sauce like Pastis Aïoli. Piled high on a plate that had been covered with a crisp white napkin, they make a scrumptious appetizer or whole meal. Serve them with very thin, crispy French fries.

1. Make the aïoli. In a medium nonreactive bowl, combine the egg yolk, garlic, Pastis, and 1 teaspoon of the lemon juice. Whisking steadily, add the oils in a thin stream to form an emulsion. Whisk in the remaining teaspoon of lemon juice, salt, and pepper.

2. Slowly add the vegetable oil to a fryer with a basket or use a deep, heavy skillet or wok. (If using a wok, make sure it is balanced securely with a wok ring or overturned burner grid.) Turn the heat under the oil to high and heat the pan to 375°F. on a frying thermometer. Have ready a large plate covered with paper toweling and a mesh skimmer if you are not using a frying basket.

3. On a large plate, combine the cornstarch, flour, and salt. Dredge the fish in the mixture, making sure they are well coated, and shake off any excess.

4. When the oil is ready, add the fish. Do not crowd; fry in batches if necessary, making sure the oil returns to 375°F. before adding more fish. Fry the whitebait until they are golden and very crisp, about 2 minutes.

5. Remove the fish, using the basket or skimmer, to the paper towel–covered plate. Drain well and serve immediately with the aïoli.

CORN-FRIED OYSTERS WITH SPICY CORN RELISH

FOR 4

RELISH

1/2 small red onion, diced

3/4 cup corn kernels (preferably fresh, but frozen work well)

4 scallions, green parts only, chopped

1 small red bell pepper, cored, seeded, and diced

1 1/2 tablespoons Champagne vinegar or other white wine vinegar

1 very small jalapeño pepper, minced

1 tablespoon olive oil

Salt and freshly ground black pepper

OYSTERS

4 cups vegetable oil, for frying

2 cups fine cornmeal

1 teaspoon cayenne pepper

1/2 teaspoon ground cumin

24 oysters, any kind, shucked and drained, bottom shells reserved

Salt

COOK'S OPTION

You can use 48 cherrystone clams in place of the oysters.

I used to be an oyster purist—only raw ones served with lemon juice or black pepper would do. Now I know better. These crunchy cornmeal-fried oysters, served with a tingling corn and red onion relish, really make the case for cooked oysters. They're crisp, sweet, and spicy all at once.

Be sure to prepare the relish in advance to give it time to develop flavor. These oysters make a fabulous hors d'oeuvre or a great snacking supper.

1. At least 2 hours and up to 24 hours in advance, prepare the relish. In a small saucepan, blanch the onion in boiling water for 1 minute. Drain well.

2. Combine the onion with the remaining relish ingredients and stir well. Refrigerate.

3. Slowly add the oil to a fryer with basket, or use a deep, heavy skillet or wok. (If you are using a wok, make sure it is balanced securely with a wok ring or overturned burner grid.) Turn the heat under the oil to high and heat it to 350°F. on a frying thermometer. Have ready a large plate covered with paper toweling for draining the oysters and a mesh skimmer.

4. On a large plate, combine the cornmeal, cayenne, and cumin. Mix well. Dredge the oysters gently in the cornmeal mixture, making sure they are thoroughly coated. Shake off excess coating.

5. When the oil is ready, add the oysters. Do not crowd them. Fry in batches, if necessary, making sure the oil returns to 350°F. before proceeding with a new batch. Turn the oysters as necessary so that they color evenly. Fry the oysters until golden, about 1 minute.

6. Remove the oysters using the frying basket or skimmer to the paper towel–covered plate to drain. Season with the salt while still hot (salt will not adhere to warm fried food) and serve immediately, in the half shells, with the relish.

WHOLE CRISPY PORGY WITH CARROT "POMMES PAILLE"

FOR 4

This is one of those the-more-fried-ingredients-the-better dishes, like the Italian *frito misto*. Here, whole porgies are deep-fried and accompanied by crisply fried julienne carrots—a take-off on the French *pommes paille*, or straw potatoes. The carrots' slight sweetness beautifully complements the crisp, sweet-fleshed fish.

1. Preheat the oven to 250°F.

2. Dry each fish well with paper toweling. Make 3 gashes about ⅛ inch deep on both sides of each fish.

3. Slowly add the oil to a wok or large Dutch oven. (If you are using a wok, make sure it is balanced securely with a wok ring or overturned burner grid.) Turn the heat to high and heat it to 360°F. on a frying thermometer. Have ready 1 large and 1 medium plate covered with paper toweling for draining the fish and carrots and a large mesh skimmer.

4. On a second large plate, distribute the cornstarch evenly. Dredge the fish in the cornstarch, shaking off all excess.

5. When the oil is ready, add a fish. Use the skimmer to keep it under the surface of the oil while cooking. Fry the fish until golden and the gashes reveal milk-white flesh that is still slightly transparent at the bone, about 4 minutes. Remove the fish to the large paper towel–covered plate to drain. Fry the remaining fish one at a time, allowing the oil to return to 360°F. between fryings. Season each fish with the salt and pepper as it is cooked. Keep fried fish warm in the preheated oven.

6. Check the temperature of the oil. Adjust the heat so the thermometer reads 340°F. Add the carrots, and fry until crisp, about 4 minutes. Remove vegetables to the remaining paper towel–covered plate to drain. Season them with the salt and pepper.

7. Place the fish on plates, accompany with the carrot "pommes paille," and serve.

4 whole porgy, 14 to 18 ounces each, cleaned, heads and tails left on

3 quarts vegetable oil, for frying

1 cup cornstarch

Salt and freshly ground black pepper

4 small carrots, peeled and julienned

COOK'S OPTION

One whole blackfish can be substituted for the porgy.

CONCH FRITTERS WITH ZESTY PINEAPPLE SALSA

FOR 6

SALSA

¼ cup sugar

2 tablespoons Champagne vinegar or rice vinegar

¾ cup pineapple juice

1 tablespoon sambal oelek
(Asian red chili paste), or 2
teaspoons Chinese chili
paste, or 1 teaspoon Tabasco
Sauce

½ cup diced pineapple (preferably fresh, but you can use
unsweetened canned pineapple packed in water and
well drained)

1 medium tomato, peeled,
seeded, and diced

1 teaspoon salt

1 tablespoon plus 1 teaspoon
cornstarch, dissolved in 2
tablespoons water

FRITTERS

2 pounds conch meat, trimmed,
if necessary, of all dark
tissue

1 medium onion, quartered

2 teaspoons salt

If you've been disappointed with conch fritters in the past, you've got to try these. Unlike the competition, you can taste the conch in these frit-ters and each mouthful is an airy poem. A batter lightened by whipped egg white ensures their delicacy. The fiery, sour-sweet salsa, bursting with fresh pineapple, is the perfect accompaniment. This recipe works well with other deep-fried seafood, too.

1. Make the salsa. In a small saucepan over high heat, melt the sugar and cook without stirring until a light brown caramel has formed, about 4 minutes. Watch the sugar carefully to make sure that it does not over-brown; remove the pan from the heat a moment before you think it is done as it will continue to cook off the stove.

2. Cool briefly, then return the sugar to the burner, add the vinegar and pineapple juice, and cook over medium heat, stirring, for 3 minutes. Add the sambal oelek and the diced pineapple and cook 2 minutes longer. Add the tomato and salt, cook for 1 minute, and stir in the cornstarch mixture. Simmer gently until the salsa is lightly thickened, about 5 min-utes. Remove from the stove and keep warm.

3. In the bowl of a food processor, combine the conch, onion, salt, pepper, parsley, and chives. Pulse until the mixture is evenly chopped. Remove to a bowl and add the egg. With a wooden spoon, incorporate the flour gradually and mix very well.

4. Slowly add the oil to a fryer with a basket, or use a deep, heavy skillet or wok. (If you are using a wok, make sure it is balanced securely with a wok ring or overturned burner grid.) Turn the heat under the oil to high and heat it to 375°F. on a frying thermometer. Have ready a large plate covered with paper toweling for draining and a mesh skimmer.

5. Beat the egg whites to soft peaks and fold gently into the conch mix-

ture. When the oil is ready, drop the fritter batter by heaping tablespoons into it. Do not crowd; fry a second batch, if necessary, allowing the oil to return to 375°F. between batches. Fry until the fritters have floated to the top of the oil and are golden, about 3 minutes. During cooking, use the mesh spoon to turn the fritters so that they brown evenly. Remove the fritters using the basket or skimmer to the paper towel–covered plate to drain. Sprinkle them with additional salt while still hot and serve immediately with the salsa.

1½ teaspoons freshly ground white pepper

2 tablespoons chopped fresh Italian (flat-leaf) parsley

1 teaspoon chopped chives

1 large egg

1 cup all-purpose flour

3 quarts vegetable oil, for frying

2 large egg whites

GROUPER BEIGNETS WITH BEET CHIPS

FOR 4

1 1/4 pounds grouper fillets,
  preferably from fish personally inspected for freshness,
  cut into strips about 2 inches
  long by 1/2 inch thick

1/2 teaspoon cayenne pepper

1/2 teaspoon salt

1/2 cup cornstarch

1/2 cup all-purpose flour

1 1/2 tablespoons unsalted
  butter, melted

1 cup lukewarm water

3 quarts vegetable oil, for frying

1 large beet, peeled

Salt

2 large egg whites

COOK'S OPTION

Tilefish can be substituted
for the grouper.

This is my version of fish and chips—puffy grouper beignets that I pair with beet chips and serve with Spicy Honey Mustard (page 78) or Best Tartar Sauce (page 79).

I love the idea of chips made from root vegetables such as beets, yucca, or celery root. Each has its own subtle flavor and characteristic bite—my particular favorite is made from beets. Because of their relatively high sugar content, these root chips last longer than those made from potatoes. (Their sugar, caramelized in cooking, hardens on cooling, making the chips less vulnerable to moisture.)

To ensure the delicacy of the beignets, make sure their batter base is lightly mixed, then fry away.

1. Season the fish with the cayenne and salt. Have ready 2 large plates covered with a layer of paper toweling for draining and a mesh skimmer. Spread the cornstarch on a third plate.

2. In a bowl, combine the flour, butter, and water. Do not overmix; the batter should have the consistency of a thick pea soup. If it seems too thick, add a bit more water. Reserve.

3. Slowly add the oil to a fryer with a basket, or use a deep, heavy skillet or wok. (If you are using a wok, make sure it is balanced securely with a wok ring or overturned burner grid.) Turn the heat under the oil to high and heat it to 350°F. on a frying thermometer.

4. With a sharp knife or mandoline, slice the beet into chips as thinly as possible.

5. Dredge the beet chips in the cornstarch and shake off all excess. When the oil is ready for frying, add the chips. Fry until crispy, about 2 minutes. Remove to a paper towel–covered plate to drain and salt immediately. Reheat the oil until the thermometer reads 380°F.

6. Whip the egg whites until stiff but still glossy. Lightly fold them into the reserved batter.

7. When the oil is ready for frying, dip the fish strips in the batter, allow to drain, and add them one by one to the oil. Do not overcrowd; fry in batches, if necessary. If frying a second batch, allow the oil to return to 380°F. before proceeding. Fry the beignets until golden, about 3 minutes. During cooking, use the skimmer to push the beignets under the surface of the oil so that all sides brown evenly.

8. Remove the beignets to the second paper towel–covered plate using the frying basket or skimmer. Make sure the beignets do not cover one another. Season with the salt. If frying a second batch, change the toweling before draining again. Serve the fish and chips together with one or more dipping sauces.

TEMPURA

FOR 4

BATTER

2 cups all-purpose flour

2 cups club soda

2 large eggs

1 teaspoon salt

4 cups vegetable oil, for frying

FOODS FOR COATING

2 pounds extra-large shrimp
(16 to 20 count), peeled and
deveined

6 catfish or grouper fillets,
preferably from fish personally inspected for freshness,
cut into strips 1¼ inches
wide by 2½ inches long

6 medium onions, sliced into
1-inch-thick rings

2 pounds whole asparagus
and/or string beans, blanched

2 pounds mushrooms

6 medium zucchini, cut diagonally into ¼-inch-thick
slices

10 medium carrots, cut diagonally into ⅛-inch-thick slices

1 medium eggplant, peeled,
halved, and cut into ¼-inch-
thick slices

Tempura, which we associate with Japan, is in fact Spanish and Portuguese in origin. Given its multinational pedigree, you won't be surprised to learn that I made my first tempura in New Orleans. I'd taken a night job at a restaurant whose chef liked to challenge his cooks. "Make a hollandaise," he'd bark at me, or, on one occasion, "Make a tempura batter." I did—and it turned out to be so good that my tormentor was silenced . . . temporarily.

Delicacy is the goal when making tempura. What you want is golden, lacy fried food with the thinnest of crusts. My untraditional batter recipe produces a fine, really crispy coating. You can use just about any fresh seafood or vegetable to make tempura—my suggestions follow. Choose any or all of these for coating, depending on your appetite and the number of people you want to feed. One recipe of batter makes any *one* of the ingredients for four; you can halve or quarter the quantity of any single ingredient to make combination plates.

Leftover steamed or blanched vegetables make excellent tempura; pat them dry with paper toweling before coating them with the batter. Accompany the tempura with Ponzu (page 79) or Orange-Lemon Hot Sauce (page 77). Beer or tea complete the feast.

1. To make the batter, combine all the ingredients in a medium bowl and blend thoroughly with a fork.

2. Slowly add the oil to a fryer with a basket, or use a deep, heavy skillet or wok. (If you are using a wok, make sure it is balanced securely with a wok ring or overturned burner grid.) Turn the heat under the oil to high and heat it to 375°F. on a frying thermometer. Have ready a large paper towel–covered plate for draining and a mesh skimmer.

3. When the oil is ready for frying, dip each item into the batter. Shake off excess and add one by one to the oil; do not crowd. Fry in batches, if necessary, making sure the oil returns to 375°F. before proceeding with

a new batch. During cooking, use the skimmer to push the tempura under the surface of the oil so it browns evenly. Fry until golden, 3 to 4 minutes.

4. Remove the tempura to the paper towel–covered plate. Use fresh paper toweling to drain a second batch. Serve immediately, accompanied by little bowls of dipping sauce.

Note: Fruit make wonderful tempura. Try coating and frying whole strawberries, 2-inch-square pineapple chunks, or ripe mango slices $3^1/_2$ inches long by 1 inch wide. Shake confectioners' sugar over the drained fried fruit and serve.

TEMPURA FRIED ICE CREAM

FOR 4

Enough round-layered or loaf-style sponge cake or Genoise, homemade or best-quality store-bought, to create four 2½-inch-square slices ⅓ inch thick

1 pint best-quality pistachio ice cream (or any flavor you like)

BATTER

2 cups all-purpose flour

2 cups plus 2 tablespoons club soda

2 large eggs

1 teaspoon salt

2 quarts vegetable oil, for frying

2 tablespoons confectioners' sugar

I swore I would resist including desserts in this book, but once I thought about making a fruit tempura, there was no holding me back. Reminiscent of dishes like baked Alaska, in which "cooked" ice cream stays hard, this fried, batter-coated sandwich of sponge cake and ice cream is perfect after a light meal. Because the sandwich must be frozen before it's fried, you can easily prepare most of the dessert in advance. This is one of those culinary reputation makers.

1. At least 1 hour in advance, cut the sponge cake into 8 sandwich loaflike slices 2½ inches square by ⅓ inch thick. If you are working with round layers, cut each layer horizontally in half and trim each slice into a square.

2. Put 4 slices of the sponge cake on your work surface. Place a scoop of the ice cream in the center of each. Cover each scoop with a remaining slice of cake and mold the slices around the ice cream. Pinch off excess cake, sealing the "sandwiches." Wrap the sandwiches in plastic film and place in the freezer until the cake becomes hard, about 1 hour.

3. Combine the batter ingredients in a large bowl and blend thoroughly.

4. Slowly add the oil to a fryer with a basket, or use a heavy, deep vessel. Turn the heat under the oil to high and heat it to 370°F. on a frying thermometer. Have ready a large plate covered with a layer of paper toweling and a mesh skimmer.

5. Unwrap the sandwiches. When the oil is ready for frying, dip each into the batter. Shake off all excess and add one by one to the oil. Do not crowd. Fry in batches, if necessary, making sure the oil returns to 370°F. before proceeding with a new batch. During cooking, use the skimmer to push the sandwiches under the surface of the oil so it browns evenly. Fry until golden, 1½ to 2 minutes.

6. Remove the sandwiches to the paper towel–covered plate. Use fresh paper toweling to drain a second batch. Sprinkle the fried ice cream with the confectioners' sugar and serve. (Or cut the sandwiches in half before serving.)

SAUTÉED COD WITH SAKE AND CHINESE BLACK BEAN SAUCE

FOR 4

This signature dish evolved casually enough. I was shopping in an Asian food store and began to fill my basket with groceries—black beans, sake, rice vinegar, soy sauce. I stopped for some cod, went home, and without really thinking about it, put everything together. Sometimes the gods smile. The dish was great. From the moment it appeared at the restaurant it was a huge success.

The dish is simple. Cod fillets are sautéed and served with a shallot-sweetened sauce made with sake, Chinese black beans, and butter. The slightly astringent saltiness of the beans plays marvelously against the mild sweetness of the cod; the sake, carried by the butter, adds its characteristic warmth. The finished dish will amaze you with the way its flavors combine.

Try to get cod fillets from small fish—they're firmer and sauté better. Served with couscous, this dish is just too good to miss.

1. In a small nonreactive saucepan, melt 1 tablespoon of the butter over medium-low heat. Add the garlic and shallots, cover, and cook without stirring until translucent, about 3 minutes.

2. Add the black beans, sake, and soy sauce and mix well. Increase the heat to medium-high and reduce the liquids by two-thirds. Remove the pan from the heat and whisk in the remaining butter by tablespoons. Add the rice vinegar gradually until the sauce has a pleasingly acidic edge. Set aside.

3. Season the fillets with the salt. In a large, heavy skillet, melt the butter over medium-high heat. When the butter begins to brown, add the fillets, skin side up. Shake the pan gently to avoid sticking. Sauté until flesh sides are golden, about 2 minutes. Turn the fillets carefully and cook until the cod is flaky, 3 to 4 minutes.

4. To serve, put a portion of couscous on each plate and smooth into a circle with the back of a tablespoon. Put the fillets on top of the couscous and spoon the sauce liberally over the fish.

SAUCE

5 tablespoons unsalted butter, cut into 5 equal pieces

2 teaspoons minced garlic

2 tablespoons minced shallots

1 tablespoon fermented Chinese black beans, rinsed and coarsely chopped

1 $1/3$ cups sake

1 tablespoon soy sauce

1 tablespoon rice vinegar, approximately

FISH

4 cod fillets (6 to 7 ounces each), preferably from small whole fish personally inspected for freshness

Salt

2 tablespoons unsalted butter

3 cups cooked couscous, for serving

SAUTÉED SOFT-SHELL CRABS WITH PINE NUTS AND SCALLION BUTTER

FOR 4

½ cup pine nuts

12 small soft-shell crabs, cleaned

2 cups milk, approximately

2 tablespoons water

½ cup Scallion Butter (page 62), at room temperature

Salt and freshly ground black pepper

Drops of fresh lemon juice

3 cups all-purpose flour, for dredging

4 tablespoons unsalted butter

4 tablespoons olive oil

One of the happier signs of spring is the arrival of soft-shell crabs in our seafood markets. These are blue crabs taken from the waters of Florida, Maryland, and the Carolinas during their molting, or soft-shell, stage. Transported quickly throughout the country, they bring with them the almost startling pleasure of their sweet flesh and bursting juiciness. In season I can eat indecent quantities; I suspect you can too, especially if you make them as I suggest here.

Soft-shells cry out for a buttery sauté, which is what I've given them in this recipe. To the crabs I've added toasted pine nuts to further enhance the marvelous "brown" flavors of sautéing, and a scallion butter sauce for a rich oniony finish. If you prefer, you may serve the butter as is, allowing slices of it to melt into the hot crabs. Accompany this lovely dish with Spaghetti Vegetables—the recipe follows.

1. Preheat the oven to 400°F.

2. Spread the nuts evenly on a medium-size baking sheet and brown until golden, 6 to 8 minutes. Check the nuts at half-minute intervals, shaking the pan so they color evenly. Remove the nuts to a small bowl. (Caution: avoid touching the nuts; their oil will be very hot.) Do not turn off the oven.

3. Submerge the crabs in milk to cover and soak for 5 minutes. (The milk bath adds sweetness and moisture to the crabs, and helps to retain their whiteness.)

4. In a small nonreactive saucepan, bring the water to the boil, remove the pan from the heat, and, piece by piece, whisk in the Scallion Butter. The sauce should be lightly creamy. Season with the salt and pepper. Add drops of lemon juice if you think the sauce needs it. Set aside.

5. Meanwhile, spread the flour on a large plate. Have a baking sheet, preferably with cake racks for drainage, ready to receive the cooked crabs.

6. Heat a 10-inch heavy skillet over medium-high heat. Add 2 tablespoons of the butter and 2 tablespoons of the oil. When the butter sizzles, remove a crab from the milk, shake off the excess, and dredge it quickly in the flour. Shake gently and slide into the hot skillet, shell side up. Repeat with 5 additional crabs. Sauté until light brown, about 2½ minutes. Turn and cook 1½ minutes more. Remove the sautéed crabs to the baking sheet or to cake racks on the sheet. Repeat the procedure with the 6 remaining crabs.

7. Put all the crabs in the oven to finish cooking, about 2½ minutes.

8. To serve, surround the crabs with the sauce, or place two ¼-inch slices of chilled Scallion Butter on each. Sprinkle the crabs with the pine nuts. Add additional scallion greens, if you wish.

SPAGHETTI VEGETABLES
FOR 4

1. With a sharp knife or using a mandoline, julienne the zucchini, carrots, and squash, making strips as long as the vegetable. Remove large seeds from the squash as you work.

2. In a medium skillet, heat the oil over medium heat. Sauté the vegetables until tender-crisp, about 3 minutes. Season with the salt and pepper. Sprinkle with the thyme and serve.

1 small zucchini

2 small carrots

1 small yellow squash

2 tablespoons olive oil

Salt and freshly ground black
  pepper

2 teaspoons chopped fresh
  thyme

SHAD ROE WITH CREAM, BACON, AND ONIONS

FOR 4

7 bacon strips (preferably applewood smoked), cut into 1-inch squares

1 medium onion, diced

2 tablespoons Champagne vinegar or cider vinegar

¾ cup heavy (whipping) cream

2 tablespoons coarsely chopped fresh tarragon leaves or whole fresh thyme leaves

1 tablespoon coarsely ground black pepper

Vegetable or olive oil

2 cups all-purpose flour, for dredging

4 medium pairs shad roe (about 6 ounces each)

3 tablespoons unsalted butter

3 tablespoons olive oil

This is *the* recipe for people who aren't yet shad roe enthusiasts. The combination of the roe and a tarragon-flavored sauce of cream, bacon, and onions is mouthwatering and will convert even the most roe-reluctant palates.

A note on purchasing: the roe—egg sacs, actually—must be rosy in color, not ruby or brown, and unbroken. If a sac is torn, it will burst during cooking. Appearance aside, the eggs can spatter the cook! This precaution taken, you should have nothing but pleasure from making and eating this wonderful, hearty dish.

1. Preheat the oven to 400° F.

2. In a medium saucepan, cook the bacon over medium heat without allowing it to color, about 4 minutes. Discard three-fourths of the accumulated fat. Reduce the heat to medium-low, add the onion, and cook until translucent, about 10 minutes. Add the vinegar and reduce slowly until the liquid has almost evaporated, about 8 minutes. Add the cream, raise the heat to medium-high, and bring to the boil, reducing the liquid by one-third, about 4 minutes. Add the tarragon or thyme and season with the black pepper. Taste and add a bit more vinegar or tarragon if needed. Reserve the sauce in a warm place.

3. Lightly oil a baking sheet with vegetable or olive oil. Pour the flour onto a large plate and delicately dredge the roe. Handle gently to avoid tearing; rather than shake off excess flour, toss the roe lightly from hand to hand, allowing excess flour to fall through your fingers. Place the floured roe on a plate.

4. Heat a heavy, medium skillet over medium heat. (Make sure the heat is no higher than medium to prevent the roe's bursting while cooking.) Add

½ tablespoon each of the butter and oil. When the butter sizzles, add 2 pairs of roe. Sauté 2 minutes, turn, and cook 1 minute more. Remove the roe to the baking sheet. Repeat the procedure with the remaining roe. Bake the roe until it is resilient to the touch, 3 to 4 minutes. Remove to serving plates, allowing 1 pair of roe for each diner. Spoon the sauce generously over the roe and serve.

VARIATION

Shad Roe with Meunière Butter Dredge and sauté the roe as above and reserve in a warm place. In a small skillet, melt 4 tablespoons unsalted butter over medium-high heat. When brown, add 2 tablespoons minced shallots, 1½ tablespoons drained crushed capers, and 4 tablespoons coarsely chopped fresh Italian (flat-leaf) parsley. Cook, shaking the pan, for 5 seconds. Add the juice of 1 small lemon and season with salt and freshly ground black pepper. Place the roe on serving plates, 1 pair per diner, and pour the meunière butter over each serving.

SNAPPER WITH HAZELNUT CRUST AND MARJORAM SAUCE

FOR 4

MARJORAM SAUCE

1/3 cup light olive oil

1 1/2 tablespoons chopped fresh
marjoram leaves

2 tablespoons fresh lemon juice

1 small garlic clove, crushed
with the flat of a knife

3 tablespoons Fish Stock
(page 67) or Chicken Stock
(page 66)

1/4 cup loosely packed fresh
Italian (flat-leaf) parsley
leaves

Salt and freshly ground black
pepper

FISH

2 cups hazelnuts

1 cup unsweetened graham
cracker crumbs

1/2 cup all-purpose flour

4 large eggs, lightly beaten

4 snapper fillets (about 1 1/2
pounds), preferably from a
whole fish personally
inspected for freshness, cut
into 4 equal portions

2 1/2 cups vegetable oil, for
shallow-frying

Toasted hazelnuts make a delicious crust for snapper, which is wonderful paired with a vinaigrettelike sauce flavored with marjoram. Cookbooks usually tell you to use marjoram with discretion, but this pungent herb blooms when brought to the foreground. The herby sauce contrasts perfectly with the crisp, nut-sweetened fillets.

1. To make the sauce, combine all the ingredients in a blender (a food processor won't do the job) and puree about 1 minute. Reserve. (The sauce may be prepared in advance. If it is, blend it again just before using.)

2. Preheat the oven to 325°F. On a medium baking sheet, spread the nuts evenly and toast until golden, about 15 minutes. Check the nuts frequently, shaking the pan so they color evenly. Remove the nuts to a clean kitchen towel. Wrap the towel to enclose the nuts and rub them in a circular motion to remove their skins.

3. Place the nuts in the bowl of a food processor. Pulse several times to break up the nuts, then process until the nuts have the texture of coarse bread crumbs, about 15 seconds. Add the graham cracker crumbs and process 15 seconds more.

4. Spread the hazelnut mixture and the flour on separate plates. Have the beaten eggs ready, as well as a paper towel–covered plate for draining the cooked fish.

5. Dredge the fish in the flour and shake off all excess. Dip each fish portion quickly in the beaten eggs, allow excess egg to drip away, and dredge in the hazelnut mixture. Make sure each portion is coated evenly.

6. Add the oil to a large, heavy skillet until it fills the pan to a depth of 1 inch. Heat the oil until it just begins to smoke. Add the fish and shallow-fry until golden, about 1½ minutes. Turn and fry 1½ to 2 minutes on the second side. (The longer frying time is required to compensate for the drop in oil temperature brought about by cooking.) The fish is done when it is golden and yields easily to a fork. Remove the portion to the paper towel–covered plate to drain.

7. Make a pool of sauce on each serving plate. Place the fish on top and serve immediately.

I've reworked this recipe for a number of food magazines, each time featuring a different fish. Though snapper is my favorite choice for this dish, you can use striped bass or black sea bass with excellent results.

STIR-FRIED SHRIMP WITH KUMQUATS, SCALLIONS, AND PLUM WINE

FOR 4

1 tablespoon vegetable oil

1¼ pounds medium shrimp (31 to 35 count)

4 scallions, green parts only, cut into 3-inch lengths

1 quarter-size slice fresh ginger, crushed with a knife handle or mallet

14 kumquats, quartered lengthwise

¼ cup plum wine, or ⅛ cup dry sherry

2 tablespoons fresh orange juice

1 tablespoon soy sauce

Tabasco Sauce, to taste

COOK'S OPTION

Bay scallops (1¼ pounds) also work well with this recipe.

This explosion of tangy-sweet taste reflects my love of the Chinese approach, both balanced and sensual, to seafood cookery. Kumquats, with their brilliant orange color and honeyed tart flesh, make a perfect match for briny shrimp and crisp green scallions. Plum wine, soy sauce, and Tabasco Sauce complete the dish, adding depth and dash.

When shopping for kumquats, look for fruit with the yielding firmness of a tangerine. Store kumquats, available fall to spring, at room temperature for a few days or in the refrigerator for up to two weeks.

Serve this dish with Spicy Stir-Fried Bok Choy with Sesame Oil—the recipe follows.

1. Heat a wok over high heat until very hot. Add the oil and tilt the wok to distribute it evenly. When the oil begins to smoke, add the shrimp and scallions and stir-fry until the shrimp are just cooked through, 1½ to 2 minutes.

2. Add the ginger and kumquats and cook until the full flavor of the fruit is released, about 30 seconds. Add the wine, orange juice, and soy sauce and season with the Tabasco. Stir to incorporate the ingredients, turn out onto a large dish, and serve immediately.

SPICY STIR-FRIED BOK CHOY WITH SESAME OIL

FOR 4

2 tablespoons vegetable oil

⅓ large bok choy, or 5 small

½ teaspoon chili paste

1 tablespoon soy sauce

2 teaspoons Asian sesame oil

1. Halve the bok choy lengthwise and cut into 2-inch ribbons.

2. Heat a wok over high heat until very hot. Add the vegetable oil and tilt the wok to distribute it evenly. When the oil begins to smoke, add the bok choy and stir-fry just until the leaves begin to wilt, about 2 minutes.

3. Add the chili paste and the soy sauce. Stir-fry for 30 seconds, then remove from the heat. Fold in the sesame oil and serve immediately.

STIR-FRIED SQUID WITH SCALLIONS AND SLICED ALMONDS

FOR 4

Seafood and almonds have had a long-standing marriage, particularly in the cooking of the Mediterranean. Squid and almonds, with their contrasting textures, are a particularly pleasing combination—and especially good when paired with crisp scallions.

Stir-frying is the perfect way to cook squid. A fast turn in hot oil followed by a momentary in-wok braise ensures properly cooked flesh. I like to increase the almond quotient by serving the dish with jasmine or regular white rice garnished with toasted sliced almonds.

1. Rinse the squid well and pat dry. Cut off tentacles and leave them whole. Cut the squid bodies in half horizontally.

2. In a medium wok or heavy skillet, heat the oil over high heat until smoking. Add the squid, scallion whites, and almonds and stir-fry just until the scallions begin to wilt, 2 minutes. Add the sesame oil, soy sauce, cornstarch mixture, red pepper flakes, and scallion greens. When the mixture is bound by the cornstarch, remove the squid immediately from the heat. Turn out into a large dish and serve immediately.

2 pounds baby squid, cleaned

1 teaspoon peanut or other vegetable oil

1 small bunch scallions, white parts cut into 1$\frac{1}{2}$-inch lengths, green parts coarsely chopped

$\frac{1}{3}$ cup sliced almonds

1 teaspoon Asian sesame oil

2 teaspoons soy sauce

1 teaspoon cornstarch, dissolved in $\frac{1}{3}$ cup water or stock

$\frac{1}{4}$ teaspoon red pepper flakes

COOK'S OPTION

Baby soft-shell crabs, about 3 inches long, make a fine substitute for the squid.

STIR-FRIED MONKFISH WITH CHILI PASTE AND GINGER

FOR 4

1 tablespoon peanut or other
vegetable oil

1 pound monkfish, cut into
bite-size pieces

1 large red bell pepper, cored,
seeded, and cut into bite-
size pieces

1 teaspoon chili paste

2 cups sugar snap peas, stringed
and tipped

1 tablespoon minced fresh
ginger

1 garlic clove, crushed with the
flat of a knife

2 tablespoons dry sherry

2 tablespoons soy sauce

COOK'S OPTION

*You can substitute extra-
large shrimp (16 to 20
count) or medium sea
scallops for the monkfish.*

Maybe it's the rhythm of stir-frying—all those quick flip-flops, turns, and sweeps—that makes the method so much fun. Stir-frying also excites my chef's imagination—I find myself devising stir-fry dishes in rapid succession, this, then this, now that. *This* chili-fired stir-fry, which combines monkfish with sugar snap peas, red bell pepper, garlic, and ginger, was creation number three one day at the restaurant when all I'd set out to do was make some lunch for the team. It was such a success it went on the menu the next day.

For an interesting change, serve this beautiful, aromatic dish over egg noodles—a delicious alternative to the usual rice.

1. In a medium wok or heavy skillet, heat the oil over high heat until smoking. Add the monkfish and stir-fry until colored, 3 to 4 minutes.

2. Add the pepper and chili paste and stir-fry until the pepper is slightly softened, about 2 minutes. Add the sugar snap peas and stir-fry for 1 minute.

3. Add the ginger and garlic, stir-fry 30 seconds, then add the sherry and soy sauce. Simmer for 1 or 2 minutes, turning the ingredients, then remove to a platter and serve immediately.

12. COOKING IN WRAPPERS

I felt like one of those cartoon characters with a lightbulb over his head when, years ago, I first "got" wrapper cookery. Before that I'd never thought about this method at all, even as I enjoyed such pursed, pillowy, or rolled treats as Chinese dumplings, calzone, crepes, and even stuffed cabbage. But I came to my senses one day when I was experimenting with phyllo dough, which I decided would make a perfect enclosure for escargots. I wrapped the escargots in little purses made from the dough, baked them golden, and served them with a creamy garlic sauce. The buttery little packages were a huge hit. After that, wrapper cookery assumed a big place in my kitchen.

My escargot dish is part of a long tradition. Wrapper cookery is as old as the need to heat food without drying it out. We're apt to think of pots with lids as the sole solution to this problem, but throughout history various wrappers have not only protected food but developed its flavor excitingly. Wrappers themselves have run the gamut from the inedible to the delicious, from the clay enclosures of English kiln workers to the savory cases that enfold the fillings of empanadas or egg rolls. The essential wrapper method—indirect cooking in sealed "packages"—was made for delicate fish and shellfish. Wrapper cookery not only produces juicy, delicious seafood but is great fun to do.

COOKING EN PAPILLOTE

When I first began to devise wrapper recipes my thoughts turned immediately to cooking *en papillote*. This classic technique, wonderfully easy and tidy, involves enclosing individual portions of fish (or other quick-cooking protein) in a tightly sealed parchment or foil package containing vegetables, wine, condiments, and a bit of butter. The packages are baked, moisture is retained, and flavors meld. The diner opening his or her package at table is greeted by an aromatic burst of steam—and fish tasting wonderfully of itself. And there's almost no cleanup.

The New Classic Pompano en Papillote provides the master recipe; you can substitute any whole fish such as snapper, porgy, fluke, halibut, mackerel, even sardines, for the pompano. I've wreathed the pompano with broccoli and button mushrooms, but you could use red or yellow pepper, zucchini, yellow squash, leeks, or onions. Just remember that the firmer the vegetable, the thinner you'll need to slice it—about ⅛ inch thick for harder vegetables like carrots, bell peppers, celery root, parsnip, and the like, ½ inch for softer vegetables like scallions, leeks, zucchini, and yellow squash, which cook more quickly. Avoid using fish larger than 2½ pounds—the package will puff before the fish is cooked through. In the master recipe I've included a number of variations on the theme that I know will spark other versions of your own.

OTHER WRAPPERS

Devising containers that provide their own flavor and texture is the real fun of wrapper cookery. Dishes such as Crispy Fried Blackfish in a Plantain Crust or Steamed Sea Bass in Bok Choy with Carrot Ginger Sauce use just such wrappers. These dishes also provide an interesting illustration of what I call split-level cooking: the method that cooks the outside of the "package" isn't the one that cooks the food inside, and you end up with a tantalizing array of tastes and textures. For example, shrimp enclosed in sautéed leek wrappers actually cook by moist heat. The chewy leek wrappers caramelize deliciously while the shrimp they enclose steam to perfection. Similarly, sautéed fish in caul fat char enticingly on the outside, roast deliciously within their packages.

Wrapper dishes also make beautiful presentations, which means they're great for company. And just about all the wrapper recipes here can be prepared ahead. Fillings can be made in advance and refrigerated, then wrapped and cooked later. The Escargots in a Phyllo Purse can be completely wrapped beforehand and cooked within minutes, as can the Pike Mousse in a Leafy Green. Remember them when you want to give people exciting food but are short on time.

I know you'll come up with your own wrapper ideas as you go along. There's something about this kind of cooking that encourages invention—and really glorifies fresh seafood.

STEAMED SEA BASS IN BOK CHOY WITH CARROT GINGER SAUCE

FOR 4

My grandmother, a really fabulous cook of the old school, would no doubt raise an eyebrow at this latter-day interpretation of stuffed cabbage—until she tasted it. Then she'd call it "dress-up cooking," her phrase for food that was delicate and important.

Here, sea bass fillets seasoned with ginger and lemon zest are wrapped in the blanched outer leaves of bok choy and then steamed. The fish packages are served with a light sauce made with more ginger and carrots, which provides delicate vegetable sweetness and warm color. The sauce deepens the subtle gingery flavor of the fish; the bok choy makes a beautiful, lightly chewy wrapper. In other words, great stuffed cabbage.

1. Make the sauce. In a medium nonreactive saucepan, melt the butter over medium-high heat.

2. Add the carrots, shallot, and ginger, reduce the heat to medium, and cook until the vegetables are soft, without coloring, 6 to 8 minutes.

3. Add the stock and wine and simmer for 15 minutes. Remove from the heat and add the vinegar. Pour into the bowl of a food processor and puree, about 2 minutes. Season with the salt and pepper and strain. Keep warm.

4. To prepare the fish, blanch or steam the bok choy until the leaves are pliable, about 3 minutes. Dry the leaves between sheets of paper toweling.

5. Place the fillets on your work surface and top with carrots, ginger, lemon, and salt and pepper. Take 2 leaves and overlap them side by side. Place a fillet near the bottom of the leaves, perpendicular to the central "seam." Fold the sides in over the fillet, then turn to enfold. The leaf wrapper will seal itself. Repeat with the remaining leaves and fillets.

6. Prepare a steamer. Steam the packages for about 8 minutes. The fish should be slightly resilient to the touch. (To check for doneness, open a package and cut into a fillet—it should be translucent at the center.)

7. Remove the packages to plates, pour the sauce over the fish packages, and serve.

SAUCE

2 teaspoons unsalted butter

5 medium carrots, peeled and minced

1 medium shallot, minced

4 quarter-size slices of fresh ginger, crushed with a knife handle or mallet

1/4 cup Chicken Stock (page 66)

1/4 cup dry white wine

1 teaspoon Champagne vinegar

Salt and freshly ground black pepper

FISH

8 outer leaves of a large bok choy (or savoy cabbage)

4 skinless sea bass fillets (about 6 ounces each), preferably from whole fish personally inspected for freshness

2 medium carrots, peeled and finely julienned

1 1/2 teaspoons minced fresh ginger

2 teaspoons grated lemon zest

Salt and freshly ground black pepper

ESCARGOTS IN A PHYLLO PURSE

FOR 4 AS AN APPETIZER (2 PURSES PER PERSON)

¾ pound snails, fresh or canned

2 cups red wine, preferably
  Burgundy

2 medium shallots, thinly sliced

6 fresh thyme sprigs, coarsely
  chopped, or ¼ teaspoon
  dried

1 garlic clove, crushed with the
  flat of a knife

2 black peppercorns

8 medium mushrooms, cleaned
  and quartered

6 sheets phyllo dough

¼ cup unsalted butter, melted

COOK'S OPTION

Sixteen bay scallops (2 per
purse) can be used in place
of the escargots. Reduce the
cooking liquid by half
before adding the scallops.
Simmer for only 1 minute.

Escargots are always popular restaurant offerings, but I was tired of the same old presentation with garlic butter, and those little shells used for serving them were driving me crazy. I set to work to create a new snail dish and here are the results: escargots cooked in wine and aromatics, enclosed in phyllo "purses," and baked until golden. You'll love this delicious, elegant reinvention of the traditional dish—each forkful is flaky and buttery.

Snails are now being farmed in America, and they're excellent. But don't knock yourself out trying to find a source—canned varieties can be excellent. Here is a case in which price correlates with quality; buy the costliest brand you can afford. The purses can be prepared a day in advance and refrigerated—great if you're entertaining but have little time to cook. Serve the purses as is, or with Creamy Garlic Sauce; the recipe follows.

1. Preheat the oven to 375°F.

2. Rinse the snails well under running water and drain. In a medium nonreactive saucepan, combine the snails with the wine, shallots, thyme, garlic, and peppercorns. Bring to a simmer and cook for 10 minutes.

3. Add the mushrooms and simmer for 3 minutes. Strain and discard the garlic and peppercorns. Allow the mixture to come to room temperature.

4. Have ready a damp kitchen towel for covering the phyllo sheets. Working quickly, place 1 phyllo sheet on your work surface. Cover the remaining sheets with the towel. Brush the exposed sheet liberally with the butter to its edges. Cover with a second sheet, brush with butter, and cover with a third. Using a small, sharp knife, divide the phyllo sheets into 4 equal squares. You now have 4 wrappers.

5. Place approximately one-eighth of the snail and mushroom mixture in the center of 1 wrapper. Gather up the 4 corners and pinch them together to form the purses. Repeat with the remaining 3 sheets of phyllo and filling. Place the purses on a nonstick baking sheet and drizzle the remain-

ing butter on top. (At this point, you can drape the purses with a piece of plastic film and refrigerate for baking the following day.)

6. Bake the purses until a deep golden brown, 10 to 12 minutes. Serve as is or spoon a small pool of the Creamy Garlic Sauce onto each plate, place a purse on top, and serve.

CREAMY GARLIC SAUCE
FOR 4

1. Combine the garlic and milk in a small nonreactive saucepan. Bring to the boil, reduce the heat, and simmer for 15 minutes. (Simmering removes the harshness.)

2. Strain the garlic and discard the milk. Rinse the garlic under running water to remove any milk residue.

3. Clean the saucepan. In it, combine the stock and thyme and reduce until about 2 tablespoons remain, about 15 minutes. Meanwhile, mash the garlic well with a fork.

4. When the stock has reduced, add the pureed garlic and cream. Bring the cream to the boil, then turn down the heat and simmer until the liquid is reduced by one-third, about 5 minutes.

5. Season the sauce with the salt, pepper, and lemon juice just before serving.

5 garlic cloves

1 cup milk

1 cup Chicken Stock (page 66)

4 thyme sprigs, or ¼ teaspoon dried

1¼ cups heavy (whipping) cream

Salt and freshly ground pepper

1 teaspoon fresh lemon juice

COLD LOBSTER SPRING ROLLS WITH CRUSHED PEANUTS

FOR 4

One 1-pound chicken lobster
(culls may be used), boiled
or steamed, meat removed

2 teaspoons Asian sesame oil

2 teaspoons soy sauce

1 teaspoon mirin (sweet sake)

1 tablespoon rice vinegar

1/8 teaspoon red pepper flakes

1/2 medium carrot, shredded

4 scallions, green parts only,
split lengthwise

1/2 head Boston or Bibb lettuce,
shredded

2 tablespoons crushed roasted
peanuts

2 large circular rice paper
sheets, each cut in half

COOK'S OPTION

*One pound of shrimp, any
size, can be substituted for
the lobster. Titi shrimp are
an economical choice.*

Whenever I'm a little down, I know I can make myself feel happier with spring rolls. They're great to eat and fun to make. But I don't always deep-fry them—or even cook them. These spring rolls are made to be eaten uncooked, so their spicy lobster, scallion, and peanut filling tastes fresh and light.

The rolls are wrapped in rice paper (see page 59), a staple of Vietnamese and other Southeast Asian cuisines. For this recipe, you'll need large round thin sheets, which keep indefinitely in a cool, dry place. They're softened to make them pliable, filled, and then rolled. The chicken lobster used for the filling provides ample meat for the rolls plus the dividend of cooked shells for future use. I serve these rolls as an appetizer, but they'd make a wonderful light supper. Pass Ponzu (page 79) for dipping.

1. To prepare the filling, dice the lobster meat and combine with all the remaining ingredients except the rice paper.

2. Soften the rice paper by putting the half-circles between very wet kitchen towels. Press the towels gently. The rice paper should be pliable within 10 to 15 minutes.

3. To make the rolls, carefully lay a softened half-circle on your work surface, curved side away from you. Place one-fourth of the filling about one-third up from the bottom of the sheet. Turn up the bottom to enclose the filling, fold in the sides, and roll somewhat tightly. The paper will adhere to itself. Repeat the procedure with the remaining half-circles and serve.

Note: You can use 1/2 teaspoon saffron or 1 teaspoon turmeric dissolved in 4 cups of water to give the rolls an attractive amber color. Soak old kitchen toweling with this solution before softening the rice paper in it. If you wish, sauté the rolls using 1 tablespoon of vegetable oil in a medium skillet (preferably nonstick) over medium heat. Sauté until golden on all sides, about 4 minutes.

THAI BROILED SCALLOPS WRAPPED IN BACON

FOR 4

Bacon isn't *really* a wrapper, of course. Nonetheless, this simply done dish of sambal-fired scallops, broiled until the bacon just crisps, is so good I've allowed myself some culinary license.

Serve the scallops with a salad of bitter greens or grilled vegetables for a quick, completely satisfying supper.

1. At least 30 minutes in advance, soak 40 wooden toothpicks in water. (This will prevent their burning when they are put under the broiler.) Preheat the broiler.

2. If you are using regular soy sauce, put it in your smallest saucepan and reduce to 2 tablespoons over medium heat; allow to cool. Combine the soy sauce with the sambal and oil in a medium bowl. Add the scallops and toss well.

3. Wrap each scallop with a piece of bacon and secure it with a toothpick. Insert a second toothpick horizontally into the scallops to stabilize them while cooking.

4. Place the scallops on a broiling tray and broil until the bacon becomes crispy, about 2 minutes per side. Remove the toothpicks and serve.

2 tablespoons dark soy sauce, or
   3 tablespoons regular
1 teaspoon sambal oelek (Asian
   red chili paste)
1 teaspoon vegetable oil
20 jumbo sea scallops (about
   1½ pounds)
20 bacon slices

CRISPY FRIED BLACKFISH IN A PLANTAIN CRUST

FOR 4

2 green plantains, as straight as
   possible
4 blackfish fillets (5 to 7 ounces
   each), preferably from a
   whole fish personally
   inspected for freshness
Salt and freshly ground black
   pepper
Pinches of cayenne pepper
Grated zest of 1 lime
2½ quarts vegetable oil, for
   frying
Chinese mustard

COOK'S OPTION

Snapper, tilefish, or halibut
also work well with this
recipe.

One of my weaknesses is plantain chips. They're greasy and salty and wonderful. I was nibbling some a while ago when I suddenly thought of using them as a crispy, moisture-protecting wrapper for blackfish fillets. The result of my experimentation is a dish of melting fish with a crunchy, slightly sweet crust.

Plantains, sometimes called cooking bananas, are a starch staple in much of the Southern Hemisphere. When cooked, they can be eaten, and vary in taste, at every stage of their development. In this recipe plantains are used green, when their flesh is mildly flavored and their texture most starchy—perfect for frying. I'm always interested in using good inexpensive fish and that's why I love delicate, economical blackfish.

Serve this dish with Chinese mustard, a perfect accompaniment.

1. Cut the ends off the plantains. Using a paring knife, peel the skin from the flesh. Put the peeled plantains in water to avoid darkening.

2. Trim the fillets to make them roughly rectangular. Season with the salt and pepper and pinches of cayenne. Sprinkle with the lime zest. Reserve.

3. Dry the plantains, and using a mandoline or thin sharp knife, slice each lengthwise into uniform strips no more than ⅛ inch thick. Cut 4 pieces of plastic film or waxed paper about 8½ by 11 inches and place 1 on your work surface.

4. Overlap 5 or 6 plantain strips on the film. Each strip should cover the preceding one halfway. The completed wrapper should be 1 to 2 inches wider than the length of the fillets. Cut 2 additional plantain strips in half and place 2 overlapping pieces on each side of the wrapper.

5. Place a fillet in the center of the plantain wrapper. Turn the horizontal plantain strips over the fillet to hold it, and using the film for support, fold up the wrapper to enclose the fillet. Once the fillet is completely enclosed, cut off any extra plantain so there is no excessive overlap. The plantain wrapper will adhere to itself, sealing the package. Repeat the procedure with the remaining fillets. Turn the packages so that the seams are on the bottom.

6. Add the oil to a fryer with a basket or use a deep, heavy skillet or wok. (If you are using a wok, make sure it is balanced securely with a wok ring or overturned burner grid.) Turn the heat under the oil to high and heat to 350°F. on a frying thermometer. Have ready a large plate covered with paper toweling and, if not using a frying basket, a large skimmer or strainer.

7. Place 2 packages seam side down in the basket or strainer or on the skimmer, and lower it just under the surface of the oil. Fry for 30 seconds to seal the packages. (If you fully submerged the packages right away, the action of the oil would open them.) Submerge the packages completely and fry until golden, about 3 minutes. Remove and drain on the paper toweling. Allow the oil to return to 350°F. and repeat the frying procedure with the remaining packages. Drain and serve all the packages immediately, accompanied by the mustard.

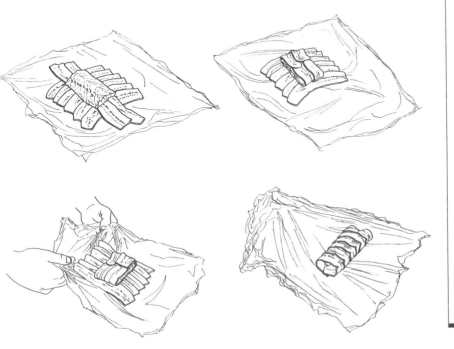

PIKE MOUSSE IN A LEAFY GREEN

FOR 4

3/4 pound pike fillets

3/4 teaspoon salt

1/4 teaspoon freshly ground black
   pepper

1 large egg

2/3 cup heavy (whipping) cream

2 teaspoons unsalted butter, at
   room temperature

Pinch of cayenne pepper

Pinch of grated nutmeg

1/3 cup chopped fresh Italian (flat-
   leaf) parsley

1 head romaine or Boston lettuce,
   collard greens, napa, or
   savoy cabbage

FOR SHALLOW POACHING

1 tablespoon unsalted butter

1 tablespoon minced shallots

1/4 cup dry white wine

3/4 cup Fish Stock (page 67)

1/4 cup heavy (whipping) cream

As a student chef I learned to prepare quenelles, those delicate souf-flélike fish dumplings of classical French cuisine. They're wonderful to eat but something of a chore to form and poach. Here's my wrapper version—easier to make and completely delicious.

A gossamer pike mousse is wrapped in leaves of romaine, shallow-poached, and served with a light buttery sauce made from the cooking liquid. The pale green leaves make a lovely, delicate enclosure for the pillowy mousse.

Although pike is traditional, you can use sole, scallops, snapper, or halibut. And feel free to vary the wrapper—leaves from Boston lettuce, collards, or green cabbage work equally well; each produces a subtly different dish. Serve the mousse bundles as a first course or light entree.

1. Place the fillets in the bowl of a food processor. Add the salt and pepper and process until smooth, about 30 seconds. Add the egg and process until incorporated, 15 seconds more. Allowing the machine to run, slowly add about one-sixth of the cream through the feed tube. Watch carefully. You want the resulting puree to have the consistency of a heavy pudding. It should hold its shape but not be too pasty. Remove the puree to a non-reactive bowl. (The puree may be prepared one day in advance and held refrigerated.)

2. Whip the remaining cream until lightly beaten. Season to taste with the cayenne and nutmeg and more salt and pepper, if necessary. (If you are hesitant about eating uncooked fish, boil 2 cups of water, drop in a tablespoon of the puree, poach for 2 minutes, and taste.) Add the parsley and stir. Cover and refrigerate.

3. Bring a large pot of salted water to the boil. Core the lettuce and separate the leaves. If using collard greens, remove any large ribs, or cut the cabbage in half. Have a bowl of cold water ready.

4. Blanch the lettuce, greens, or cabbage until the leaves just wilt, 30 seconds for the lettuce or greens, 2 minutes for the cabbage. The leaves should be pliable but not mushy. Remove to the cold water.

5. When cold, drain the leaves and pat dry with paper toweling. (If any thick ribs remain, shave them to the surface of the leaf with a sharp knife.)

6. To make the mousse packages, choose 12 good-size leaves. Spread a leaf on your work surface, rounded side toward you. Place 1 tablespoon of the chilled mousse at the center of the leaf. Turn the leaf edges over the mousse and wrap it up in the leaf. The leaf will adhere to itself, sealing the package. Prepare the remaining packages. (The packages may be made in the morning for poaching at night; store them, covered, in the refrigerator.)

7. To shallow-poach the packages, melt the butter in a 10-inch nonreactive skillet, preferably with straight sides. Add the shallots and sweat them without coloring, about 1 minute. Add the white wine and the stock. Bring to the boil, then reduce the heat so the liquid simmers.

8. Add the mousse packages. The liquid should cover one-half to two-thirds of the packages; if not, add more stock. Simmer until the packages are firm, about 5 minutes. Remove the packages and keep warm.

9. Reduce the cooking liquid by half. Add the cream and reduce the sauce over high heat until it coats a spoon lightly, 3 to 5 minutes. Place 3 packages on each plate, spoon the sauce over them, and serve.

VARIATION

Pike Mousse in Salmon Paupiettes Season 12 slices of fresh uncooked salmon about 5 inches long by ⅛ inch thick with salt and freshly ground white pepper. Make paupiettes by putting 2 tablespoons of the mousse in the center of each slice of salmon, turning the edges of the salmon inward and rolling the salmon to enclose the pike mousse. Squeeze the rolls gently to distribute the mousse toward the sides of the packages, but leave a little hump in the center. Shallow-poach the paupiettes slowly, using the ingredients and method above. Cook until the packages are firm but still resilient, about 4 minutes. Remove the paupiettes and keep warm. Prepare the sauce as above and serve.

SAUTÉED TILEFISH IN CAUL FAT WITH ORZO AND SCALLIONS

FOR 4

About 1 pound caul fat, rinsed
and squeezed dry

8 bay leaves

8 fresh thyme sprigs, or
2 teaspoons dried

4 tilefish fillets (6 to 7 ounces
each), preferably from a
whole fish personally
inspected for freshness

Salt and freshly ground black
pepper

2 tablespoons olive oil

2 teaspoons unsalted butter

2 bunches scallions, cut into
1-inch lengths

1 cup heavy (whipping) cream or
half-and-half

2 tablespoons vegetable oil, for
sautéing

1¼ cups orzo

COOK'S OPTION

Grouper can be used in
place of the tilefish.

Tilefish fillets are delicous sautéed until golden and sauced with a reduction of leeks, scallions, and cream. Add orzo, toasted to make it nutty tasting, and you've got a great meal.

Caul fat? Even before I joined the ranks of serious cooks, I was an aficionado of this webbed membrane that lines the visceral cavity of the pig. It makes a perfect natural wrapper; when heated, it melts into the food it encloses, adding a rich, meaty taste. It's particularly delicious with mild, sweet seafood like tilefish.

Caul fat is available at butcher shops that make their own sausages, specialize in pork products, or have a European clientele. It freezes beautifully for up to two months—get several pieces while you're at it. Then make this delicately rustic seafood dish.

1. Preheat the oven to 400°F.

2. Spread the caul fat on your work surface. With a sharp knife or scissors, cut rectangular pieces roughly twice the width of the fillets and 2 inches longer at each side. If there are holes in the membrane or if you tear it, patch it with excess fat.

3. Along the middle of each rectangle distribute evenly 2 bay leaves and 2 sprigs of thyme (or ½ teaspoon dried). Leave the 2-inch border uncovered—it will be folded over the fillets.

4. Place a fillet "skin side" (red side) up over the center of each rectangle. Salt and pepper the fillets generously. Fold the sides of the caul fat over the fillets and wrap them in the fat. Turn so that the skin side is down. The fat will adhere to itself, sealing the packages. Reserve.

5. In a medium saucepan, heat the oil and butter over medium heat. Add the scallions and season with salt. Cover and sweat the scallions until they are soft, about 2 minutes. Add the cream, bring to the boil, then

reduce the heat and simmer until the cream has reduced by one-half. Correct the seasoning. (You can make this reduction up to 2 days in advance and refrigerate it. When ready to use, warm it in a saucepan over low heat.)

6. Heat a large, heavy ovenproof skillet over high heat. When the skillet is very hot, add the vegetable oil. Allow the oil to become hot and add the fish packages seam side up. (Depending on the size of your skillet, this may have to be done in batches.) Sauté until golden, about 3 minutes. Turn the packages gently with a spatula and sauté the seam side until golden. Remove the skillet to the oven and cook until the packages feel lightly springy to the touch, about 3 minutes. (If you have sautéed the packages in batches, transfer all the packages to a heavy baking sheet and put it in the oven.)

7. Meanwhile, in a medium dry skillet over medium-high heat, toast the orzo, stirring constantly, until it is a light nutty brown, about 5 minutes. Cook the orzo in plenty of boiling salted water until al dente, about 10 minutes. Drain the orzo, return it to the pot, and add the sauce. Cook over low heat until the sauce has been almost entirely absorbed by the orzo, about 3 minutes.

8. Divide the orzo among 4 plates. Slide a fillet package over each portion and serve.

SALMON STEAMED IN KONBU

FOR 4

1 package pliable sheets of
konbu, 6 by 7 inches
Four 6- to 7-ounce portions of
skinless salmon fillet
1/2 cup soy sauce
Salt and freshly ground black
pepper
12 fresh dill sprigs
Additional soy sauce, lemon
juice, or hot Asian sesame
oil, for serving

COOK'S OPTION

*Snapper also works well
with this recipe. Steam it
for 7 to 8 minutes only.*

My interest in cooking with konbu—or kelp—goes back to my first visit to Hawaii. Using konbu and other sea leaves for cooking is as commonplace on the islands as it is in Japan, where konbu is one of the basic ingredients in the stock called dashi. Here it is used to wrap fresh salmon portions that are then steamed and splashed with soy or lemon juice, or drizzled with hot sesame oil. You can't imagine how good this dish is; it's all pure sweet ocean freshness.

You'll need moist konbu, available packaged in pliable sheets from Asian markets. They come in various dimensions; you want the smaller sheets (as opposed to those used for making dashi), roughly 6 by 7 inches in size. (You may be able to get fresh konbu from your fish seller.) Served with rice, the salmon packages make a perfect light meal.

1. Refresh 4 sheets of konbu by swishing in tepid water.
2. Place the salmon portions in a baking dish just large enough to hold them and add the soy sauce. Marinate for 10 minutes at room temperature.
3. Prepare a steamer.
4. Spread the sheets of konbu on your work surface. Remove a salmon portion from the marinade, shake off the excess soy sauce, and place it in the center of a konbu sheet. Repeat with the remaining portions. Season the salmon lightly with the salt and more abundantly with the pepper and arrange 3 dill sprigs on top of each. Turn the outside edges of the konbu inward over the portions and wrap, enclosing them in a single konbu layer. Trim excess konbu to prevent overlapping. The konbu will adhere to itself, sealing the packages.
5. Steam the packages, in batches if necessary, until they are softly resilient to the touch, about 12 minutes. Remove the packages to plates and serve with any of the suggested accompaniments.

SNAPPER WITH CELERY LEAVES IN FOIL POUCHES

FOR 4

I can't imagine an easier or more satisfying *en papillote* recipe than this dish of sweet snapper fillet prepared with celery leaves, olive oil, and a bit of lemon. It's also versatile—you can steam, grill, or bake the foil-wrapped fillets; you can even cook them over charcoal or wood embers.

Perfect for dieters and nondieters alike, this is yet another example of the advantages of sealed-package cooking.

1. Preheat the oven to 400°F., fire a grill until the embers are ash-covered, or prepare a steamer. Cut 4 sheets of foil about 7 inches square.

2. Place a fillet in the center of each sheet of foil. Mold the foil up around the fillets so that added liquid will be contained.

3. Season the fillets evenly with the salt, pepper, celery salt, and lemon juice. Add 1 teaspoon of oil and 2 teaspoons of water to each packet. Distribute the celery leaves evenly over the fillets.

4. Close and seal the packages tightly by folding top edges over themselves and turning the sides inward. Cook by steaming, baking, or grilling for about 15 minutes or in live embers for 5 minutes. The fish is done when it is fairly resilient to the touch. It should be medium-rare—pink—inside.

5. Transfer the packages to plates and serve. Allow the diners to open the packages themselves.

4 snapper fillets (about 6 ounces each)
1 teaspoon kosher or sea salt
1/2 teaspoon freshly ground white pepper
1 1/2 teaspoons celery salt
Juice of 1 lemon
4 teaspoons olive oil
8 teaspoons water
1 cup loosely packed celery leaves, preferably the tender yellow leaves at the center of the head

COOK'S OPTION

Striped bass, sea bass, or blackfish are also good with this recipe.

NEW CLASSIC POMPANO EN PAPILLOTE

FOR 2

1 whole pompano (about 1¼
   pounds), gutted only, or 2
   pompano fillets (6 to 8
   ounces each), preferably
   from a whole fish personally
   inspected for freshness

1 cup bite-size broccoli florets

Squeeze of fresh lemon juice

4 fresh thyme or oregano sprigs,
   or ¼ teaspoon dried, or 2
   teaspoons chopped chives

12 button mushrooms, or 1½
   cups mushrooms sliced
   ¼ inch thick

1 tablespoon unsalted butter or
   olive oil (optional)

⅓ to ½ cup dry white wine,
   Fish Stock (page 67), or
   water

Salt and freshly ground black
   pepper

When I think of *en papillote* cooking—oven-steaming in a sealed, moisture-protecting parchment or foil pouch—I smile to myself. I feel like the keeper of a special secret: am I the only one who knows how great this low-fat method is for preparing seafood? It produces juicy whole fish or fillets that taste absolutely of themselves; it's easy, fast, and makes an appetite-whetting presentation as the package is opened at table. It's perfect for the way we cook and eat today.

And it's versatile. The possibilities are endless. Pompano—a gorgeous silver, yellow, and blue ocean fish with sweet firm flesh—makes a lovely *en papillote* dish but you can use many other fish (suggestions appear at the beginning of this chapter). I call for butter or oil here, but their use is optional—great news for dieters. If you do use butter, emulsification will take place and you'll end up with a lovely, light sauce; olive oil won't emulsify *en papillote* and works as a tasty seasoning.

I've included some special ideas at the end of the recipe for delicious variations, but you should be able to come up with your own in no time. *En papillote* cooking inspires creativity.

1. Preheat the oven to 400° F.

2. Cut a piece of foil 2 inches longer than and twice as wide as the fish or fillets. Fold the foil in half and seal 1 long and 1 short side by crimping the edges well. You will have a pouch, open at one short side.

3. Slide the fish or fillets into the pouch. Add the broccoli, lemon juice, herbs or chives, mushrooms, and butter or olive oil, if using. If using button mushrooms, pour in ⅓ cup wine, stock, or water (½ cup if using sliced mushrooms). Sprinkle with salt and pepper, then seal the remaining side of the pouch tightly.

4. Place the pouch on a baking sheet. Put the baking sheet on top of the stove over medium-high heat for 3 minutes to start cooking, then transfer to the oven and bake until the foil has puffed, 15 to 20 minutes.

5. Remove the pouch from the oven. Put it on a serving plate and bring to table. Slit it open with a small, sharp knife, transfer the contents to individual plates, and spoon the sauce or liquid over all.

VARIATIONS

Add 2 bay leaves to the pouch and/or 1 tablespoon pitted Gaeta, Niçoise, or Kalamata olives. You can add lemon, lime, or grapefruit slices, if you wish. For an unexpectedly lovely flavor, add ¼ vanilla bean.

Any herbs—sage, marjoram, or dill, for example—can replace the thyme. Try using walnut, hazelnut, or toasted peanut oil (available at Asian markets) instead of the olive oil or butter. For heat, add 1 jalapeño, seeded and minced.

SCALLOPS IN BANANA LEAVES WITH VANILLA

FOR 4

4 banana leaves (page 58), cut
into 8 rectangles approximately 4 by 6 inches

1 tablespoon unsalted butter,
softened

1 pound sea scallops

Salt

2 vanilla beans, quartered

1 lime, peeled, seeded, and
cut into small dice

8 allspice berries, cracked

2 scallions, green parts only,
minced

1/2 teaspoon red pepper flakes

COOK'S OPTION

Sixteen jumbo shrimp,
peeled except for the tail
and butterflied, also work
well with this recipe. Steam
for only 8 minutes.

One day I found myself thinking about creating a dish with vanilla beans and scallops—vanilla lends a deliciously subtle taste to all shellfish—when I discovered a stash of banana leaves in a corner of the restaurant kitchen. Banana leaves mean tamales to me and tamales mean an aromatic steaming. The day before I had been shopping at a Japanese department store, where I marveled at the many beautifully wrapped items, all tied with natural materials like raffia or jute. It wasn't long before I devised these tamales—packages of scallops, scallions, and vanilla beans brightened with lime, heated with red pepper, and secured with a natural banana leaf "string." Quickly steamed, these tamales are as good as they look. They also make a great dish for company.

1. Prepare a steamer.

2. Place the banana-leaf rectangles on your work surface. Spread the butter evenly over them.

3. Place equal portions of the scallops in the center of each rectangle. Season with salt. Distribute the remaining ingredients over the scallops.

4. Fold the sides of the rectangles over the fillings and roll once to form packages. Secure the packages with ribbons cut from the banana leaf remains, or with kitchen string.

5. Steam the packages approximately 10 minutes. Divide among plates and allow diners to open them in order to enjoy their aromatic steam.

Note: Foil can be used in place of banana leaves. The cooking time is the same as for packages prepared with the leaves.

SEAFOOD TAMALE IN BANANA LEAVES

FOR 4 (2 TAMALES EACH)

I encountered my first banana-leaf-wrapped tamale in Florida, when I was researching the menu for Tropica. If you've never had a tamale wrapped in banana leaves, you're missing a culinary pleasure long enjoyed in Mexico, the Caribbean, and Latin America.

Though people can become pretty doctrinaire about the proper filling for tamales, almost anything that is good to eat can be used. For this great tamale, I've chosen a garlicky filling of shrimp and bay scallops enclosed in a light "dough" made from plantains—a departure from the usual (and somewhat heavy) corn-flour casing. The dough-wrapped filling is then enclosed in the leaves and steamed. The result is wonderfully good.

1. Prepare a steamer. Steam the plantains over boiling water for 10 minutes to loosen the peel and remove it with a sharp knife. Return the plantains to the steamer and cook until almost soft, about 35 minutes.

2. While still warm, cut the plantains into rough pieces and place in the bowl of a food processor. Process until pureed, 3 to 4 minutes. With the machine running, slowly add the oil through the feed tube until the mixture forms a smooth, heavy dough, 3 to 4 minutes. Season with the salt and cumin.

3. In a bowl, combine the shrimp, scallops, sambal oelek, cilantro, garlic, and cumin. Season with the salt and mix well.

4. To make the tamales, place the banana-leaf rectangles on your work surface, ends to the side. With moist hands, spread the plantain dough over the rectangles, leaving an uncovered border. The dough should be spread about ¼ inch thick.

5. Spread one-fourth of the seafood mixture evenly over the plantain dough and roll the tamales, tucking the sides under each roll. The rectangles will adhere to themselves to seal the packages. Steam the tamales for 7 minutes. Split them open with a sharp knife and serve.

DOUGH

2 green plantains
⅓ cup olive oil
Salt
1 teaspoon ground cumin

FILLING

¾ pound small shrimp, peeled, deveined, and cut into bite-size pieces
½ pound bay scallops, halved
1 teaspoon sambal oelek (Asian red chili paste), or ½ teaspoon Chinese chili paste
1 tablespoon coarsely chopped fresh cilantro (coriander)
1½ teaspoons minced garlic
½ teaspoon ground cumin
Salt

1 large banana leaf, fresh or frozen, cut into 8 rectangles roughly 4½ by 6 inches (see Note, opposite)

SHRIMP SAUTÉED IN LEEK WRAPPERS

FOR 4, AS AN APPETIZER

4 large leeks

8 jumbo shrimp, peeled and
deveined

Salt and freshly ground black
pepper

1 teaspoon unsalted butter

Leeks, once called the asparagus of the poor, have a restrained yet earthy goodness. They're sweet and oniony, and are therefore a perfect match for most seafood. Here, leek-wrapped shrimp are sautéed. The sautéing caramelizes the leeks deliciously while the shrimp within steam to perfect doneness.

Enjoy this dish with a potato puree made with Chive Butter (page 63).

1. In a large pot, bring plenty of salted water to the boil. Have ready a bowl of cold water and 8 wood or metal skewers. (If you are using wood skewers, soak them in water for 30 minutes to avoid burning them.)

2. Slice the root ends from the leeks. Trim each leek so the white parts are the same length as the shrimp. Slit these leek sections lengthwise just to the center; each layer will open into a flat sheet.

3. Add the leeks to the boiling water. After 2 minutes, check them with a pair of tongs. If they feel soft, remove them to the bowl of water; if not, cook 1 or 2 minutes longer and remove them to the water. Allow the cooking water to return to the boil.

4. Peel the softened layers from the leeks and reserve in the water. (Inner layers may require another minute or so.) Cool in the water.

5. Thread each shrimp on a skewer, from head end through tail. (This prevents curling while cooking.) Season the shrimp with the salt and pepper.

6. Cut 4 pieces of foil long enough to enclose the skewered shrimp and 4 inches wide. Remove the leek layers from the water and pat dry with paper toweling. To form the leek wrappers, place the foil rectangles on your work surface. On each, shingle 3 leek layers long edge to long edge, overlapping each layer halfway over the previous one to create a large rectangular sheet. It should enclose 2 skewered shrimp completely; overlap more leek layers, if necessary.

7. Place 2 skewered shrimp head to tail at the bottom of each leek sheet.

Trim the sides of each sheet, if necessary, so that only the skewer ends will protrude when the shrimp are wrapped.

8. Using the foil for support, roll each leek sheet around the shrimp to make a rectangular package, peeling off the foil as you go. The leeks will adhere to themselves, sealing the packages.

9. In a heavy 10-inch skillet, melt the butter over medium-low heat. Add the leek packages, seam side up. Using the tongs to check for doneness, sauté until the undersides are golden, 2 to 3 minutes. Turn and sauté the second side until golden. Remove the packages from the pan, and holding down one side of each package, remove the skewers from the shrimp.

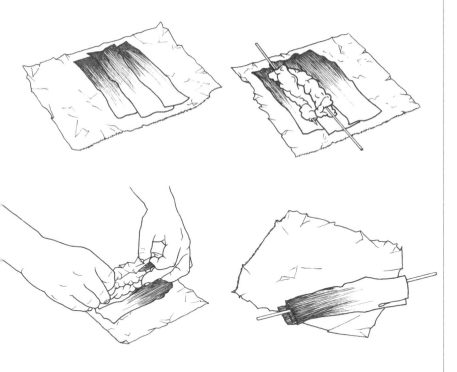

STRIPED BASS WITH POTATO SCALES IN A RED WINE SAUCE

FOR 4

SAUCE

½ cup (1 stick) unsalted butter plus 1 tablespoon, at room temperature

1 bottle rich, dry red wine, such as Pinot Noir, Cabernet Sauvignon, or Barolo

1 medium shallot, minced

¾ cup Fish Stock (page 67)

6 fresh thyme sprigs, or ½ teaspoon dried

1 bay leaf

FISH AND POTATOES

2 large Russet potatoes, peeled

4 sea bass fillets (6 to 7 ounces each), preferably from a whole fish personally inspected for freshness

Salt and freshly ground black pepper

2 tablespoons vegetable oil, for frying

COOK'S OPTION

Snapper or sea bass can be substituted for the striped bass.

I was preparing some vegetable chips one day when I realized I could use thinly sliced potatoes to make a crispy, scalelike coat for striped bass fillets. I prepared a buttery, deep-flavored wine sauce to accompany the crispy fish and voilà—this good dish.

This is not after work cooking, but a rewarding exercise of your culinary powers when you have time to make something truly special. You should have no difficulty sautéing the potato-covered fillets if you cut the potatoes thin enough—they'll cling to the fillets like a second skin.

1. Make the sauce. Cut the stick of butter into 8 equal pieces. In a medium saucepan, reduce half of the wine over medium heat until syrupy, about 15 minutes; reserve.

2. Meanwhile, in a second medium saucepan, melt the tablespoon of butter over medium heat. Add the shallot, cover, and cook without coloring, about 3 minutes. Add the stock, thyme, bay leaf, and remaining wine. Reduce until syrupy, about 15 minutes. Away from the heat, whisk in the stick of butter, piece by piece. The butter should not melt into the sauce but create a creamy emulsion.

3. Strain the sauce and stir in the wine reduction. (Reducing the wine in 2 steps produces a glossier sauce.) Keep the sauce warm, avoiding direct heat. (The sauce may be made 2 to 3 hours in advance.)

4. Preheat the oven to 475°F. With a paring knife, trim the sides of the potatoes to make them roughly cylindrical. As you work, put the potatoes into a bowl of cold water to avoid discoloration. Have ready a large spatula and a baking sheet large enough to hold all the fillets.

5. Using a mandoline or thin knife, cut the potatoes into slices roughly ⅛ inch thick.

6. Season the fillets with the salt and pepper. Place 2 of the fillets on your work surface and shingle rows of potato slices over each, overlapping slices by one-third.

7. In a 12-inch nonstick ovenproof skillet, heat 1 tablespoon of the oil over medium heat. When hot, bring the pan to the potato-covered fillets. Tilt the pan, resting its edge on a heatproof surface, such as a trivet. Slide the spatula under 1 fillet and quickly invert it into the pan. There should be no difficulty if you keep the pan close to the fillet and flip it rapidly. Repeat with the second fillet and sauté both until the potatoes are golden, about 4 minutes. Remove each to the baking sheet as soon as the potatoes are golden. Shingle the remaining fillets, add 1 tablespoon more oil to the pan, and repeat the sautéing process. Remove the second batch of sautéed fillets to the baking sheet.

8. Bake the fillets until the flesh turns very white but is still soft to the touch, about 6 minutes. Transfer the fillets to plates and serve with the sauce poured around them.

13. DUMPLINGS, FISH CAKES, AND CROQUETTES

I feel particularly close to the dishes in this chapter. They're all deeply satisfying, seafood soul food. Many of them evoke the home cooking of my boyhood—potluck dishes no less delicious for being improvisations.

Dumplings are food with a long past. Dropped, filled, or fritterlike, they've been belly- and soul-satisfying staples from earliest times. They're marvelous in their original, starchy versions or gussied-up, like pike quenelles. Fancy or down-to-earth, they never fail to please.

I'm also passionate about fish cakes, dumplings' culinary cousins. They're as adaptable as dumplings—which doesn't mean they can be concocted carelessly. I've encountered too many leaden fish cakes consisting of who-knows-what, and I'm sure you have, too. You'll never wonder what's in "All Crabmeat" Crab Cakes—they're loaded with sweet crabmeat so that's what you taste. And the Sunday Supper Fish Cakes with Horseradish Cream are baked to ensure their delicacy. Both these dishes, as well as Big Danny's Thai Fish Cakes, reflect the ongoing refinement of dumplings and fish cakes through the years.

The croquette, which I define as a hand-formed dumpling made with mashed potatoes, also lacks a fancy pedigree but is wonderfully good when prepared with care. Dad's Salmon Croquettes with Day-Old Spaghetti has found its way into the permanent repertoires of many friends to whom I've given the recipe. Everyone cherishes its kitchen-table savoriness.

Dumplings, fish cakes, and croquettes are food to *use.* They can be served as hors d'oeuvres, appetizers, or main or side dishes. And talk about preparation potential! All the dishes here can be made wholly or partly in advance. Many welcome leftovers or otherwise unemployable fish scraps—Fresh Salmon Cakes are a good example. And most can be on the table—start to finish—in 30 minutes. They're versatile, too. The Shrimp Spaetzle work as a starter, main course, or as an accompaniment. The Seafood Wontons are great in broth, miso, or chicken soup. Or fry them to serve as a tempting appetizer with Ponzu (page 79) for dipping.

The simple universality of this food has meant that many of us have put it aside in favor of "finer" dishes. But what could be finer than this plain food? My seafood versions are light and up-to-date, but they also seem like old friends. They're full of feeling—of meals shared over time and appetites really satisfied.

BIG DANNY'S THAI FISH CAKES

FOR 4

Big Danny, so-called to distinguish him from another, shorter Danny, who also cooked with me, invented this great dish. With the addition of Thai red curry paste and kaffir leaf, Big Danny brought shrimp and snapper fish cakes to vivid life This dish is easily done. I like to serve it for lunch with whole peeled sweet potatoes cooked in coconut milk.

1. In the bowl of a food processor, combine the fish and shrimp and pulse until well ground but not pureed, about 1 minute.

2. Add the egg and curry paste and process 30 seconds more. Transfer to a nonreactive bowl and fold in the green beans and kaffir leaf (or grated lime peel). Season with the salt and pepper.

3. Make 4 fish cakes about the size of a thin hamburger. In a shallow skillet, heat the oil over high heat until hot. Sauté the fish cakes until golden on both sides, about 1½ minutes per side. Drain on paper toweling and serve.

¾ pound skinless snapper fillet

½ pound shrimp, any size, peeled and deveined

1 large egg

2 tablespoons Thai red curry paste

½ cup julienned green beans

1 kaffir leaf, finely chopped, or ½ teaspoon grated lime peel

Salt and freshly ground black pepper

2 tablespoons vegetable oil, for sautéing

COOK'S OPTION

You can substitute ¾ pound scallops for the shrimp.

DAD'S SALMON CROQUETTES WITH DAY-OLD SPAGHETTI

MAKES 8 CROQUETTES

About 3 cups leftover or fresh
tomato-sauced spaghetti

1 pound cooked or canned
salmon

1½ cups mashed potatoes

1 tablespoon chopped fresh
Italian (flat-leaf) parsley

1 teaspoon chopped fresh chives

1 teaspoon chopped fresh dill

¼ teaspoon cayenne pepper

¼ cup heavy (whipping) cream

Salt

2 cups bread crumbs, preferably
homemade

2 cups all-purpose flour

4 large eggs, beaten

1 tablespoon unsalted butter

1 cup grated cheddar or
American cheese

COOK'S OPTION

*You can also use 1 pound of
cooked cod in place of the
salmon.*

This was Dad's specialty—a family dish of salmon croquettes served with spaghetti that we all loved. I still remember the green Pyrex bowl that came to the table, overflowing with bubbly baked spaghetti. It had absorbed a rich tomato sauce overnight and was now crusty with golden cheddar. The salmon croquettes, made with fresh or leftover mashed potatoes, were crisp on the outside and delicately yielding within.

I've doctored Dad's recipe a little, but this remains simple, no-fuss cooking. Canned salmon works beautifully, and if you haven't got the spaghetti, feel free to substitute another starch, like rice.

1. Preheat the oven to 375°F. Pack the spaghetti into an ovenproof casserole and refrigerate for at least an hour. (This can be done 24 hours in advance.)

2. In a nonreactive bowl, combine the salmon, potatoes, herbs, cayenne, cream, and salt. On separate large plates, evenly distribute the bread crumbs and flour. Have the beaten eggs ready in a medium bowl.

3. Form 4 croquette patties by hand, about the size of a hamburger. Dredge each patty lightly in the flour, shaking off the excess. Dip each quickly into the beaten egg, allowing the excess to drip away, then dredge in the bread crumbs until evenly coated.

4. In a medium skillet, preferably nonstick, melt the butter over medium heat. When the butter sizzles, add the croquettes and sauté on both sides until golden, about 2 minutes per side. Remove the croquettes to a baking sheet. (The croquettes may be prepared up to 1 hour in advance.)

5. Distribute the pieces of cheddar evenly on top of the spaghetti and cover the casserole with foil. Bake until hot, about 20 minutes. Turn the temperature up to 425°F., remove the foil, and slide the croquettes into the oven on a lower rack. Cook until the cheese has melted and a slight crust forms around the edges of the casserole and the croquettes are hot, 8 to 10 minutes. Remove and serve the croquettes and spaghetti side by side.

GOLDEN TUNA CORNMEAL DUMPLINGS

FOR 4

I first prepared these spicy, golden dumplings at Marie-Michelle, a New York restaurant where I was chef in the early nineties. Officially, they should be called dropped dumplings; but instead of using boiling water or soup as their cooking medium, these dumplings are deep-fried, like fritters, until brown and crispy. Best Tartar Sauce on page 79 is just the right accompaniment.

1. In a medium bowl, soak the bread in the milk until it is fully softened, about 10 minutes. Squeeze gently to remove excess milk. Place the tuna in the bowl of a food processor and pulse until coarsely chopped, about 45 seconds.

2. Combine the tuna with the bread and cream and season with the cumin, cayenne, and salt. Mix until all the ingredients are well blended, about 2 minutes.

3. Slowly add the oil to a fryer with a basket or use a deep, heavy skillet or wok. (If you are using a wok, make sure it is balanced securely with a wok ring or overturned burner grid.) Turn the heat under the oil to high and heat it to 360°F. on a frying thermometer. Have ready a large plate covered with paper toweling and a mesh skimmer. On a second large plate, distribute the cornmeal for dredging.

4. Wet a teaspoon and use it to form small oval dumplings from the tuna mixture. Roll the dumplings in the cornmeal and shake off all excess.

5. When the oil is ready for frying, add the dumplings. Do not crowd. Fry the dumplings in batches, if necessary, making sure the oil returns to 360°F. between batches. Fry the dumplings until golden, 3 to 4 minutes. During cooking, use the skimmer to push the dumplings under the surface of the oil so that they brown evenly.

6. Remove the dumplings to the paper towel–covered plate to drain. Serve immediately with tartar sauce.

3 slices best-quality white
   bread, crusts removed
1 cup milk
1 pound raw tuna
2 tablespoons heavy (whipping)
   cream
1 teaspoon ground cumin
$\frac{1}{4}$ teaspoon cayenne pepper
Salt
4 cups vegetable oil, for frying
2 cups yellow cornmeal
Best Tartar Sauce (page 79)

COOK'S OPTION

You can substitute salmon for the tuna.

"ALL CRABMEAT" CRAB CAKES

MAKES 8 CAKES

1½ cups cornflake crumbs

1 pound jumbo lump crabmeat

1½ teaspoons Homemade
   Mayonnaise (page 71), or
   best-quality store-bought

1½ teaspoons Old Bay
   seasoning

⅓ teaspoon cayenne pepper

1 large egg yolk

1 tablespoon red bell pepper,
   cored, seeded, and finely
   diced (optional)

1 tablespoon yellow bell pepper,
   cored, seeded, and finely
   diced (optional)

1½ teaspoons chopped fresh
   chives

¼ teaspoon minced jalapeño
   pepper

2 teaspoons unsalted butter

True Orange Sabayon (page 76),
   Best Tartar Sauce (page 79),
   or Spicy Honey Mustard
   (page 78)

Crab cakes are one of those deeply American dishes that can be really satisfying—or so blandly pasty you wonder why they were invented at all. This recipe makes the best crab cakes you'll ever eat. In place of the usual moistened bread or bread crumb binder I use a single egg yolk, so the crabmeat taste really comes through. Cayenne, chives, and jalapeño add just enough zip and there's no frying at all—the cakes are coated in cornflake crumbs (a perfect complement to the crab) and *baked*. Although other ingredients are present, the impression these cakes make is of crab alone. And that is what a good crab cake is all about.

1. Preheat the oven to 375°F. Distribute the cornflake crumbs on a platter.
2. Combine all the remaining ingredients except the butter and accompaniment in a nonreactive bowl and toss gently until well blended. Make 8 crab cakes no more than 3 inches thick, pressing the ingredients together well.
3. Place the cakes on the crumbs and coat lightly on all sides. Put the cakes on a baking sheet and dot each with a bit of the butter.
4. Bake the cakes until just hot, about 6 minutes, and serve with one of the accompaniments.

FRESH SALMON CAKES

FOR 4

These salmon cakes have been called salmon burgers by their fans so often that even *I* forget their true name. They began in an attempt to make an unbreaded, featherlight fish cake—which is what they turned out to be. Label them as you please, these salmon burgers combine the ease and straightforwardness of a traditional burger with the delicacy and refinement of a fish cake.

Make them from fresh salmon bought specifically for the purpose or from fish scraps you've wisely saved—they're great either way.

1. Put the fish in the bowl of a food processor and puree until smooth, about 1½ minutes.
2. Remove the puree to a bowl and mix in the cream, scallions, and Tabasco. Season with the salt and pepper. Mix in the egg white vigorously.
3. Form 4 patties and refrigerate to firm them, 15 to 20 minutes.
4. Put the oil in a medium skillet. Sauté the patties over medium-high heat until just cooked through, about 3 minutes per side.

1 pound raw salmon or other oily fish

⅔ cup heavy (whipping) cream

½ bunch scallions, green parts only, chopped

2 teaspoons Tabasco Sauce

Salt and freshly ground black pepper

1 large egg white, beaten to a light froth

1 tablespoon vegetable oil

COOK'S OPTION

Tuna also works well with this recipe.

SUNDAY SUPPER FISH CAKES WITH HORSERADISH CREAM

FOR 4

HORSERADISH CREAM

1 1/2 cups sour cream

2 tablespoons prepared white
horseradish

1 teaspoon Tabasco Sauce

Juice of 1/2 lemon

2 tablespoons coarsely chopped
fresh dill

Salt

FISH CAKES

1 1/4 pounds cooked fish, any
kind

3 tablespoons Homemade
Mayonnaise (page 71), or
best-quality store-bought

1/8 teaspoon cayenne pepper

2 celery stalks, minced

2 tablespoons chopped fresh Italian
(flat-leaf) parsley

1 large egg yolk

1/2 teaspoon Old Bay seasoning

Salt and freshly ground black
pepper

2 cups fresh bread crumbs,
preferably homemade

1 tablespoon unsalted butter

Every time I serve these homey fish cakes to friends or family I delight in watching their reaction. Although the trend to "back-to-basics" cuisine has reminded them of how good simple food can be, my guests often remain fish-cake phobic—until they give these a taste. These fine, light fish cakes, deftly seasoned, are baked, which ensures their delicacy. Served with a zesty dill- and horseradish-flavored cream, they make the perfect informal supper, brunch, or buffet centerpiece.

1. Preheat the oven to 375°F.

2. In a medium bowl, combine the ingredients for the sauce and refrigerate while preparing the fish cakes.

3. Make the fish cakes. In a medium bowl, combine all the ingredients except the bread crumbs and butter and mix well. Spread the bread crumbs evenly on a large plate.

4. Form the fish cake mixture into 4 patties, pressing the ingredients together firmly. Press the patties into the bread crumbs on all sides to coat evenly. Shake off any excess.

5. Place the patties on a baking sheet and dot them with the butter. Bake until just hot, 8 to 10 minutes. Remove and serve with the Horseradish Cream.

Note: If you wish, sauté the patties in 1 tablespoon of butter until golden, 3 to 4 minutes per side.

SHRIMP SPAETZLE

FOR 6 AS AN ACCOMPANIMENT

When I prepare these delicious spaetzle, made with pureed shrimp and cream bound with an egg, I'm reminded of quenelles, the air-light seafood dumplings of classical French cooking. The basic method for the two is the same—a mousselike paste is briefly poached and served hot in a light sauce. Formed in the same way as traditional spaetzle, my shrimp version are really delicate mini-dumplings that make an elegant accompaniment or first course. Serve with browned butter.

1. Place the shrimp in the bowl of a food processor. Pulse until chopped and then run the machine until the shrimp are pureed, about 1½ minutes.

2. Remove the puree to a nonreactive bowl. Add the remaining ingredients. Stir for 2 minutes to blend very well. Refrigerate until well chilled, about 2 hours.

3. In a large soup pot, bring 2 quarts of salted water to a boil. Reduce the heat until the water just simmers.

4. Place a spaetzle mill or large-hole colander over the pot. Add the mousse and turn the handle of the mill, or push the mousse through the colander using a large spatula or wooden spoon.

5. Simmer for 1 minute. Do not boil.

6. Remove with a large skimmer or strainer and drain in a colander.

7. In a small saucepan, melt the butter over medium heat. Reduce the heat somewhat and continue to cook until the butter is nut-colored.

8. Toss the spaetzle with the browned butter and serve in small bowls.

1 pound shrimp, any size
1 large egg
¾ cup heavy (whipping) cream
½ teaspoon salt
⅛ teaspoon cayenne pepper
½ cup (1 stick) unsalted butter

COOK'S OPTION

You can substitute 1 pound sea scallops for the shrimp.

GRANDMA MINNIE'S GEFILTE FISH

MAKES 10 PIECES

GEFILTE FISH

1¼ pounds whitefish fillet, preferably from a whole fish personally inspected for freshness

1½ pounds pike fillet, preferably from a whole fish personally inspected for freshness

½ pound carp fillet, preferably from a whole fish personally inspected for freshness

1 small onion

2 large eggs

1½ tablespoons matzoh meal

2 tablespoons cold water, approximately

Kosher salt and freshly ground black pepper

POACHING LIQUID

3 pounds bones, including heads, and skin from the fish

1 medium onion, cut into eighths

2 celery stalks, quartered

2 medium carrots

1½ tablespoons kosher salt

2 pinches of thread saffron

My grandma Minnie was a wonderful cook. She occupied her kitchen in a way we seldom see today; it was her domain, the room she was happiest in. We, her grandchildren, felt a real pleasure watching her cook. She could do anything, from peeling an apple so the skin hung in one continuous curl, to rolling sheets of noodle dough sheer enough to read through. She had a generous, uncomplicated mastery of cooking, the result of a practiced hand and an open heart. We loved her because she created a charmed circle, welcomed us in, then fed us her food.

One of Grandma Minnie's best dishes was gefilte fish. This delicacy, synonymous with Jewish cuisine, is prepared with a variety of freshwater fish because it was made first by inland peoples. *Gefilte* means stuffed and the traditional recipe calls for the fish skin to be stuffed with the ground fish flesh. These days, the fish is usually prepared as a "naked" dropped dumpling, a homier version of the French quenelle. If you've had only gefilte fish from the delicatessen or the supermarket shelf, I urge you to try Grandma Minnie's recipe served with freshly made horseradish. You'll understand why this Sabbath specialty has been so deeply loved for so long. And you'll feel as close as I do to Grandma Minnie.

1. Chill a nonreactive bowl. Pass the fish through the finest disk of a grinder or chop it finely by hand. (A food processor will not do as it creates too homogeneous a consistency). Remove the mixture to the bowl.

2. Grind the onion in a food processor and add to the fish mixture. Mix well with a wooden spoon.

3. Add the eggs and incorporate them completely, 2 to 3 minutes. Add the matzoh meal and stir to blend. Begin to add the water, stirring, until you have a light, soft mixture that will still hold its shape when formed. Add additional water, if necessary. Season well with the salt and pepper.

4. Cover the bottom of a large soup pot with the fish bones, heads, and skin. Add a layer of onion, celery, and carrots and sprinkle with the salt.

5. Wet your hands and form the fish mixture into oval dumplings about 4 inches long and 2½ inches wide. Place the gefilte fish on the vegetables. Add water to cover the fish by about 2 inches. Add the saffron.

6. Bring the liquid to a simmer and cook gently until firm, about 1 hour.

7. Remove the gefilte fish to a deep serving dish. Cut the carrots into slices about 1 inch thick. Sprinkle them over the fish.

8. Strain the liquid and pour it over the fish to just cover. Refrigerate until the liquid has jellied, about 12 hours. Serve the fish with its carrot garnish and about 2 tablespoons of the jelly per portion.

MRS. WINOGRAD'S HORSERADISH
FOR ABOUT 2 CUPS

To make sure the flavor of the horseradish has developed fully, begin at least 8 hours or more in advance.

1. Simmer the beet in plenty of water until soft, 15 to 20 minutes. Place in the bowl of a food processor and process until pureed, about 1½ minutes.

2. Combine all the ingredients in a nonreactive bowl. Correct with additional salt, sugar, or vinegar, as necessary. May be stored refrigerated for at least 1 month.

1 small beet, peeled

2 pounds fresh horseradish, peeled and finely grated

1 tablespoon kosher salt

2 teaspoons sugar

2 tablespoons distilled white vinegar

SEAFOOD WONTONS

MAKES 18 WONTONS

FILLING

1/4 pound shrimp or scallops,
   or a combination

2 tablespoons water

1 teaspoon Asian sesame oil

1 tablespoon chopped scallion
   green

1 teaspoon soy sauce

1/2 teaspoon finely grated
   fresh ginger

Pinch of freshly ground white
   pepper

SEALING PASTE

3 tablespoons flour

4 tablespoons water

18 square wonton skins

Next time you order wonton soup, take a look at the wontons. Yes—they're dumplings. Because I've always loved the slippery texture and chewy bite of wontons, I set about making a really superior seafood version. This is it—juicy little wontons, made with shrimp or scallops or a combination, full of the taste of sesame and fragrant ginger. Boil and serve them in soup or dashi, or pass them as is with Spicy Honey Mustard (page 78).

1. Bring a soup pot full of Fish Stock (page 67), Dashi (page 70), or salted water to the boil. Meanwhile, place the shrimp or scallops in the bowl of a food processor. Pulse until chopped and then run the machine until the seafood is pureed, about 1 1/2 minutes. Remove the puree to a mixing bowl and add the remaining ingredients. Mix them thoroughly until well blended.

2. Put the flour in a small bowl and blend in the water gradually, stirring with a fork, until a smooth paste is formed.

3. Place 6 wonton skins on your work surface with corners near you. With your finger, dab a bit of the sealing paste along the edges of the skins. Place 1/2 teaspoon of the filling about 1 1/2 inches above the bottom corners of each skin. Form the wontons by folding the bottom corners up over the filling to meet the top corners, making a triangle. Press to seal the edges. Fold in the bottom side corners forward and down so they overlap at the center of the bottom edge and use a dab of the paste to seal them. Repeat the procedure with the remaining wonton skins.

4. Cook the wontons in the boiling stock, dashi, or water for 3 to 4 minutes. Serve in the soup or dashi, or remove from the water, drain, and serve with the mustard.

14. PASTA, NOODLES, AND RICE

When I travel in Italy, I'm constantly excited by the variety of seafood dishes made with pasta and rice I encounter. I wish we had the same large repertoires here. Notwithstanding dishes like jambalaya, linguine with clam sauce, and various fish and noodle casseroles, we all too rarely combine seafood with pasta or rice.

Perhaps this is because we lack the pasta- or noodle-making tradition the Italians or Chinese have. We do enjoy those great Creole jambalayas, but they've remained stubbornly regional, close to the Southern fields where rice first grew in America. This is a real pity and one I want to help correct. Now that we have the world's pasta and rice at our fingertips, we can explore the many opportunities available for combining them with sparkling seafood.

I love pasta cooked in broth, Asian style. As a nation, we have yet to explore with any seriousness these meal-in-a-bowl delights. Japanese "Oishii" Noodles, served in dashi, is a pure brothy dinner; Penne with Scallops, Broccoli Rabe, and Roasted Red Pepper could be converted into a meal-in-broth by increasing the stock required and decreasing the amount of oil; the shrimp-filled Chinese Ravioli are delicious served in a rich chicken stock. There's deep pleasure to be had in slurping steaming pasta from a fortifying bowl of broth.

We've also neglected soba noodles from Asia. With their deep buckwheat savor and soft texture they're wonderfully good—and excel in dishes like the tingling Thai-inspired Spicy Shrimp with Lime and Soba Noodles or Spicy Buckwheat Noodles with Shrimp. This explosive sweet-and-sour dish, related to the "small eats" of China, is another great showcase for the way soba's rich nuttiness combines with seafood.

Sticking closer to home, I've taken the much-abused linguine with clam sauce and devised what I think is the ultimate version—pasta, Manila clams, and cockles in a rich, creamy sauce flecked with fresh marjoram and oregano. Farfalle with Creamy Oysters and Smoked Salmon is another reworking of an old favorite that pairs the fanciful pasta bows with a luscious salmon-laced sauce, briny oysters, lemon, and fresh dill. These new-old pasta and seafood dishes work equally well for intimate dinners or for entertaining a food-loving crowd.

Rice is another great vehicle for flavors, and especially those of seafood. Of the world-famous rice and seafood dishes, paella has got to be near the top of my list. Unfortunately, it's often overcooked so the seafood becomes flavorless and rubbery. In All-Seafood Paella everything steams together at the last minute in the oven, so the shellfish are perfectly done.

Cajun dirty rice is another dish I love. It always contains chicken livers—the "dirt"—and usually pork; my version features sweet catfish, a regional favorite now widely farmed. And, of course, there's risotto with seafood—the crowning glory, I think, of all seafood and grain cookery.

BUYING PASTA . . .

In the early 1980s, when fresh pasta began to move out of ethnic markets and appear more generally, we all felt that we could toss our boxed pastas aside. In fact, there is a time and place for both fresh and dried pastas.

Fresh pasta — undried pasta usually made with eggs — is richer than factory-made boxed pastas and has a softer bite. It's closest to homemade. I prefer fresh pasta for noodle dishes, in broth, or with a light cream sauce.

Dried pasta, a commercial invention of the early nineteenth century, is another animal entirely. It should be made of durum wheat — Italian packages call it pure semolina. Check the label. Dried pasta has a firm bite and a mellow, wheaty goodness all its own. More and more supermarkets carry imported dried pastas as well as the familiar domestic brands. American dried pastas can be excellent. (In fact, at a recent blind tasting of commercial pastas, many pasta experts chose American brands over the imported competition.) Some pasta shapes, like orzo, can only be purchased dried.

For most seafood dishes I prefer dried pasta made without eggs. Its "hard" texture and pronounced wheatiness combine beautifully with seafood. Actually, I've become something of a hard pasta junkie; I even allow fresh pasta to dry before cooking it to give the finished dish a greater chewiness. Cook any pasta you're using until it's *just* al dente. Naturally soft fish and shellfish require an accompaniment with body.

Fresh pasta is now widely available in supermarkets, encased in plastic packages and nitrogen treated to prevent oxidation, which leads to spoilage. These pastas can be good, but don't really compare to those freshly prepared and cut in gourmet or ethnic shops. (I've found that boiled packaged fresh pastas often go from rubbery to overcooked in an instant; watch them carefully when you prepare them.)

Store dried pastas on the shelf, where they will last indefinitely. To keep fresh unpackaged pasta, place it on a plastic-wrap-lined cookie sheet, drape the pasta with a slightly damp towel, then cover the towel with additional film. Or place the pasta in a resealable plastic bag and refrigerate. Using either method, the pasta will last for two to three days. Or freeze fresh pasta for up to three months. Fresh pasta may also be dried in an airy place, bagged and stored as you would regular dried pasta. I've noticed no difference in the taste or texture of fresh pasta previously frozen as opposed to dried. I call for a number of pastas you may not be familiar with—orzo, buckwheat noodles, and ramen among them.

A great favorite of the Greeks, orzo has a particularly pleasing consistency and bite. Though used traditionally in soup, I love to serve orzo as an accompaniment. Like other miniature pastas, it can be cooked in a relatively small amount of water or stock, which the pasta absorbs in the process. I prefer to prepare it in abundant salted water until just soft. Though orzo has less tendency to become gummy than rice, this method ensures separate "grains."

A number of cultures have produced buckwheat noodles, which are undoubtedly Asian in origin. You are probably most familiar with the Japanese soba, considered a northern or cold climate specialty there. Thin, flat, and brownish gray in color with a light wheaty taste, soba are often eaten plain with accompanying broth, or cold with soy sauce and scallions. They are sold dried in cellophane packages in Asian groceries and health food stores, or fresh in vacuum-sealed packages. Dried are fine, and are the buckwheat noodles of choice for the recipes in this book.

Ramen are spaghettilike egg noodles, now hopelessly overpopulating supermarket shelves as part of "instant" soup meals. They are ever so much better fresh, sold in plastic bags in Asian food markets. Chinese groceries seem to be the best source for these fresh noodles, known as lo mein. Because of their delicate flavor, ramen work very well with seafood. Prepare ramen as you would any fresh pasta, and serve it al dente; as they are made from a "hard" dough, they are less inclined to overcook than other pastas. All the rules that apply to the storage of fresh and dried Italian pasta are applicable to ramen.

... AND RICE

When we think of rice, we are usually thinking of the long-grain kind, the most popular American grain. Converted rice, another American standby, is polished rice that has had the nutrients that were removed in its processing "reinstated." When making traditional American fare such as dirty rice, long-grain is the kind to choose. Other dishes demand other rices. Although you may not wish to stock as many rices as I do at home—I rarely have fewer than seven types including standard long-grains, risotto rices, basmati, and sushi rice—a variety of rices really gives you culinary scope.

Most of us know that the rice of choice for making risotto is the short-grain Italian arborio. There's a reason for its use in this delicious dish, which requires that individual rice kernels retain some bite while cohering in a creamy mass. When cooked by the risotto technique, the small, fat grains of arborio do not become mushy as other rices might. This is due to arborio's well-balanced starch content.

Traditionally packed in cotton bags, arborio is now widely available in one-pound boxes. Other rices suitable for making a risotto—vialone nano and carnaroli—may be found in Italian markets and gourmet shops. Vialone nano, a favorite of Venetian cooks, has a plumper grain than arborio and is particularly quick cooking; full-grained carnaroli, the rarest and most esteemed of risotto rices, has a marvelous, subtle flavor and a perfect "cling." If you can find it and wish to splurge a bit, by all means buy it.

Jasmine rice, a sweetly fragrant long grain with a naturally tender texture, makes a perfect accompaniment to Asian dishes, and is also good for rice desserts. For those of us who have found the usual Chinese rice lacking in interest, jasmine is just what the doctor ordered. My supermarket stocks a domestic brand of jasmine that is delicious. If you can't find jasmine in your local supermarket, try gourmet stores and, of course, Asian grocers.

PERFECT RISOTTO

I'm seldom happier than with a dish of creamy, steaming seafood risotto in front of me. Its success, however, depends on observing a few easy risotto-cooking rules.

What you're aiming for when making a risotto is a creamy emulsion in which every grain of rice, though cooked, is still firm to the bite. You must, therefore, first choose an Italian short-grain rice like arborio, which produces enough starch to create velvety creaminess, but not so much that the rice becomes gummy. Cooking time is also of the essence. The trick is knowing just when the risotto is ready. There is a window of perfection, a longish 1½ to 2 minutes, at which time the rice is both creamy and tender-firm.

Be sure, always, to follow your recipe to a T, making certain that the stock or liquid you use is deeply flavored, hot, and at hand. Keep stirring the rice to avoid sticking and *keep tasting*. If you continue to taste, you will know when the rice is ready. Add more stock, if necessary, by cupfuls. The risotto tasting tells you when the rice is done; remove from the stove *immediately*, add any additional ingredients—and enjoy.

PENNE WITH SCALLOPS, BROCCOLI RABE, AND ROASTED RED PEPPER

FOR 6

The produce manager of my local supermarket tells me that he can barely keep broccoli rabe in stock. Great! Delicious in itself, this pleasingly bitter relative of the turnip is perfectly suited to accompany mild foods such as pasta. Combined here with penne, sea scallops, garlic, and red bell pepper, it makes a deeply satisfying dish.

Remember that broccoli rabe (also known as broccoli raab or broco-letti di rape) cooks quickly. Though Italians, who love the vegetable, would undoubtedly call our briefly blanched greens uncooked, you want it crunchy for this zesty, lightly sauced dish.

1. Blanch the broccoli rabe in plenty of boiling salted water until tender-crisp, about 2 minutes. Drain but save the cooking water, allowing it to return to the boil. Add the penne and cook until al dente, 8 to 10 minutes. Drain the pasta and return to the cooking pot. Mix in 1 tablespoon of the olive oil to prevent sticking. Reserve.

2. Dry the scallops with paper toweling. In a large sauté pan, heat the remaining oil over high heat. Add the scallops and cook, turning occasionally, until lightly colored, about 2 minutes.

3. Add the broccoli rabe, red peppers, garlic, scallions, and stock. Bring to the boil, then reduce the heat and simmer until the liquid is slightly thickened, 2 to 3 minutes.

4. Add the pine nuts and the pasta. Toss and cook until the pasta is hot, about 1 minute. Season with the salt and pepper and serve.

1 small bunch broccoli rabe

$3/4$ pound penne

3 tablespoons olive oil

1 pound medium sea scallops

2 small red bell peppers, roasted, cored, seeded, and cut into large dice

3 garlic cloves, crushed with the flat of a knife and minced

2 tablespoons minced scallions, white parts only

1 cup Chicken Stock (page 66)

2 tablespoons pine nuts, toasted

Salt and freshly ground black pepper

COOK'S OPTION

You can use extra-large shrimp (16 to 20 count), peeled except for the tail and butterflied, in place of the scallops.

FRESH EGG PASTA WITH WHITE BEANS, TOMATOES, AND CALAMARI

FOR 6

1/4 cup dried small white beans
   or navy beans, or 1 cup
   canned, well rinsed
1/2 cup plus 1 tablespoon olive
   oil
18 garlic cloves
2 medium tomatoes, cored,
   seeded, and cut into large
   chunks
1/2 bunch fresh oregano, stems
   removed
Pinch of hot red pepper flakes
1 cup Fish Stock (page 67),
   Chicken Stock (page 66), or
   water
Fresh egg pasta (recipe follows),
   or 1 pound best-quality
   store-bought fettuccine
1 pound squid, tentacles
   removed, the bodies cut into
   1 1/2-inch-wide rings
Salt

COOK'S OPTION

*You can use 1 pound peeled
medium shrimp (31 to 35
count) in place of the squid.
Cook for 2 minutes.*

This dish, with its pure Mediterranean flavors, proves once again how good pasta and bean dishes can be. Besides tasting wonderful together, the pasta and bean textures contrast perfectly and combine to create a healthy, whole-protein starch.

Calamari is, of course, the Italian word for squid. We're likely to think of calamari as deep-fried rings; here the rings are gently simmered in a sauce made with tomatoes, beans, and sweet roasted garlic. I usually like an eggless pasta with seafood, but this zesty sauce really requires a richer, "softer" taste. Fresh pasta is available widely, but I've included a recipe here for those who would like to make their own.

Serve this robust, deliciously garlicky dish with crusty bread and a big red wine.

1. If using dried beans, soak in the refrigerator for 24 hours in sufficient water to cover. Change the water and simmer the beans until tender, about 45 minutes.

2. In a small skillet, heat 1/2 cup of the oil over medium heat. Add the garlic and cook until golden and soft, stirring frequently, 8 to 10 minutes. If the garlic seems to be browning too quickly, reduce the heat. (The garlic may be prepared in advance.)

3. Bring plenty of boiling water to the boil. Meanwhile, in a medium skillet, heat the tablespoon of oil over medium heat. Add the tomatoes and garlic and sauté 2 minutes. Add the oregano, pepper flakes, and stock or water. Bring to a simmer, add the beans, and simmer 2 minutes.

4. Meanwhile, add the pasta to the boiling water and cook until al dente, 2 to 3 minutes. When the pasta is cooked, drain well and place in a large bowl.

5. Add the squid rings and tentacles to the skillet and cook for 1 minute. Season with the salt. Add the sauce to the pasta and toss well. Serve immediately.

FRESH PASTA

F O R 6

Plan to make this pasta a day or so in advance of serving it.

1. Add all the ingredients to the bowl of a food processor fitted with a plastic blade. Process until the dough forms a ball, about 3 minutes. Work in more flour if the dough seems sticky. Refrigerate the dough for 1 to 5 days. (You may get away with 2 hours refrigeration if you are pressed for time.)

2. Scatter semolina flour on your work surface to avoid sticking. Coat a rolling pin with semolina and roll out the dough from center to sides until you have a sheet about 1/8 inch (thinner if you like your pasta more gossamer). Roll loosely. (The rolled-up pasta can be made up to a day in advance. Wrap it in waxed paper, cover the roll with moist paper toweling, then wrap again in plastic film. Refrigerate.)

3. Cut the rolled sheet into strips about 1/2 inch wide.

1 1/2 cups semolina flour, plus
  more for sprinkling
1 1/2 cups all-purpose flour
4 large eggs
1/2 teaspoon salt
1 tablespoon water
1 tablespoon olive oil

ANGEL HAIR PASTA WITH BAY SCALLOPS, WILD MUSHROOMS, AND SUN-DRIED TOMATOES

FOR 6

2 ounces unreconstituted sun-
   dried tomatoes

2 teaspoons olive oil

$1/8$ pound fresh wild mushrooms,
   such as shiitake, portobello,
   cremini, or chanterelles, cut
   into bite-size pieces

2 small garlic cloves, minced

$3/4$ cup Fish Stock (page 67)

$1/2$ pound dry angel hair pasta

$1^1/2$ pounds bay scallops,
   drained

$1/2$ cup Red Pepper Butter
   (page 63)

Salt and freshly ground
   black pepper

COOK'S OPTION

*You can substitute 1 pound
squid, tentacles removed,
bodies cut into 1½-inch-
wide rings, for the scallops.
Cook for 1½ minutes.*

Angel hair pasta, or *capelli d'angelo*, is actually eaten more frequently in America than it is in Italy. I love the pasta when it isn't buried under heavy sauces. In fact, one of the best "sauces" of all for this pasta is just a fruity olive oil or good fresh butter. For this dish I use a flavored butter for the sauce, as well as sweet bay scallops, wild mushrooms, and unmarinated sun-dried tomatoes. These ingredients are tasted bit by bit as you eat, but also all at once, in every bite—my idea of the ideal pasta-eating experience.

1. Reconstitute the tomatoes in 3 cups of hot water, about 10 minutes. Drain and reserve.

2. In a medium skillet, heat the oil over medium-high heat. Add the mushrooms and sauté until softened, about 2 minutes. Add the garlic, tomatoes, and stock and simmer until the flavors are blended, about 10 minutes. Reserve.

3. Bring plenty of salted water to the boil. Add the pasta and cook until al dente, 5 to 7 minutes. Drain well.

4. Bring the mushroom mixture to the simmer, then add the scallops and pepper butter. Stir and cook until the scallops are white and firm (they will be slightly translucent at the center), about 2 minutes. Add the pasta, toss well, season with salt and pepper, and serve.

SPICY SHRIMP WITH LIME AND SOBA NOODLES

FOR 4

I'm devoted to soba noodles. Their earthy buckwheat goodness makes a perfect backdrop in spicy noodle meals like this.

This recipe uses two ingredients that may be new to you. One is the Thai fish sauce called *nam pla*, a seafood-based flavoring ingredient as popular in Southeast Asia as is soy sauce in China or Japan. The other is kaffir leaf, a delightfully aromatic edible leaf used often in Thai cooking. The fermented fish sauce, which is actually quite mild, adds a subtle sea taste to the noodles. The kaffir leaf enhances the dish with its delicate lime-like perfume. Both may be bought in Asian markets.

The soba cook relatively quickly, so keep an eye on them while you prepare the spicy sauce.

1. Cook the soba in plenty of boiling salted water until al dente, 5 to 7 minutes.

2. Meanwhile, in a large saucepan over medium heat, bring the stocks, shrimp, lime juice, and kaffir or grated lime to the simmer. Continue to cook until the flavors have blended, about 3 minutes.

3. Add the fish sauce, butter, and red bell pepper flakes. Bring to the boil.

4. Drain the noodles and add to the sauce. Mix well. Season with the salt and pepper and serve.

$^1/_2$ pound soba (buckwheat) noodles

$^3/_4$ cup Chicken Stock (page 66)

$^3/_4$ cup Fish Stock (page 67)

1 pound small shrimp, peeled and deveined

Juice of 1 lime

1 kaffir leaf, julienned finely, or 1$^1/_2$ teaspoons grated lime peel

4 teaspoons nam pla (Thai fish sauce)

2 tablespoons unsalted butter

$^1/_4$ teaspoon red pepper flakes

Salt and freshly ground black pepper

COOK'S OPTION

One pound of bay scallops also work well with the recipe. You can also substitute capellini for the soba noodles.

LINGUINE WITH CLAM SAUCE

FOR 4

½ pound linguine

1 tablespoon olive oil

1 medium shallot, minced

3 garlic cloves, crushed with the flat of a knife and peeled

¾ pound Manila clams, well washed

¾ pound cockles, well washed

¼ cup dry white wine

½ cup Fish Stock (page 67) or water

¼ teaspoon red pepper flakes

1¼ cups heavy (whipping) cream

¼ pound cooked periwinkles (optional; see Note)

2 level teaspoons finely grated lemon zest

1 tablespoon coarsely chopped fresh marjoram, or 2 teaspoons dried

2 teaspoons chopped fresh oregano, or ½ teaspoon dried

Salt and freshly ground black pepper

Linguine with clam sauce (white or red!) is one of the warhorses of Italian-American cuisine. It's been botched so often—flour-based sauces, chewy clams—that it's hard to remember how good the dish can be. I think you'll find this version, which uses Manila clams and cockles, a happy reintroduction to a true classic.

Though you may use whatever clams are readily available, the thin-shelled Manilas, native to the Pacific, are worth seeking out. Cockles, found in Maine and Washington state waters, have lots of plump, clean-tasting meat and are available in specialty seafood stores. I've included periwinkles optionally, but these lovely little snails, native to the Atlantic, appear at fish markets with increasing regularity. Oregano, marjoram, and a good shake of hot red pepper add kick and herby greenness.

1. Cook the pasta in plenty of boiling salted water until al dente, 9 to 11 minutes; drain.

2. Meanwhile, prepare the sauce. In a medium saucepan, heat the oil over medium-high heat. Add the shallot and garlic and sauté gently without allowing them to color, about 2 minutes.

3. Add the clams, cockles, and wine and cook, covered, until the wine bubbles, about 1 minute. Add the stock or water and the red pepper flakes and cook until the shellfish open, about 1 minute. Remove the shellfish and reserve.

4. Add the cream, bring to the simmer, and reduce until lightly thickened, 2 to 3 minutes.

5. Add the periwinkles, if using, the lemon zest, and the herbs. Season with the salt and pepper. Return the shellfish to the saucepan.

6. Drain the pasta and divide it among serving bowls. Ladle on the sauce, avoiding the contents at the very bottom of the saucepan, which may contain sand. Serve immediately.

Note: To prepare the periwinkles, wash them well in 2 changes of water. In a medium soup pot, bring 2 quarts of salted water to a boil, add the periwinkles, and boil for 2 minutes. Drain and cool until they can be handled, about 10 minutes. Using a straight pin, remove the meat from each shell and reserve.

FARFALLE WITH CREAMY OYSTERS AND SMOKED SALMON
FOR 4

Farfalle, which means "butterflies," are small pasta bows. I use them often. Besides being fun to look at, farfalle catch sauce nicely and work perfectly with a cream-based sauce full of briny oysters and smoked salmon ribbons. This dish is done in a few minutes and makes a lovely first course.

1. Cook the pasta in plenty of boiling salted water until al dente, 10 to 12 minutes; drain.

2. Meanwhile, prepare the sauce. In a medium saucepan, melt the butter over medium heat. Add the shallot and sauté without coloring until soft, 2 to 3 minutes.

3. Add the cream, allow it to come to the boil, then reduce the heat and simmer until it coats a spoon lightly, about 4 minutes. Add the salmon, oysters, dill, and lemon and simmer just until the edges of the oysters curl and the flavors are blended, 1 minute. Remove immediately from the heat, season with the salt and pepper, pour over the drained pasta, and serve.

$^1\!/_2$ pound farfalle

1 teaspoon unsalted butter

1 large shallot, minced

2 cups heavy (whipping) cream

2 ounces smoked salmon, cut
   into $1^1\!/_2$ by $1^1\!/_2$-inch pieces

12 oysters, any kind, shucked

1 tablespoon chopped fresh dill

2 teaspoons fresh lemon juice

Salt and freshly ground black
   pepper

COOK'S OPTION

You can substitute 20 shucked littleneck clams for the oysters. Cook just until their edges curl.

CHINESE RAVIOLI

FOR 2

½ pound sea scallops, diced

Salt

¾ bunch fresh thyme, chopped

1 package (18 count) round
   wonton skins

2¼ cups Beurre Blanc
   (page 76), with 1 tablespoon
   chopped fresh thyme
   (optional)

COOK'S OPTION

Fresh pasta sheets can be
used in place of wonton
skins. Use a 3½-inch cookie
cutter to create dough cir-
cles, or cut circles using a
glass top and a sharp-
pointed knife.

I first got the idea for these scallop-filled ravioli when I apprenticed for the great French chef Alain Senderens, who has masterfully reenvisioned many traditional recipes.

Unlike their Italian namesake, these ravioli are made with wonton skins (or *gyoza* in Japanese). Prepared with or without eggs, the skins are also available commercially round or square, thick or thin. For this recipe you want the round, thin, and eggless kind—those made with only flour, salt, and water. The skins are available in Asian markets and in some supermarkets.

Serve the ravioli in soup or broth as you would a dumpling, or with a Beurre Blanc to which you've added some chopped fresh thyme.

1. Two hours in advance, season the scallops with the salt and sprinkle with the thyme. Place the scallops in a colander and fit the colander into a bowl. Refrigerate for 2 hours. (The scallops will lose excess water, which will drain into the bowl.)

2. To make the ravioli, lay 2 wonton skins on your work surface. Using your fingertips or a fine paintbrush, moisten the edge of the skins. Place ½ teaspoon of the scallop mixture in the center of each skin. Place 1 more skin on top of each ravioli and press firmly around the edges to seal. (You can prepare the ravioli up to 24 hours in advance. Store, covered, in the refrigerator.)

3. Bring plenty of salted water to the boil. Add the ravioli and cook until they float, 2 to 3 minutes.

4. Drain and serve as is or with the optional Beurre Blanc.

JAPANESE "OISHII" NOODLES

FOR 4

Oishii means "delicious" in Japanese—a perfect description of the sustaining noodles that have long been part of the Japanese diet. Though we're probably most familiar with soba noodles, made from buckwheat, "white" wheat noodles, associated with southern Japan, are also traditional. Both kinds are eaten plain or in broth and, as custom demands, happily slurped.

For this recipe, ramen noodles are served in dashi, the Japanese stock made with kelp (konbu) and dried bonito flakes (katsuo-bushi) and then garnished with shrimp, spinach, and shiitake mushrooms. This pure noodle meal is particularly welcome when we hunger for simple, pure flavors.

1. Cook the ramen in plenty of boiling salted water until al dente, 3 to 5 minutes. Drain and hold at room temperature. (The noodles will not stick together.)

2. Cut the spinach crosswise into 3-inch lengths. Bring the dashi to the boil and add the shrimp. Cook for 2 minutes. Add the spinach and mushrooms and cook for 1 minute more. Add the noodles, soy sauce, and scallions, ladle into bowls, and serve.

$1/4$ pound ramen noodles (preferably fresh), available at Asian markets

$1/4$ pound spinach, well washed, stems removed

4 cups Dashi (page 70)

16 extra-large shrimp (16 to 20 count), peeled except for tails

$1/2$ cup julienned fresh shiitake mushrooms

2 teaspoons soy sauce

1 bunch scallions, green parts only, coarsely chopped

COOK'S OPTION

Watercress makes an interesting substitution for the spinach.

SPICY BUCKWHEAT NOODLES WITH SHRIMP

FOR 6

SAUCE

1/2 cup roasted peanuts

3 tablespoons soy sauce

1 tablespoon honey

1 tablespoon rice vinegar

1 teaspoon Chinese chili paste

1 cup peanut oil

2 tablespoons water

SHRIMP

1 tablespoon peanut oil

2 pounds medium shrimp
(31 to 35 count), peeled

2 garlic cloves, minced

1/3 teaspoon Chinese chili paste

3 tablespoons finely chopped
roasted peanuts

NOODLES

8 ounces buckwheat (soba)
noodles

1 small cucumber, peeled, split
lengthwise, seeded, and
juilenned

1 small carrot, peeled and
julienned

1/2 cup loosely packed fresh
cilantro (coriander) leaves

This exceptionally good noodle dish, related to the dishes called "small eats" in China, is full of multilayered flavor. It uses peanuts in an uncooked sauce and then again as part of a shrimp sauté. It plays raw cucumber and carrot, cool and sweet, against honey, chili paste, and soy.

Quick to prepare, this is a perfect cold dish when you want something fast and filling that also tastes sprightly.

1. Make the sauce. Place all the ingredients except the oil and water in the bowl of a food processor. Pulse until well pureed, 4 to 5 seconds.

2. With the machine running slowly, add the oil and then water through the feed tube until incorporated, about 1½ minutes. Reserve.

3. Prepare the shrimp. In a wok or medium skillet, bring the oil to the smoking point over high heat. Add the shrimp and stir-fry until the shrimp are orange and just cooked through, about 2 minutes. Add the remaining ingredients and cook 30 seconds more. Reserve.

4. Have ready a large bowl of ice water. Cook the noodles in plenty of salted boiling water until al dente, 3 to 5 minutes. Drain the noodles and add to the ice water. When cold, drain again and return to the bowl with the cucumber, carrot, and cilantro. Toss the noodles with half the dressing, adding more as needed until they are well coated. Adjust the seasoning with additional vinegar and/or soy sauce.

5. Divide the noodles among 6 plates. Surround with the shrimp, drizzle them with additional sauce, and serve.

ORZO WITH MUSSELS AND CILANTRO

FOR 6

No one seems indifferent to the taste of cilantro. For some people it's a real no-no; personally, I can't get enough of it.

Though we usually associate this musky herb with Asian or Latin American cooking, it's actually a native of the Mediterranean. Cilantro is a perfect match for the mussels in this recipe, whose cooking broth makes a delicious sauce for the pasta.

For cilantro lovers, I've created a cilantro double whammy here. Cilantro Butter is used for the "sauce," and a cilantro garnish tops the steaming pasta.

1. Cook the orzo in plenty of boiling salted water until al dente, 10 to 12 minutes. Drain and reserve.

2. In a large nonreactive pot over medium-high heat, combine the shallots and vermouth. Simmer until the shallots soften, about 3 minutes.

3. Add the mussels, cover, and simmer until they open, 2 to 3 minutes. Remove from the heat and pour the cooking liquid into a bowl slowly to ensure that any sand remains in the pot. Remove the mussels to a bowl and wash the pot well.

4. Remove the meat from the mussels and return it to the pot. Place the pot over medium heat and add the orzo and Cilantro Butter. Stir until the pasta is warm and creamy. Add the cilantro leaves, season with the salt and pepper, and serve.

2 cups orzo

3 medium shallots, thinly sliced

1/2 cup dry vermouth

3 pounds mussels (preferably cultivated), cleaned and bearded

1/2 cup Cilantro Butter (page 63)

1/2 cup loosely packed fresh cilantro (coriander) leaves

Salt and freshly ground black pepper

ALL-SEAFOOD PAELLA

FOR 4

1 tablespoon olive oil

1 medium onion, diced

1 small red bell pepper, cored, seeded, and diced

1 garlic clove, minced

1 medium tomato, cored, seeded, and diced

$1/2$ teaspoon saffron threads

$1^1/_4$ cups long-grain rice

1 cup water

$2/_3$ cup Fish Stock (page 67)

12 littleneck or cherrystone clams, cleaned

8 extra-large shrimp (16 to 20 count), unpeeled

24 mussels (preferably culti-vated), cleaned and bearded

8 medium sea scallops

12 best-quality Spanish or Tunisian green olives, pitted

Salt

There are many delicious all-seafood paella recipes, but I think my version is hard to beat. Full of clams, mussels, shrimp, and scallops folded into a rich, saffron-flavored rice, it's a particularly great choice for a gathering.

Paella isn't hard to do, so I'm constantly amazed when the ones I'm served are dry, characterless, or full of chewy seafood. I guarantee a perfect dish if you follow this method, which involves steaming all the seafood together in the oven at the last minute.

You can use any ovenpoof casserole to make this dish, but a traditional paella pan works best. Besides being attractive to bring to the table, its large surface area and relative shallowness encourage proper cooking. If you find yourself craving paella often or enjoy serving it to guests, the proper pan is a good investment.

1. Preheat the oven to 375°F.

2. In a traditional paella pan or ovenproof casserole, heat the oil over medium heat. Add the onion and red pepper and sauté until the onion is translucent, 2 to 3 minutes.

3. Add the garlic and tomato and sauté 1 minute longer.

4. Add the saffron and rice and mix well. Add the water and stock, bring to the boil, and reduce the heat to medium-low so the mixture just simmers. Cover with foil and simmer slowly for 10 minutes.

5. Remove the foil and arrange all the seafood and olives evenly over the rice. Season with the salt. Recover with the foil, place in the oven, and oven-steam until the clams have just opened and the scallops are milk-white but not firm, about 15 minutes. (If some clams have not opened, try to open them gently with a fork. If they do not respond to prodding, discard.) Bring the dish to the table and serve.

LOBSTER FRIED RICE

FOR 4

When was the last time you went to a Chinese restaurant and ordered fried rice? If you're like me, it's been a long while. Usually bastardized, fried rice gets short shrift in even the best Chinese restaurants. Properly done, it can become a standard in your repertoire.

The secret of this delicate and savory fried rice is rapid cooking of the highest-quality ingredients. Lobster fried rice is a special treat that sounds extravagant but isn't—a chicken or cull lobster is all you need. Make sure not to overcook the egg finish; it should remain at the trembling stage, suave and golden.

1. In a wok or large skillet, heat the oil over medium-high heat. When it is very hot, add the celery, pepper, and scallion stalks. Stir-fry until the scallions are wilted, about 3 minutes. Add the garlic, sesame oil, soy sauce, chili paste, and lobster. Sir-fry for 30 seconds.

2. Break the eggs directly into the mixture. Stirring vigorously, cook until the eggs are just set, about 15 seconds. Add the rice and toss well. Sprinkle with the scallion greens and serve.

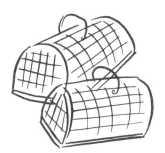

2 teaspoons peanut oil

2 celery stalks, peeled and cut diagonally into pieces about $^1/_8$ inch thick

1 medium red bell pepper, cored, seeded, and cut into strips about 1 by $^1/_4$ inch

$^1/_2$ bunch scallions, white parts cut into 2-inch lengths, green parts coarsely chopped

1 garlic clove, minced

1 teaspoon Asian sesame oil

2 tablespoons soy sauce

$^1/_3$ teaspoon Chinese chili paste

2 chicken lobsters or small culls, boiled or steamed, meat removed and cut into bite-size pieces

2 large eggs

$2^1/_2$ cups cooked white rice, cooled

COOK'S OPTION

Use $^1/_4$ pound cooked medium shrimp (31 to 35 count) in place of the lobster.

RISOTTO WITH OCTOPUS, ROOT VEGETABLES, AND RED WINE

FOR 4

1 precooked or frozen raw baby
octopus, about 1 pound
(see Note)

1 bottle red Burgundy or Barolo

2 cups Chicken Stock
(page 66)

1 cup Fish Stock (page 67)

3 tablespoons unsalted butter

1 small onion, minced

2 cups arborio rice or other
short-grain Italian rice

1 medium carrot, peeled and
finely diced

1 small celery root, peeled and
finely diced

2 bay leaves

3 tablespoons grated Asiago or
Romano cheese

Salt and freshly ground
black pepper

Because of the root vegetables and red wine, I think of this dish as a winter risotto, but it's marvelous at any time of year. The recipe uses an interesting seasoning technique you should keep in mind. Red wine is first reduced to concentrate its full-bodied flavor, then added to the risotto just before you serve it as a seasoning. The rice is lightly tinted and has a subtle, earthy bouquet.

Try to get fresh baby octopus, which weigh about a pound each; they're available precooked in East Coast markets in November and December; on the West Coast in September. They're also sold frozen raw, or partly cooked and then frozen.

1. Cut the octopus into bite-size pieces.

2. In a medium saucepan over medium-high heat, simmer the wine until it is reduced to about ¾ cup, about 15 minutes. Pour into a bowl and reserve. In the same saucepan, combine the stocks and bring to the simmer over medium-high heat.

3. In a large saucepan over medium heat, melt 1 tablespoon of the butter. Sauté the onion until soft without allowing it to color, about 2 minutes. Add the rice and cook, stirring, until the rice has become opaque, about 1 minute.

4. Add about 1¼ cups of the combined stocks to the rice and cook, stirring, until the liquid is absorbed, about 6 to 8 minutes. Add the carrot, celery root, bay leaves, and another 1¼ cups of stock, cooking and stirring until it is absorbed. Continue to add stock until the rice is tender-firm and coheres in a creamy mass, 15 to 20 minutes. If necessary, add additional stock.

5. Add the octopus, the remaining butter, and the cheese and stir well. Add the reduced wine and season with the salt and pepper. Serve immediately in bowls.

Note: To prepare frozen raw octopus, simmer first in boiling water until tender, 12 to 15 minutes.

RISOTTO WITH LOBSTER AND SHRIMP

FOR 4

I had my first seafood risotto years ago in an Italian restaurant in New York and it was just awful. I couldn't identify any of the shellfish in the dish because everything had the same rubbery texture. I knew I could do better and this recipe is the result.

Although this version is deluxe in both taste and feeling, it's easy on the pocketbook. I've combined creamy rice with sweet shrimp and bite-size pieces of lobster, then finished the dish with Parmesan, chives, and a little optional truffle oil. I can't imagine a more elegant dish that is quicker to prepare. It makes a marvelous starter for guests or a main dish for a special supper with your significant other.

1. In a medium saucepan, melt 1 tablespoon of the butter over medium heat. Sauté the onion without allowing it to color, about 2 minutes.

2. Add the rice and cook, stirring, until the rice has become opaque, about 1 minute.

3. Mix the stocks and add about 1¼ cups to the rice. Cook and stir until the liquid has been absorbed. Add another 1¼ cups, allowing it to become absorbed. Repeat the procedure until you have used all the stock. The rice should be tender-firm and cohere in a creamy mass. If it is still undercooked, add more stock. After about 14 minutes of cooking, add the shrimp and cook until they become just firm and orange colored, about 6 minutes.

4. Add the lobster and cook 30 seconds to warm. Add the remaining butter, cheese, chives, and optional truffle oil and stir to blend. Season with the salt and pepper and serve in small bowls.

3 tablespoons unsalted butter

1 small onion, minced

2 cup arborio or other short-grain Italian rice

2 cups Chicken Stock (page 66)

1 cup Fish Stock (page 67)

¹/₂ pound medium shrimp (31 to 35 count), peeled and deveined

One 1¹/₂-pound lobster, steamed or boiled, meat removed and cut into bite-size pieces

3 tablespoons grated Parmesan cheese

1¹/₂ tablespoons chopped fresh chives

2 teaspoons truffle oil (optional)

Salt and freshly ground black pepper

COOK'S OPTION

The recipe can be made with only shrimp. Increase the quantity to 1 pound.

FAT TUESDAY CATFISH WITH DIRTY RICE

FOR 4

DIRTY RICE

1/4 pound chicken livers

2 tablespoons unsalted butter

2 tablespoons brandy

1 small red bell pepper,
    seeded, cored, and cut into
    small dice

2 cups cooked white rice

CATFISH

8 cups vegetable oil, for frying

1 1/2 pounds catfish fillets, cut
    into 1 by 3-inch strips

2 cups yellow cornmeal

2 teaspoons cayenne pepper

Salt

1 bunch scallions, green
    parts only

2 teaspoons Worcestershire
    sauce

1/2 teaspoon Tabasco Sauce

Salt

COOK'S OPTION

*You can substitute cooked
wild rice for one half of the
white rice.*

Where did a nice Jewish boy from New Jersey first encounter dirty rice, the great Southern dish so-named because of the chicken livers it contains? In New Orleans, of course, when I was young and could afford to eat only inexpensive dishes. Actually, dirty rice is one of the world's great simple and filling meals, on a par with the greatest peasant dishes of Europe and Asia.

For this recipe I've paired a dirty rice containing scallions and red bell pepper with golden fried catfish, another Southern staple. Traditionally associated with the poor, catfish have entered American folklore through the "fries" recalled in works like *Porgy and Bess*. Nowadays, the fish are widely farmed and are, as ever, tremendously good eating. The catfish and dirty rice make a great combination. Like paella, this dish makes a great party centerpiece and can be doubled or tripled, as you like.

1. Make the rice. Dry the chicken livers well with paper toweling. In a medium skillet over high heat, melt 1 tablespoon of the butter and add the livers; avoid crowding. Sauté the livers until fork-tender, about 1 minute per side. Add the brandy, avert your face, and ignite. Remove the livers from the skillet and reserve.

2. Add the remaining butter to the skillet, reduce the heat to medium, and add the pepper. Sauté until just cooked through, 2 to 4 minutes.

3. Meanwhile, gently break up the livers with a fork. Return them to the pan with the pepper and add the rice. Stir and remove from the heat. Reserve.

4. Slowly add the oil to a fryer with a basket or use a deep, heavy skillet or wok. (If you are using a wok, make sure it is balanced securely with a wok ring or overturned burner grid.) Turn the heat under the oil to high and heat it to 375°F. on a frying thermometer. Have ready a large plate covered with a layer of paper toweling and a mesh skimmer.

5. On a second large plate, mix the cornmeal, cayenne, and salt. Dredge the fish strips in the cornmeal mixture.

6. When the oil is ready for frying, shake any excess cornmeal mixture from the strips and add them one by one to the oil. Do not overcrowd. Fry a second batch, if necessary, allowing the oil to return to 375°F. before proceeding. Fry the fish until golden and flaky when broken into with a fork, about 3 minutes.

7. Remove the fish using the basket or skimmer. Drain on the paper towel–covered plate. Make sure the fish pieces do not cover one another.

8. Return the rice to the stove. Warm over medium heat. Add the scallions and season with the Worcestershire, Tabasco, and salt. Stir and serve immediately with the catfish.

15. PO' BOYS AND SNAPPER SANDWICHES

I love sandwiches—they remind me of home. And sandwiches that pair bread with seafood can be magically good. As a kid, my approach to sandwich making was to "put everything in." Now I'm more discriminating. Every sandwich included here has its own logic.

Each element in the sandwich should do something for the others. The Grilled Snapper Sandwich with Guacamole and Tomatillo Salsa illustrates this culinary theory of relativity. The mild sweet snapper needs enrichment, which is provided by a buttery guacamole. The astringency of the tomatillos in the salsa balances the lushness of the avocado, which in turn "absorbs" the tomatillo's bite. Tabasco Sauce adds fire and the chewy wheatiness of the semolina baguette anchors everything deliciously.

What makes a great sandwich great? My checklist begins with great bread—bread with a definite flavor and texture. It must taste like the grain from which it is made. Like ripe fruit, good bread smells wonderfully of itself—of yeast and flour and baking.

My second sandwich requirement is a protein. While I enjoy an occasional vegetarian sandwich, ultimately I find those containing meat or seafood most satisfying. One of the pleasures of seafood sandwiches is that they take you away from the standard sandwich repertoire based on poultry, beef, ham, or salami. Seafood provides a versatile, flavorful, and low-calorie alternative to traditional protein fillings.

Next, sandwiches need condiments—flavor exciters. Spreads often act as condiments; mustard, mayonnaise, and other dressings—including vinaigrettes—add moisture and zip. I like to use flavored oils in sandwiches and also the unexpected. The tart and voluptuous Lobster and Yogurt Salad in a Pita Pocket uses yogurt, an unconventional sandwich ingredient.

Last, the interesting X ingredient. Here's where I have the most fun. The X ingredient provides that taste or texture that adds punch, consistency, even passion to a sandwich. It's the watercress in the Poached Sole Sandwich with Watercress and Mom's Thousand Island Dressing, the shredded cabbage in the Corn Fried Oyster Po' Boy, the scallions in the Smoked Salmon Sandwich with Scallion Cream Cheese on Thin Rye Toast.

I also have my sandwich "can't stands." I can't stand eating a sandwich and not being able to tell what it is I'm eating. (I had my first and last gyro sandwich three years ago—no thank you.) Great ingredients on bad bread is another no-no; ditto sandwiches that are made ahead, refrigerated, and then served cold. If you must store sandwiches, or if you're traveling with them, keep them breathing and at room temperature in punctured resealable plastic bags. And don't be overgenerous with ingredients. Sandwiches thicker than 2½ inches are difficult to put in your mouth and the contents go flying when you chomp down.

Often I eat traditional seafood sandwiches—my wife, for example, fixes a great tuna salad on white with Hellmann's mayonnaise—and later find myself reinventing it. Tuna salad made with freshly poached fish, homemade mayo, and tub olives is spectacular when layered with sliced onion and served on fragrant black bread. The grilled cheese sandwich, another favorite of mine, takes a giant step forward when it becomes Grilled Crab 'n' Cheddar on White.

I rely on the refrigerator for sandwich-making treasures. A little leftover salmon, some mayonnaise flavored with tarragon or chives, a few slices of raw zucchini, a crispy baguette—voilà, a great lunch or light supper. Or think of sandwiches for easy entertaining. Most sandwiches, when scaled down, make perfect hors d'oeuvres. The Belgian Mussel Tartines—small sandwich gratins of Gruyère and mussels—work perfectly this way. When I'm having friends over I often make several kinds of sandwiches, cut them in quarters or halves, and create a beautiful platter. I add some homemade pickles and serve 'Nilla Wafers for dessert—my preferred sandwich "finish" when I was a kid. And everyone is happy.

SEARED SALMON SANDWICH ON SOURDOUGH BREAD
WITH CHARMOULA AND ZUCCHINI

FOR 4

CHARMOULA

1 small onion, grated

2 medium garlic cloves, crushed
with the flat of a knife

¼ teaspoon Chinese chili paste

¼ teaspoon cracked black
peppercorns

1 teaspoon best-quality paprika

¼ teaspoon ground cumin

½ teaspoon salt

5 tablespoons olive oil

7 tablespoons water

2 medium zucchini, ends removed
and each cut lengthwise
into 6 strips

2 teaspoons unsalted butter, softened

One ¼-pound salmon fillet, cut on
the diagonal into ¼-inch slices

8 slices loaf-style sourdough bread
(preferably thick-crusted)

1 lemon, halved

Fresh cilantro leaves

COOK'S OPTION

Tuna also works well with

this recipe.

I discovered fiery charmoula—a wonderfully spicy Moroccan marinade—while traveling in the Mediterranean. I use it here as a bath in which zucchini are cooked. The remaining charmoula is drizzled over smoky seared salmon and the zucchini, topped with fresh coriander and served in chewy sourdough. I love the idea of cooking with a marinade and then using it as a flavor-enhancing condiment.

1. Preheat the oven to 350°F.

2. In a small nonreactive bowl, combine the charmoula ingredients and mix well.

3. Arrange the zucchini strips in a single layer in an ovenproof casserole. Pour the charmoula over the zucchini and bake until just tender, about 15 minutes. Allow to cool.

4. In a large cast-iron skillet, melt 1 teaspoon of the butter over high heat until it sizzles. Sear half the fish strips for 1 minute on each side and remove. (You can sear the salmon longer if you like it cooked through.) Repeat the procedure for the remaining fish.

5. To assemble the sandwich, divide the fish among 4 slices of the bread. Add 3 slices of zucchini to each. Drizzle the charmoula and its liquid over the zucchini. Squeeze lemon juice on top and garnish with 5 or 6 cilantro leaves per sandwich. Top with the remaining bread slices and serve.

POACHED SOLE SANDWICH WITH WATERCRESS AND MOM'S THOUSAND ISLAND DRESSING

FOR 4

Sole, watercress, and rye toast make one of those inspired combinations that come under the heading of why-didn't-I-think-of-it-myself? And Thousand Island dressing, a victim of commercial overkill, can be really great when handled with care. I've loved my mother's version for years; its sweet-and-sour spiciness adds real dash to the deliciously mild fish. This goes well with sweet potato fries.

1. In a medium bowl, combine the dressing ingredients and stir well.

2. Top 4 slices of the bread with the watercress and fish. Spoon on the sauce, top with the remaining slices of bread, and serve.

DRESSING

3 tablespoons Homemade Mayonnaise (page 71), or best-quality store-bought

1 tablespoon best-quality ketchup

1 tablespoon chopped sweet pickle relish

6 dashes of Tabasco Sauce

1 tablespoon chopped fresh Italian (flat-leaf) parsley

8 slices rye bread, toasted

1 large bunch watercress, bottom third of stems removed, washed and dried

1/4 pound poached sole or leftover fish, poached, baked, or broiled

COOK'S OPTION

Cod or snapper can be used in place of the sole.

CLAM ROLLS ON TOASTED GARLIC BUNS

FOR 4

12 garlic cloves

1 cup milk

4 individual hero rolls or hot
   dog buns

1 quart vegetable oil, for frying

2 cups all-purpose flour

3 cups fine dry bread crumbs

4 large eggs

1 pound strip clams, or 48
   cherrystone clams, shucked

I thank two people for making this recipe possible—my grandmother and Howard Johnson. The former would take me to the restaurant of the latter in Asbury Park, New Jersey, when I was a kid. As any Easterner knows, the Howard Johnson chain made the best clam rolls ever—a buttery split of white bread brimming with crisply fried clams and creamy tartar sauce.

I've tried to improve on the best. I call for top-quality rolls, toasted and spread with a pungent garlic puree. Chowder clams were the Howard Johnson seafood of choice—they're big, cheap, and tasty—but I recommend strip clams, which come precut to the proper size and are available fresh at fish stores. Unfortunately, I can't provide the Asbury Park bumper cars—or Grandma.

1. Preheat the oven to 400°F.

2. In a medium saucepan, combine the garlic and milk. Bring to the boil, reduce the heat, and simmer until the garlic is very soft, 10 to 15 minutes. Drain the garlic and rinse it well under cold running water. Discard the milk.

3. Add the garlic to the bowl of a food processor and process until very smooth, scraping the sides of the bowl as necessary, about 45 seconds. Split the rolls, if necessary, leaving the halves attached, and spread the insides thinly with the garlic puree. Place the buns on a cookie sheet and toast them in the oven until golden, about 2 minutes.

4. Meanwhile, slowly add the oil to a fryer with a basket or use a deep, heavy skillet or wok. (If you are using a wok, make sure it is balanced securely with a wok ring or overturned burner grid.) Turn the heat under the oil to high and heat it to 365°F. on a frying thermometer.

5. Have ready a large plate covered with paper toweling and a mesh skimmer. On a second plate, distribute the flour for dredging, and on another the bread crumbs. In a medium bowl, beat the eggs lightly.

6. Dredge the clams in the flour, shaking off all excess. Dip each clam quickly in the beaten egg, shake to drain all excess, and roll in the bread crumbs. Shake off excess and place on another plate.

7. When the oil is ready for frying, add the clams. Each clam should be "consumed" by the oil and rise immediately to the surface. If bubbling doesn't occur or if a clam sinks to the bottom of the fryer, stop and remove it. This means the oil's heat has been lowered by the clams. Fry this and other clams, if any, in a second batch, making sure the oil returns to 365°F. before proceeding. Fry the clams until golden, 1 to 1½ minutes.

8. Remove the clams using the basket or skimmer. Drain on the paper towel–covered plate. Make sure the clams do not overlap one another or they will become soggy.

9. Divide the clams among the toasted rolls and serve.

GRILLED SNAPPER SANDWICH WITH GUACAMOLE AND TOMATILLO SALSA

FOR 4

SALSA

2 tablespoons minced Vidalia
    onion or red onion

1 small red bell pepper, cored,
    seeded, and diced

6 tomatillos, husks removed,
    cut into small dice

1/4 cup loosely packed fresh
    cilantro (coriander) leaves

1 tablespoon fresh lime juice

2 scallions, green parts
    only, chopped

1 tablespoon olive oil

Red pepper flakes

Salt and freshly ground black
    pepper

GUACAMOLE

1 medium, very ripe avocado,
    peeled and pitted

1 small ripe tomato, cored,
    seeded, and diced

1 garlic clove, put through a
    garlic press

1 tablespoon olive oil

6 dashes of Tabasco Sauce

1 teaspoon fresh lime juice

Salt

At first glance it might seem that you could make a sandwich out of just about anything that goes with bread. Actually, a little more attention to ingredients is required. A good sandwich must be thought out—a fact I had to learn through trial and error.

Composing this sandwich, I first tried any number of mayonnaise-based accompaniments to delicate grilled snapper, but everything tasted too "soft." Finally, I paired the fish with a cumin-spiked guacamole and a piquant tomatillo and Vidalia onion salsa. I chose semolina bread for its wheaty goodness and its illusion of sweetness, a nice contrast to the nip of the spices. The result is a super sandwich, great for supper or a lunch with friends.

1. At least 12 hours in advance, make the salsa. Place the onion in a strainer and run it under hot water for 1 minute to remove its raw taste. Bring a medium saucepan of water to the boil and blanch the red bell pepper for 1 minute.

2. In a medium nonreactive bowl, combine the onion and red pepper with the tomatillos, cilantro, lime juice, scallions, and olive oil. Season with the red pepper flakes, salt, and pepper. Reserve in the refrigerator up to 3 days.

3. Make the guacamole. In a small nonreactive bowl, combine the ingredients and mash with a large fork until the guacamole has a medium-smooth texture.

4. Preheat a ridged iron grill pan for 3 minutes. Season the fish with the salt, pepper, and olive oil. Grill the fish until softly resilient, 2 to 2½ minutes per side.

5. To assemble the sandwich, place tomato slices on the bottom half of each baguette segment, then add the fish. Spoon on the guacamole and the salsa. Top with the remaining bread and serve.

Note: You can put a dollop of sour cream on top of the guacamole before serving the sandwich.

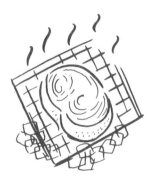

SANDWICH

1¼ pounds skinless snapper
   fillet, cut into 4 equal-size
   pieces
Salt and freshly ground black
   pepper
2 tablespoons olive oil
1 large beefsteak tomato, cored
   and sliced
1 semolina baguette, split
   lengthwise and cut into 4
   equal pieces

COOK'S OPTION

*Striped bass, or a 1¼-
pound fillet of mahi-mahi,
cut into 8 pieces, can
be used in place of the
snapper.*

REAL TUNA SALAD ON BLACK BREAD

FOR 4

SALAD

1 pound fresh tuna, poached and
 flaked

3½ tablespoons Homemade
 Mayonnaise (page 71), or
 best-quality store-bought

1 celery stalk, minced

12 Kalamata, Niçoise, or other
 brine-cured black olives,
 pitted and chopped

Pinch of red pepper flakes

Salt

8 slices black bread, about
 ½ inch thick

1 small red onion, sliced
 ¼ inch thick

COOK'S OPTION

*You can use leftover grilled
tuna for a deliciously
smoky filling.*

There's nothing like *real* tuna salad—salad made with freshly poached tuna combined with homemade mayonnaise (or the best mayonnaise you can buy) plus Kalamata, Niçoise, or other "tub" olives. Served with slices of red onion on black bread, this salad makes a sandwich that's very, very special.

Keep this sandwich in mind when you next poach tuna. Cook extra and the salad (which may also be plated) can be put together.

1. In a medium nonreactive bowl, combine the salad ingredients. If you are not going to use the salad immediately, store it in the refrigerator, where it will keep for 2 days.

2. To assemble the sandwich, spread one-fourth of the salad on each of 4 slices of bread. Add a layer of the sliced onion to each and cover with the remaining bread. Serve the sandwich with additional olives for nibbling.

BELGIAN MUSSEL TARTINES

FOR 4 AS A MAIN COURSE, 8 AS AN HORS D'OEUVRE

These grilled cheese and mussel sandwiches, which may also be served as hors d'oeuvres, are traditional Belgian fare. If you've ever had Coquilles St. Jacques, that luscious gratin of Gruyère and scallops, you know how good shellfish with melted cheese can be. Served with beer, as they are in Belgium, the tartines make a marvelous Sunday supper.

1. Preheat the broiler.

2. In a medium nonreactive pot, combine the mussels, wine, and bay leaf. Steam over high heat just until the mussels open, about 5 minutes.

3. Drain the mussels and cool to room temperature. Remove the meat from the shells and reserve. (The mussels may prepared a day in advance and refrigerated.)

4. Toast the bread lightly, 1 to 2 minutes per side. Distribute the mussels evenly on the toast and sprinkle with the cheese. Place the bread under the broiler 6 to 8 inches from the heat source and heat until cheese has just melted, about 3 minutes. Serve as is or cut each slice into 4 pieces on the diagonal.

1 pound mussels (preferably cultivated), cleaned and bearded

½ cup dry white wine

1 bay leaf

4 slices Kosher-style rye bread, sliced about 1½ inches thick

1¼ cups grated Gruyère cheese

COOK'S OPTION

Black bread can also be used with this recipe.

LOBSTER AND YOGURT SALAD IN A PITA POCKET

FOR 4

¾ pound cooked lobster meat (from a 1¾- to 2-pound lobster), cut into bite-size pieces

3 tablespoons low-fat yogurt

1 teaspoon fresh lime juice

⅓ teaspoon Tabasco Sauce

½ bunch watercress, washed, dried, and coarsely chopped

Salt

1 medium tomato, cored and diced

½ cup loosely packed alfalfa sprouts

4 pita pockets

Like everyone else, there are days I step on the scale and just wish I hadn't. What do I do when I want to keep the calories down *and* dine royally? Make myself happy with a dish like this one—a luxurious, low-calorie feast of fresh lobster with a light, creamy yogurt salad, served in a pita pocket.

These refreshing sandwiches, with their watercress, alfalfa sprout, and tomato filling, would make fabulous picnic fare or a great late supper for two. Though rich-sounding, they're really not extravagant at all—just one lobster serves four.

1. In a small nonreactive bowl, combine the lobster with the yogurt, lime juice, Tabasco, and watercress. Mix well. Season with the salt.

2. Slice the top one-fourth off each pita pocket. Stuff one-fourth of the salad into each pocket. Distribute the tomato and sprouts on top of the salad. Cover with the pita tops and serve.

Note: Try adding tobiko (Japanese flying fish roe) to the salad for great added flavor and texture.

SMOKED SALMON SANDWICH WITH SCALLION CREAM CHEESE ON THIN RYE TOAST

FOR 4

I've always enjoyed bagels with cream cheese and lox—surely one of the greatest of all sandwiches. This is my good-for-a-crowd version—thin toasted rye with smoked salmon, scallion cream cheese, and just enough Bermuda onion. Now the sandwich has delicacy as well as soul.

Make sure the bread is very thin, as thin as you can buy or slice it, and the cream cheese tip-top—avoid brands with fillers. Whip the cheese until it's really fluffy, spread it on the bread very lightly, and enjoy!

1. Toast the bread until golden. In the bowl of a food processor, combine the cream cheese, scallions, dill, capers, and Tabasco. Process until the cheese is fluffy, stopping the machine from time to time to scrape down the sides of the bowl, about 2 minutes.

2. Spread the cream cheese mixture on 4 slices of the bread. Top each with a slice of fish, distribute the onion, and cover with the remaining bread. Cut each sandwich as you wish (when divided in eighths they make great hors d'oeuvres) and serve.

8 slices very thin rye bread
$1/3$ pound best-quality cream cheese
$1/2$ bunch scallions, minced
1 tablespoon chopped fresh dill
1 tablespoon chopped capers
6 dashes of Tabasco Sauce
8 slices smoked salmon
4 thinly cut slices Bermuda onion

COOK'S OPTION

Smoked sturgeon works very well with this recipe.

SOFT-SHELL CRAB CLUB SANDWICH

FOR 4

1 medium red onion or Vidalia
onion, sliced

1/4 cup vegetable oil

1 tablespoon unsalted butter

8 small soft-shell crabs, cleaned

8 bacon slices, preferably
thick-cut

1/2 cup Homemade Mayonnaise
(page 71), or best-quality
store-bought

2 tablespoons chopped fresh
tarragon

12 slices loaf-type sourdough
bread, cut about 1/8 inch thick

3/4 cup loosely packed alfalfa
sprouts

1 medium tomato, cored and
cut into 8 slices

1 small head Boston or Bibb
lettuce, washed and separated
into leaves

With their hearty fillings and frill-topped toothpicks, club sandwiches make great eating and always seem a bit festive. For this version I've replaced the customary chicken with quickly sautéed soft-shell crabs, then added caramelized onion rings and crispy sprouts. A true club sandwhich uses two rather than three slices of bread, but you need the full bread complement here for chewiness and to sop up the good juices from the crabs.

Serve these with crispy, delicate Belgian Fries—the recipe follows. The frilly toothpicks are optional.

1. Preheat the broiler. Place the onion slices on a broiling sheet and brush with the oil. Broil the slices until lightly caramelized, 3 to 4 minutes. Reserve.

2. In a heavy, medium skillet, melt the butter over high heat. When the butter sizzles, add the crabs and sauté until just heated through, about 1 minute per side. Remove to a plate.

3. In the same skillet, sauté the bacon over high heat until crispy. Remove to paper toweling to drain.

4. Combine the mayonnaise and the tarragon. Toast the bread.

5. To make the sandwiches, place 4 slices of the bread on your work surface. Spread each with one-third of the herb mayonnaise. Distribute the sprouts evenly on top and add 2 slices of tomato. Top each sandwich with a second slice of bread. Spread the bread with more herb mayonnaise and cover each slice with 1 crab, lettuce, bacon, and grilled onion. Spread the remaining slices of bread with the last of the mayonnaise and complete each sandwich. Cut the sandwiches in quarters diagonally and secure them with toothpicks.

BELGIAN FRIES

FOR 4

Homemade fries can't be beat. Yet people shrink from preparing them, afraid of messiness and unpalatable results. Once you have your fryer and frying thermometer set up, however, there's nothing to achieving great fries if you fry the potatoes in the hot oil twice, as the Belgians do. The first frying cooks the potatoes, the second turns them crisp and golden. You can do the cooking part a day or two in advance, if you like; the final frying takes no more than 3 to 4 minutes.

Traditionally eaten from a paper cone or newspaper, these fries would be perfect with a mayonnaise made with one of the flavored oils (page 59). For drinking, serve lots of ice-cold beer.

2 large Idaho potatoes

1 quart vegetable oil, for frying

1 tablespoon red wine vinegar

1 teaspoon ground sea salt or kosher salt

1. Cut the potatoes into fingers about 2½ inches long by ¼ inch wide. Put them in a colander under cold running water and rinse for 3 to 5 minutes to remove all surface starch.

2. Slowly add the oil to a fryer with a basket, or use a deep, heavy skillet or wok. (If you are using a wok, make sure it is balanced securely with a wok ring or overturned burner grid.) Turn the heat under the oil to high and heat to 340°F. on a frying thermometer. Have ready 2 large plates, both covered with paper toweling, and a mesh skimmer.

3. Drain the potatoes and dry them thoroughly with paper toweling. Add them to the hot oil and fry until limp, about 3 minutes. Remove the potatoes using the skimmer and turn them out onto a plate. (This step may be done up to 2 days in advance. To hold the potatoes, place them on a nonstick baking sheet, or a regular sheet covered with waxed paper or plastic film, drape film over them, and refrigerate. You do not need to bring the potatoes to room temperature before finishing their cooking.)

4. Raise the oil temperature to 375°F. Cook the potatoes until they are golden and crisp, 3 to 4 minutes. Drain on the paper towel–covered plate. Sprinkle with the vinegar and salt, toss well, and serve.

GRILLED CRAB 'N' CHEDDAR ON WHITE

FOR 4

8 slices white sandwich bread

2 teaspoons Dijon mustard

1 pound jumbo lump crabmeat, shell or cartilage removed

2 scallions, minced

$\frac{1}{2}$ teaspoon coarsely ground black pepper

1 cup grated sharp cheddar cheese

2 tablespoons unsalted butter, softened

When Ann Cartwright, my chief tester, made this sandwich, she handed it to me with a grin on her face. "Amazing," was all she said. This is such a homey creation, I couldn't imagine what her excitement was about. Then I tried it and all *I* could say was—well, I couldn't say anything, I was too busy eating.

You shouldn't miss this simple mixture of cheddar, mustard, scallion, and crabmeat spread on the kind of white bread Mom used to buy, then grilled in butter. When the cheese has melted and the sandwich is golden, the dish is done. And the eating begins.

1. Place 4 slices of the bread on your work surface. Spread with the mustard and distribute the remaining ingredients except the butter evenly on top. Cover the sandwiches with the remaining bread. Spread the butter very thinly on both top and bottom of each sandwich.

2. Place a large nonstick skillet over medium-high heat. When the skillet is hot, add the sandwiches and cook until golden and the cheese is melted, 2 to 3 minutes per side. If the sandwiches seem to be browning too quickly, reduce the heat. Serve immediately, with cold beer and a crisp green salad.

ANNIE ROSNER'S WORLD-FAMOUS KOSHER DILL PICKLES

MAKES 8 TO 12 PICKLES

I'm exaggerating: my friend Annie Rosner's pickles are not world famous—yet. Annie passed this recipe on to her son who, at my insistence, gave it to me. I had to include it in this chapter.

Pickling may seem an elaborate procedure, but time and the refrigerator do most of the work. In short order you'll have the most marvelous sour dills, the kind you can get only in Old World delis. Annie's pickles are, of course, the natural accompaniment to a good sandwich and are particularly good with seafood sandwiches.

1. Place the garlic, bay leaves, dill, spices, and pepper, if using, at the bottom of a quart-size plastic or glass jar or container with a tight lid. Pack with as many cucumbers as will fit, leaving 2 inches of space at the top for expansion.

2. Bring the water to a boil and add the vinegar and salt. Pour this mixture directly over the cucumbers and let stand until the liquid has come to room temperature. Seal the container tightly and refrigerate for 5 to 7 days. Every other day, turn the jar upside down, then right side up, to make sure the brine is well distributed. After about a week the pickles will be ready to eat. They will continue to sour, however, refrigerated, though at a slower rate.

2 garlic cloves

5 bay leaves

1 dill sprig

1 teaspoon pickling spices

1 hot pepper (optional)

8 to 12 Kirby cucumbers

4 cups water

3 teaspoons Champagne or white wine vinegar

2$\frac{1}{2}$ tablespoons kosher salt

CORN-FRIED OYSTER PO' BOY

FOR 4

½ cup chopped ripe tomatoes

2 cups shredded green cabbage

1 cup Best Tartar Sauce
   (page 79)

½ small red onion, diced

½ quart vegetable oil,
   for frying

1½ cups yellow cornmeal

24 large oysters, shucked
   and drained

Salt

2 medium baguettes

COOK'S OPTION

*You can substitute 36
cherrystone clams for the
oysters.*

Whether you call them po' boys, hoagies, heroes, or grinders, these full-meal sandwiches can be really delicious—or not worth the time they take to assemble. Everything depends on the quality of their ingredients and the care with which they're combined.

I use only the best for this fried-oyster po' boy, which I learned when I cooked in a New Orleans seafood house. To make it, cornmeal-coated oysters are quickly fried, then combined with shredded cabbage, chopped tomato, and a lemony tartar sauce. Served on a chewy baguette, the result is the real thing—a stupendous sandwich meal.

1. In a medium bowl, combine the tomatoes, cabbage, tartar sauce, and onion. Toss well to blend.

2. Slowly add the oil to a fryer with a basket, or use a deep, heavy skillet or wok. (If you are using a wok, make sure it is balanced securely with a wok ring or overturned burner grid.) Turn the heat under the oil to high and heat it to 360°F. on a frying thermometer. Have ready a large plate covered with a layer of paper toweling for draining and a mesh skimmer.

3. Spread the cornmeal on a second large plate. Dredge the oysters in the cornmeal. When the oil is ready for frying, shake off excess cornmeal from the oysters and add them one by one to the oil. Do not overcrowd. Fry the oysters in 2 batches, if necessary. Fry oysters until golden, about 2 minutes.

4. Remove the oysters using the basket or skimmer. Drain them on the paper towel–covered plate. Make sure the oysters do not cover one another or they will become soggy. Salt them generously while still hot.

5. Slice each baguette horizontally, allowing bread to remain "hinged" on one long side. Open the bread like a book and remove half of the soft interior from each loaf. Lay 12 oysters end to end along the bottom of each baguette. Cover with half of the tartar sauce mixture and close the sandwich. Repeat with the remaining baguette and oysters. Cut each baguette in quarters and serve.

SMOKED SHRIMP AND AVOCADO SALAD FOCACCIA

FOR 4

This simple sandwich begins with a traditional focaccia and then just takes off. The focaccia is split and filled with smoked shrimp and avocado. The combination is great and the stuffed focaccia, with its topping uppermost, looks beautiful. I sometimes cut the sandwich into squares and serve it as an hors d'oeuvre.

You'll need to buy prepared individual focaccia, available at Italian bakeries and gourmet shops (or make your own). Choose focaccia with tomato, onion, or garlic toppings, or any combination thereof. Before assembling the sandwich, you can drizzle Basil Oil (page 60) on the focaccia and then toast it. This makes a good thing even better, but the sandwich is perfectly delicious without it.

1. Split the focaccia horizontally. In a medium nonreactive bowl, combine the remaining ingredients. Mix lightly to bind the ingredients.
2. Distribute the filling on the bottom half of each focaccia. Top with the remaining halves, cut into wedges or 2-inch squares, and serve.

Note: Smoked shrimp are available, usually canned, in seafood stores and supermarkets.

4 individual focaccia — tomato, onion, or garlic, or a combination

¾ pound any size smoked shrimp (see Note)

1 very ripe avocado, peeled, pitted, and cut into medium dice

1 medium tomato, cored, split, seeded, and cut into small dice

Juice of ½ lime

COOK'S OPTION

This recipe also works well with any size cooked unsmoked shrimp.

Appendixes

QUICK-REFERENCE RECIPE LISTINGS

QUICK TO DO\EASY TO DO

No-Fail Boiled Shrimp

Shallow-Poached Bluefish in Leek Broth with Mushrooms

Shallow-Poached Snapper with Baby Shrimp, Thyme, and Lime

Sizzle-Plate Steamed Mussels

Sizzle-Plate Poached Bay Scallops with Mushrooms

Shallow-Poached Sole Véronique

Broiled Scallop Gratin with Leeks and Crème Fraîche

Quick-Broiled Jumbo Shrimp in the Shell with Tarragon, Garlic, and Pernod

Open-Faced Brook Trout

Broiled Halibut with Caramelized Leeks

"All Crabmeat" Crab Cakes

Sautéed Soft-Shell Crabs with Pine Nuts and Scallion Butter

Stir-Fried Shrimp with Kumquats, Scallions, and Plum Wine

Grilled Bass with Fennel, Balsamic Vinegar, and Basil Oil

Grilled Pomano with Garlic and Rosemary Tomatoes

Grilled Mahi-Mahi with Mango and Black Bean Salsa

Farfalle with Creamy Oysters and Smoked Salmon

Scallop and Frisée Salad with Tomato Shallot Dressing

Ultimate Salad Niçoise

Sunday Night Fish Salad

Baby Shrimp Salad with Zesty Papaya-Mint Dressing

Poached Sole Sandwich with Watercress and Mom's Thousand Island Dressing

Real Tuna Salad on Black Bread

Belgian Mussel Tartines

Absolutely Simple Oyster Stew

Curried Mussel Soup

Chilled Tomato Soup with Basil and Crabmeat

Thai Broiled Scallops Wrapped in Bacon

Snapper with Celery Leaves in Foil Pouches

COOKING FOR ONE

No-Fail Boiled Shrimp

Creamy Hacked Braised Lobster

Whole Flounder Steamed with Soy, Ginger, and Scallions

Shallow-Poached Bluefish in Leek Broth with Mushrooms

Sizzle-Plate Steamed Mussels

Sizzle-Plate Poached Bay Scallops with Mushrooms

Best Broiled Lobster Ever

Broiled Scallop Gratin with Leeks and Crème Fraîche

Broiled Scallops on a Rosemary Skewer

Quick-Broiled Jumbo Shrimp in the Shell with Tarragon, Garlic, and Pernod

Mort's Port Broiled Snapper

Open-Faced Brook Trout

Broiled Salmon with Tomatoes, Basil, and Mint

Broiled Halibut with Caramelized Leeks

Sauce Lover's Scrod

Dad's Salmon Croquettes with Day-Old Spaghetti

"All Crabmeat" Crab Cakes

Sautéed Soft-Shell Crabs with Pine Nuts and Scallion Butter

Stir-Fried Shrimp with Kumquats, Scallions, and Plum Wine

Stir-Fried Squid with Scallions and Sliced Almonds

Stir-Fried Monkfish with Chili Paste and Ginger

Sesame-Grilled Baby Squid with Snow Peas

Herb-Grilled Mahi-Mahi

Grilled Marlin with Bacon and Endive

Grilled Bass with Fennel, Balsamic Vinegar, and Basil Oil

Seared Swordfish with Coriander and Beet Juice Oil

Grilled Pompano with Garlic and Rosemary Tomatoes

Salmon and Scallop Brochettes on Rosemary Branches

Penne with Scallops, Broccoli Rabe, and Roasted Red Pepper

Linguine with Clam Sauce

Farfalle with Creamy Oysters and Smoked Salmon

Japanese "Oishii" Noodles

Spicy Buckwheat Noodles with Shrimp

Angel Hair Pasta with Bay Scallops, Wild Mushrooms, and Sun-Dried Tomatoes

Scallop and Frisée Salad with Tomato Shallot Dressing

Squid with Basil, Mint, and Buckwheat Noodles

Baby Shrimp Salad with Zesty Papaya-Mint Dressing

Poached Sole Sandwich with Watercress and Mom's Thousand Island Dressing

Grilled Snapper Sandwich with Guacamole and Tomatillo Salsa

Real Tuna Salad on Black Bread

Lobster and Yogurt Salad in a Pita Pocket

Smoked Salmon Sandwich with Scallion Cream Cheese on Thin Rye Toast

Belgian Mussel Tartines

Grilled Crab 'n' Cheddar on White

Smoked Shrimp and Avocado Salad Focaccia

Absolutely Simple Oyster Stew

Scallop Vegetable Soup with Shiitake Mushrooms

Cucumber Yogurt Soup with Lobster

Chilled Tomato Soup with Basil and Crabmeat

Thai Broiled Scallops Wrapped in Bacon

Snapper with Celery Leaves in Foil Pouches

New Classic Pompano en Papillote

Children Will Enjoy . . .

Shallow-Poached Snapper with Baby Shrimp, Thyme, and Lime

Sizzle-Plate Steamed Mussels

Best Broiled Lobster Ever

Mort's Port Broiled Snapper

Dad's Salmon Croquettes with Day-Old Sapghetti

"All Crabmeat" Crab Cakes

Popcorn Shrimp

Conch Fritters with Zesty Pineapple Salsa

Tempura

Rock-Seared Chinese Barbecue Scallops

Buried Coal-Cooked Lobsters in the Shell

Barbecued Shrimp on Sugarcane Skewers with Ginger-Lime Sauce

Seared Tuna Loin with Chive Butter Sauce

Risotto with Lobster and Shrimp

Chinese Ravioli

Fat Tuesday Catfish with Dirty Rice

Lobster Fried Rice

Poached Sole Sandwich with Watercress and Mom's Thousand Island Dressing

Grilled Crab 'n' Cheddar on White

Clam Rolls on Toasted Garlic Buns

Crab and Corn Soup with Red Pepper Cornbread

Fisherman's Chowder

Crab and Avocado Roll

Oshi Sushi

Crispy Fried Blackfish in a Plantain Crust

Low-Calorie/Low-Fat

No-Fail Boiled Shrimp

Whole Flounder Steamed with Soy Sauce, Ginger, and Scallions

Shallow-Poached Snapper with Baby Shrimp, Thyme, and Lime

Shallow-Poached Tilefish with Port, Onions, and Carrots

Poached Whole Bass with New Potatoes and Spring Vegetables

Poached Joint of Cod

Sizzle-Plate Steamed Mussels

Roasted Monkfish with Balsamic Vinegar and Shallots

Best Broiled Lobster Ever

Broiled Scallops on a Rosemary Skewer

Open-Faced Brook Trout

Broiled Salmon with Tomatoes, Basil, and Mint

Grandma Minnie's Gefilte Fish

Stir-Fried Shrimp with Kumquats, Scallions, and Plum Wine

Stir-Fried Monkfish with Chili Paste and Ginger

Sesame-Grilled Baby Squid with Snow Peas

Herb-Grilled Mahi-Mahi

Grilled Red Snapper with Shallots and Cassis
    Marmalade

Rock-Seared Chinese Barbecue Scallops

Seared Swordfish with Burgundy

Grilled Bass with Fennel, Balsamic Vinegar,
    and Basil Oil

Seared Swordfish with Coriander and
    Beet Juice Oil

Buried Coal-Cooked Lobsters in the Shell

Grilled Pompano with Garlic and
    Rosemary Tomatoes

Grilled Mahi-Mahi with Mango and
    Black Bean Salsa

Salmon and Scallop Brochettes on
    Rosemary Branches

Penne with Scallops, Broccoli Rabe, and
    Roasted Red Pepper

Spicy Shrimp with Lime and Soba Noodles

Chinese Ravioli

All-Seafood Paella

Japanese "Oishii" Noodles

Spicy Buckwheat Noodles with Shrimp

Angel Hair Pasta with Bay Scallops, Wild Mushrooms,
    and Sun-Dried Tomatoes

Crabmeat Salad with Pickled Fennel and Carrots

Oriental Shrimp and Cabbage Salad

Scallop and Frisée Salad with Tomato
    Shallot Dressing

Ultimate Salad Niçoise

Monkfish Salad with Roasted Red and
    Yellow Peppers

Moroccan Lobster Salad

Squid with Basil, Mint, and Buckwheat Noodles

Baby Shrimp Salad with Zesty
    Papaya-Mint Dressing

Squid Salad with Jicama and Orange Vinaigrette

Lobster and Yogurt Salad in a Pita Pocket

Seared Salmon Sandwich on Sourdough Bread with
    Charmoula and Zucchini

Miso Soup with Shrimp

Scallop Vegetable Soup with Shiitake Mushrooms

Matelote of Monkfish

Caribbean Bouillabaisse with Long Croûtes

Spicy Conch Chowder with Okra, Chayote,
    and Tomatoes

Pumpkin Soup with Bay Scallops and Mushrooms

Fisherman's Chowder

Chilled Tomato Soup with Basil and Crabmeat

Nigiri Sushi

Seared Spanish Mackerel Nigiri

Cured Salmon-Belly Nigiri

Maki Sushi

Spicy Tuna Roll

Crab and Avacado Roll

Oshi Sushi

Battera Sushi

Vegetable Roll with Cucumber, Daikon, and Pickled
   Plum Mayonnaise

Steamed Sea Bass in Bok Choy with Carrot
   Ginger Sauce

Salmon Steamed in Konbu

Snapper with Celery Leaves in Foil Pouches

New Classic Pompano en Papillote

ONE-POT DISHES

No-Fail Boiled Shrimp

Whole Flounder Steamed with Soy Sauce,
   Ginger, and Scallions

Creamy Hacked Braised Lobster

Shallow-Poached Bluefish in Leek Broth
   in Mushrooms

Shallow-Poached Snapper with Baby Shrimp, Thyme,
   and Lime

Shallow-Poached Tilefish with Port, Onions,
   and Carrots

Sizzle-Plate Steamed Mussels

Sizzle-Plate Poached Bay Scallops with Mushrooms

Shallow-Poached Sole Véronique

Broiled Scallop Gratin with Leeks and
   Crème Fraîche

Stir-Fried Shrimp with Kumquats, Scallions,
   and Plum Wine

Stir-Fried Squid with Scallions and
   Sliced Almonds

Stir-Fried Monkfish with Chili Paste and Ginger

All-Seafood Paella

Absolutely Simple Oyster Stew

Miso Soup with Shrimp

Scallop Vegetable Soup with Shiitake Mushrooms

Matelote of Monkfish

Spicy Conch Chowder with Okra, Chayote,
   and Tomatoes

Pot au Feu du Pecheur

Cucumber Yogurt Soup with Lobster

Fisherman's Chowder

Chilled Tomato Soup with Basil and Crabmeat

Snapper with Celery Leaves in Foil Pouches

New Classic Pompano en Papillote

BEST FOR USING LEFTOVERS

Dad's Salmon Croquettes with Day-Old Spaghetti

Big Danny's Thai Fish Cakes

Golden Tuna Cornmeal Dumplings

Sunday Supper Fish Cakes with Horseradish Cream

Tempura

Risotto with Lobster and Shrimp

Ultimate Salad Niçoise

Sunday Night Fish Salad

Poached Sole Sandwich with Watercress and Mom's
   Thousand Island Dressing

Real Tuna Salad on Black Bread

Smoked Salmon Sandwich with Scallion Cream Cheese
   on Thin Rye Toast

Grilled Crab 'n' Cheddar on White

ESPECIALLY GOOD FOR ENTERTAINING

Whole Flounder Steamed with Soy Sauce, Ginger, and
Scallions

Poached Whole Bass with New Potatoes and
Spring Vegetables

Best Broiled Lobster Ever

Roasted Oysters Buried in Seaweed with Allspice

Roasted Whole Grouper with Garlic,
Potatoes, and Bacon

Broiled Scallops on a Rosemary Skewer

Quick-Broiled Jumbo Shrimp in the Shell with Tarragon,
Garlic, and Pernod

Big Danny's Thai Fish Cakes

"All Crabmeat" Crab Cakes

Grandma Minni's Gefilte Fish

Sautéed Soft-Shell Crabs with Pine Nuts
and Scallion Butter

Fried Whitebait with Pastis Aïoli

Popcorn Shrimp

Whole Crispy Porgy with Carrot "Pommes Paille"

Tempura

Rock-Seared Chinese Barbecue Scallops

Grilled Marlin with Bacon and Endive

Buried Coal-Cooked Lobsters in the Shell

Barbecued Shrimp on Sugarcane Skewers with Ginger-
Lime Sauce

Salmon and Scallop Brochettes on
Rosemary Branches

Seared Tuna Loin with Chive Butter Sauce

All-Seafood Paella

Fat Tuesday Catfish with Dirty Rice

Lobster Fried Rice

Lobster and Caviar Salad

Ultimate Salad Niçoise

Grilled Snapper Sandwich with Guacamole and
Tomatillo Salsa

Lobster and Yogurt Salad in a Pita Pocket

Soft-Shell Crab Club Sandwich

Smoked Salmon Sandwich with Scallion Cream Cheese
on Thin Rye Toast

Belgian Mussel Tartines

Grilled Crab 'n' Cheddar on White

Crab and Corn Soup with Red Pepper Cornbread

Curried Mussel Soup

Miso Soup with Shrimp

Scallop Vegetable Soup with Shiitake Mushrooms

Caribbean Bouillabaisse with Long Croûtes

Spicy Conch Chowder with Okra, Chayote,
and Tomatoes

Lobster Bisque

Best Cajun Gumbo

Pot au Feu du Pecheur

Pumpkin Soup with Bay Scallops and Mushrooms

Fisherman's Chowder

Chilled Tomato Soup with Basil and Crabmeat

Nigiri Sushi

Seared Spanish Mackerel Nigiri

Cured Salmon-Belly Nigiri

Maki Sushi

Spicy Tuna Roll

Crab and Avocado Roll

Vegetable Roll with Spinach, Sweet Potato, and Red Pepper

Vegetable Roll with Scallions, Pickled Squash, and Sesame Seeds

Oshi Sushi

Battera Sushi

Vegetable Roll with Cucumber, Daikon, and Pickled Plum Mayonnaise

Escargots in a Phyllo Purse

Cold Lobster Spring Rolls with Crushed Peanuts

Crispy Fried Blackfish in a Plantain Crust

Snapper with Celery Leaves in Foil Pouches

Scallops in Banana Leaves with Vanilla

Seafood Tamale in Banana Leaves

NONFISH-LOVERS WILL ENJOY . . .

No-Fail Boiled Shrimp

Whole Flounder Steamed with Soy Sauce, Ginger, and Scallions

Shallow-Poached Snapper with Baby Shrimp, Thyme, and Lime

Poached Joint of Cod

Shallow-Poached Sole Véronique

Lobster with Vanilla Sauce

Mort's Port Broiled Snapper

Sauce Lover's Scrod

Dad's Salmon Croquettes with Day-Old Spaghetti

Big Danny's Thai Fish Cakes

Golden Tuna Cornmeal Dumplings

"All Crabmeat" Crab Cakes

Sautéed Cod with Sake and Chinese Black Bean Sauce

Stir-Fried Shrimp with Kumquats, Scallions, and Plum Wine

Popcorn Shrimp

Stir-Fried Monkfish with Chili Paste and Ginger

Snapper with Hazelnut Crust and Marjoram Sauce

Conch Fritters with Zesty Pineapple SalsaGrouper Beignets with Beet Chips

Tempura

Herb-Grilled Mahi-Mahi

Rock-Seared Chinese Barbecue Scallops

Seared Swordfish with Burgundy

Buried Coal-Cooked Lobsters in the Shell

Barbecued Shrimp on Sugarcane Skewers with Ginger-Lime Sauce

Seared Tuna Loin with Chive Butter Sauce

Penne with Scallops, Broccoli Rabe,
  and Red Pepper

Spicy Shrimp with Lime and Soba Noodles

Risotto with Lobster and Shrimp

Linguine with Clam Sauce

Chinese Ravioli

Japanese "Oishii" Noodles

Spicy Buckwheat Noodles with Shrimp

Fat Tuesday Catfish with Dirty Rice

Angel Hair Pasta with Bay Scallops, Wild Mushrooms,
  and Sun-Dried Tomatoes

Lobster Fried Rice

Scallop and Frisée Salad with Tomato Shallot Dressing

Moroccan Lobster Salad

Poached Sole Sandwich with Watercress and Mom's
  Thousand Island Dressing

Seared Salmon Sandwich on Sourdough Bread with
  Charmoula and Zucchini

Belgian Mussel Tartines

Grilled Crab 'n' Cheddar on White

Clam Rolls on Toasted Garlic Buns

Corn-Fried Oyster Po' Boy

Crab and Corn Soup with Red Pepper Cornbread

Miso Soup with Shrimp

Spicy Conch Chowder with Okra, Chayote,
  and Tomatoes

Lobster Bisque

Best Cajun Gumbo

Cucumber Yogurt Soup with Lobster

Pumpkin Soup with Bay Scallops and Mushrooms

Spicy Tuna Roll

Crab and Avocado Roll

Vegetable Roll with Spinach, Sweet Potato,
  and Red Pepper

Vegetable Roll with Scallions, Pickled Squash,
  and Sesame Seeds

Vegetable Roll with Cucumber, Daikon, and
  Pickled Plum Mayonnaise

Cold Lobster Spring Rolls with Crushed Peanuts

Crispy Fried Blackfish in a Plantain Crust

Shrimp Sautéed in Leek Wrappers

Seafood Tamale in Banana Leaves

"NEW" SEAFOOD TO TRY

Nothing is worse than finding a seafood recipe that really excites you, then discovering that the fish or shellfish called for isn't available where you live. So in planning this book, I made sure to offer recipes for only the most readily obtainable seafood.

Still, there are many delicious "new" fish and shellfish you should ltry. Here is a selection of recently rediscovered varieties that have begun to receive mass-market attention. Take note of their leanness/fattiness ratio, as well as their firmness and flavor, so you can make wise substitutions for the seafood called for in this book.

Tilapia. A versatile freshwater fish that is bred throughout the world and domestically in such southern states as Arizona, Texas, and Florida. Tilapia have lovely mottled black and white or pink skin, which should be featured when prepared, and weigh about 3 pounds in the market. Their flesh is quite firm, lean, and mild. Tilapia are particularly good when sautéed or broiled.

Corvina. A member of the weakfish genus (so-named because of their delicate mouth structure), corvina, or corbina, are greatly esteemed in Central and South America. Fish for our consumption come from the waters of California down to Chile and are available weighing 1 to 6 pounds. Corvina have firm, relatively fatty flesh and a pleasingly pronounced flavor. They are best seared, grilled, or sautéed.

Red Drum. Also known as channel bass or redfish (and made prominent due to Chef Paul Prudhomme's blackened redfish), red drum occur along the southern Atlantic Coast and in the Gulf of Mexico. Four to 6 pounds are the prime size of this fish named for drumlike noise it emits—the sound of its gas bladder contracting. The fish has lean, firm, and relatively mild flesh that is delicious when sautéed, grilled, or broiled.

Redfish. Not to be confused with the red drum also called redfish (see above), these members of the rockfish family are better known as ocean perch. They are caught off our northeastern coast and in Canada. The average market weight of these fish is three pounds, and their flesh is lean, flaky, and mild. The fillets are best sautéed.

Stone Bass. Sometimes called wreckerfish because of their alleged propensity to nibble on the flotsam and jetsam of lost seacraft, stone bass are taken from the waters of our northeast coast. An average fish weighs twelve pounds. Stone bass are lean and mild and delicious to eat when grilled or sautéed.

Sturgeon. Best known as the source for the world's finest caviar and widely enjoyed when smoked, this large fish (40 to 50 pounds is average, but some fish grow to 350 pounds) is excellent cooked. Sturgeon are fished from fresh and saltwaters from the St. Lawrence River to South Carolina and into the Gulf of Mexico, and from Alaska to central California. They have relatively mild, firm flesh that is fatty in lake species, lean in ocean varieties. Though generally scarce, the fish are farmed in California. Their fillets are delicious sautéed or grilled.

Rock Shrimp. Formerly discarded, these hard-shelled brownish shrimp with red or purple appendages are now regularly available. This turnabout is due to the invention of a peeling device that handles the shrimps' tough coat. Rock shrimp come from Florida and Mexican waters and have lean, mild, lobsterlike flesh that is best when sautéed or simply broiled.

The Chart—A Guide to the Seafood Discussed in This Book

	SPECIES INCLUDE	WEIGHT/SIZE	MOST AVAILABLE FORM(S)	FAVORITE COOKING METHODS	PREFERRED DONENESS	FLAVOR 1-3 1=MILD
BLACKFISH a.k.a. tautog, black trout, Chinese steelhead	-----	3–4 lbs. avg., up to 25 lbs.	Whole, fillets	Sauté, steam	Cooked 95% through	1
BLUEFISH a.k.a. bulldog of the ocean	-----	3–6 lbs. avg., up to 27 lbs.	Whole, fillets	Sauté, bake, broil	Cooked 80–85% through	Small-fish: 1 Large fish: 3
CATFISH	Bullhead, channel catfish, white catfish	2–3 lbs. avg., up to 40 lbs.	Fillets	Fry, sauté, broil	Cooked 100% through	1
CLAMS	Quahogs (hard-shell) a.k.a. cherrystones, little-necks (P{acific), littlenecks (Atlantic); soft-shell a.k.a. steamers; razor, manila, geoduck, cockle	1–6 inches avg., up to 18 inches	Fresh live, shucked, shucked frozen	Raw, steam, roast, bake	Raw or cooked 65% through	2
COD a.k.a. bacalao (salt cod), black cod (actually sablefish), blue cod (actually cabezon)	Atlantic cod, Arctic cod, burbot, haddock, Pacific cod, pollack (a.k.a. green cod), red hake, walleye pollock (a.k.a. Alaskan pollack), white hake	3½– 10 lbs. avg., up to 100 lbs.	Whole, steaks, fillets	Poach, roast, steam, sauté	Cooked 95% through	1

LEANNESS 1-3 1=LEAN	FLESH COLOR AND TEXTURE RAW	TEXTURE WHEN COOKED	KEEPING PROFILE	HEALTH ISSUES	SUBSTITUTIONS, IF ANY	COMMENTS
1	Opaque; very firm	Tight flakes	2–3 days whole, 2 days for fillets	-----	Bass, snapper	Mild but tasty; not for sushi or sashimi
Small fish:1 Large fish: 2	Gray or blue; soft	Long loose flakes	1–2 days whole and fillets	Smaller less likely to carry parasites	Mackerel, rainbow runner	Rich; smaller fish most flavorful; not for sushi or sashimi
1	Pale white; firm	Firm	3–5 days	Farm-raised are safest	-----	Fine, firm flesh; prefer cultivated for their cleaner taste; not for sushi or sashimi
2	Pink/ white; resilient	Firm, chewy	Live: 2–3 days, shucked: 4–5 days	To avoid risk, must be alive and closed when bought; smell before eating	-----	Littleneck and cherry-stone preferred for their higher meat to shell ratio
1	Opaque; firm	Large flakes	2 days whole and fillets	Sometime parasite carrier	Haddock, hake	Deliciously sweet flesh; low in fat; cheeks and tongues are excellent; not for sushi or sashimi

	SPECIES INCLUDE	WEIGHT/SIZE	MOST AVAILABLE FORM(S)	FAVORITE COOKING METHODS	PREFERRED DONENESS	FLAVOR 1–3 1=MILD
CONCH, WHELKS	Conch: helmuts, queen conch, samba; whelks: waved whelk, knobbed whelk	Flesh from each 2–7 inches	Partly cooked frozen	Raw (soups, chowders), fry (fritters)	Raw or cooked 100% through	1
BLUE CRAB Hard- and soft-shell	-----	Hardshells: 6–10 ounces; soft-shells: 3–4 ounces	Live whole, lump meat	Hard-shell whole: boil; soft-shell: sauté, fry	Cooked 100% through	2
ESCARGOTS (snails)	Petits gris, vine-yard snail	1–2 inches	Canned, live	Boil, bake, broil	Cooked 100% through	2
FLOUNDER (also sold by species name) all halibut are flounder, see entry below)	American plaice (a.k.a. dab, sea dab), Arrowtooth flounder, plaice, starry flounder, summer flounder (a.k.a. fluke), turbot, window-pane, winter flounder (all flatfish from U.S. waters sold as sole are flounder	3 lbs. avg., up to 700 lbs. (Atlantic halibut)	Whole, fillets	Sauté, broil, fry	Cooked 85% through	1
GROUPER (also sold by species name; all are members of the sea bass family)	Black grouper, broomtail grouper, comb grouper, gag, Jewfish (a.k.a. giant sea bass), Nassau grouper, red grouper, scamp, warsaw grouper, yellow-mouth grouper	5–35 lbs. avg., up to 700 lbs.	Whole, steaks, fillets	Sauté, grill	Cooked 85% through	2

LEANNESS 1-3 1=LEAN	FLESH COLOR AND TEXTURE RAW	TEXTURE WHEN COOKED	KEEPING PROFILE	HEALTH ISSUES	SUBSTITUTIONS, IF ANY	COMMENTS
1	Grayish white; firm but pliable	Chewy	2 days fresh, 3 months frozen	Buy frozen raw or cooked to ensure wholesomeness	-----	Intriguing smoky-sweet flesh; conch preferable to whelk for raw preparations like ceviche
1	Opaque; firm but pliable	Delicate lumps	Live: 1–2 days, cooked meat: 1–2 days	Buy alive or cooked	Dungeness crabmeat will work	Exceptional tender flesh; jumbo lump best—contains less shell
2	Dark brown; rubbery	Very chewy	Live: 1 day, in opened can: 1 week	Safest to buy in cans	-----	Land mollusk; domestically farmed very successfully; canned quite good
1	Opaque; firm	Soft, flaky	2–3 days whole, 2 days for fillets	-----	Lemon sole, fluke, et al.	Cooks beautifully on the bone; very versatile
1	White; very firm	Firm	2 days whole, 2–3 days for fillets	Fish from deepest waters most desirable	Tilefish	Excellent flesh, low fat; enjoy the cheeks; good for sushi or sashimi

	SPECIES INCLUDE	WEIGHT/SIZE	MOST AVAILABLE FORM(S)	FAVORITE COOKING METHODS	PREFERRED DONENESS	FLAVOR 1-3 1=MILD
HALIBUT	Atlantic, California, Greenland, Pacific halibut	2–10 lbs. avg., up to 700 lbs.	Whole, steaks, fillets	Poach, sauté, braise	Cooked 90% through	1
LOBSTER a.k.a. American lobster, Maine lobster	Northern lobster	Chicken: 1 lb., eighths: $\frac{1}{8}$–$1\frac{1}{4}$ lbs., quarters: $1\frac{1}{4}$–$1\frac{1}{2}$ lbs., large: $1\frac{1}{2}$–2 lbs., jumbo: over 2 lbs.	Live whole, frozen tails, cooked meat	Grill, steam, roast	Cooked 85% through	1
MAHI-MAHI a.k.a. dolphin-fish, dorado	-----	10 lbs. avg., up to 20 lbs.	Steaks, fillets	Grill, sear, broil	Cooked 80% through	2
MARLIN	Blue marlin, striped marlin	175–300 lbs. avg., up to 1 ton	Steaks, loins	Grill	Cooked 70% through	1
MONKFISH a.k.a. Anglerfish, bellyfish, goosefish, lotte, sea devil		9 lbs. (headless) avg., up to 20 lbs.	Cleaned, boneless tail meat	Roast, stir-fry	Cooked 85% through	1

LEANNESS 1-3 1=LEAN	FLESH COLOR AND TEXTURE RAW	TEXTURE WHEN COOKED	KEEPING PROFILE	HEALTH ISSUES	SUBSTITUTIONS, IF ANY	COMMENTS
1	White, greenish tint; semi-firm	Soft, flakable	2 days whole, 2–4 days for fillets	-----	Turbot, flounder, fluke	Flesh texture makes it good for brochettes; also good for sushi or sashimi
2	Opaque; firm but pliable	Firm to the bite but not rubbery	2 days alive, 2 days for cooked shelled meat	To avoid risk, must be bought alive and cooked as soon as possible or buy cooked	Spiny lobster	Always buy alive; choose females for their coral; when buying unshelled cooked lobster, be sure tail is curled, an indication that the lobster was alive when cooked
2	Beige; firm	Flaky but remains intact	2 days whole	-----	Dorado	Meat cooks quickly; may be used for sushi or sashimi
1	Whitish with pink tint; resilient	Almost firm	2–3 days	Can carry parasites	Swordfish	Lean flesh benefits from marinating; striped marlin is the best imported variety
1	White; quite firm	Soft	1–2 days	Spoils quickly— buy it fresh and use it quickly	-----	Notoriously ugly (the head is removed before marketing), insatiable scavenger with excellent flesh, newly popular in U.S.; lobsterlike texture; does not flake easily so good for stews; smaller fish most desirable; not good for sushi or sashimi

	SPECIES INCLUDE	WEIGHT/SIZE	MOST AVAILABLE FORM(S)	FAVORITE COOKING METHODS	PREFERRED DONENESS	FLAVOR 1-3 1=MILD
MUSSELS	Blueshell mussels Green lipped (a.k.a. New Zealand mussels)	1½–6 inches in length	Whole live, cleaned, cooked	Steamed	Cooked 95% through	2
OCTOPUS **a.k.a.** devil-fish, tako, pulpo	-----	3½ lbs. avg. up to 16 feet in length	Whole cooked, frozen	Sliced for salads	Cooked 100% through	1
OYSTERS	Atlantic, Olympia, Pacific oyster(s)	1½–4 inches wide avg., up to 18 inches	Live or shucked	Raw, roast	Cooked 65% through	2
PERIWINKLES **a.k.a.** sea snails, winkles	-----	1 inch	Live	Boil	Cooked 100% through	2

LEANNESS 1-3 1=LEAN	FLESH COLOR AND TEXTURE RAW	TEXTURE WHEN COOKED	KEEPING PROFILE	HEALTH ISSUES	SUBSTITUTIONS, IF ANY	COMMENTS
2	Creamy orange; slippery	Chewy but tender	2 days alive, 2–3 days cooked	To avoid risk, must be alive and closed when bought; mussels that do not open when cooked should be discarded	-----	Blue shells from Prince Edward Island superior; cultivated mussels have excellent meat to shell ratio and require less cleaning
1	White with violet (domestic) or red and orange membrane (Japanese); slippery	Firm and pleasantly chewy	3–4 days cooked fresh, 6 days frozen	If concerned about risk, buy cooked or frozen	-----	Precooked may be used as is for sushi and sashimi; Japanese variety called tako best available
2	Grayish; slippery	Soft	2–3 days alive; 2–3 days shucked stored in their liquor	To avoid risk, must be alive (shells are tightly closed) when bought; order them in reputable restaurants only; sniff before eating	-----	Though everyone has favorites, Atlantic and Pacific oysters equally excellent; West Coast waters on the whole purer, however; many fine oysters commercially grown; do not overlook Chilean oysters, if available
2	Brownish or grayish black; resilient	Chewy	2–3 days raw, 3–4 days cooked	To assure freshness, should smell briny when buying	-----	Good in soups and salads or as tasty garnish for other dishes

	SPECIES INCLUDE	WEIGHT/SIZE	MOST AVAILABLE FORM(S)	FAVORITE COOKING METHODS	PREFERRED DONENESS	FLAVOR 1-3 1=MILD
PIKE **a.k.a.** Chain pickerel (yellow pike and blue pike actually walleye)	Muskellunge, pickerel	Pike: 4–10 lbs., muskellunge: 10–30 lbs., pickerel: 2–3 lbs.	Whole, fillet	Quenelles, gefilte fish	Cooked 100% through	1
POMPANO (permit called pompano erroneously)		2½ lbs. avg., up to 5 lbs.	Fillets, whole	Grill, sauté, sear	Cooked 85% through	2
PORGY **a.k.a.** sea bream (also sold by species name)	Grass porgy, jolt-head porgy, Northern porgy (a.k.a. scup), Pacific porgy, pluma, red porgy, roundspot, saucereye porgy, sheepshead, whitebone porgy	½–3 lbs. avg., up to 20 lbs.	Whole, fillets	Fry, sauté	Cooked 85% through	1
RED SNAPPER	One member of the snapper family that includes cubera snapper, gray snapper, lane snapper, mutton snapper, yellow-tail snapper	2 to 8 lbs. avg., up to 35 lbs.	Whole, fillets	Grill, broil	Cooked 85% through	1
SALMON	Atlantic coho (a.k.a. silver), chum, chinook (a.k.a. king), pink, sockeye salmon	10–12 lbs. avg., up to 20 lbs.	Steaks, whole, fillets	Grill, broil, poach	Cooked 80% through	2

LEANNESS 1-3 1=LEAN	FLESH COLOR AND TEXTURE RAW	TEXTURE WHEN COOKED	KEEPING PROFILE	HEALTH ISSUES	SUBSTITUTIONS, IF ANY	COMMENTS
1	White, firm	Flaky, soft	2–3 days whole or fillets	-----	Whiting	Perhaps because of boniness, pike has been traditionally used ground to make quenelles or gefilte fish; not for sushi
2	Beige; very firm	Firm	2 days whole or fillets	-----	Permit	Gorgeous yellow- and blue-tinged silver fish with lovely sweet flesh; few scales; not for sushi or sashimi
1	White; very firm	Soft, flaky	2–3 days whole or fillets	-----	Brill	Economical; flavorful flesh; not for sushi or sashimi
1	White, semi-firm	Long flakes	2 days whole or fillets	-----	Tilefish, bass	Wonderful flesh; many pretenders: look for bright red skin without yellow striping, intact gills; look-alikes not as good
2	Orange, firm	Flakable	2–4 days whole, fillets or steaks	Can carry parasites; farm-raised fish are safest	Various salmon varieties for one another	Rich, buttery flesh delicious smoked or cured; belly strips good cured and are economical; not for sushi or sashimi

	SPECIES INCLUDE	WEIGHT/SIZE	MOST AVAILABLE FORM(S)	FAVORITE COOKING METHODS	PREFERRED DONENESS	FLAVOR 1-3 1=MILD
SCALLOPS	Bay, calico, sea scallops	Bay: ½–¾ inches, 100 per lb.; sea: 1½–2 inches, 20 to 30 per lb.	Shucked	Bay: bake in gratin, stir-fry; sea: grill	Cooked 75% through	1
SCROD a.k.a. young cod, schrod	-----	3 lbs. or less	Fillets	Broil	Cooked 90% through	1
SEA BASS	Black sea bass, Chilean sea bass, rock bass, striped bass (see below), white sea bass (includes all groupers)	1–3 lbs. avg., up to 5 lbs.	Whole, fillets	Grill, sauté	Cooked 80% through	1
SEA BREAM (see porgy)						
SHAD ROE	-----	4–6 ounces per pair	Fresh pairs: regular: 2–4 ounces, medium: 4–5 ounces, large: over 6 ounces	Sauté	Cooked 90% through	2

LEANNESS 1-3 1=LEAN	FLESH COLOR AND TEXTURE RAW	TEXTURE WHEN COOKED	KEEPING PROFILE	HEALTH ISSUES	SUBSTITUTIONS, IF ANY	COMMENTS
1	Pale beige to creamy pink; resilient	Firm, yielding to the bite	1–2 days raw	-----	-----	New Bedford sea scallops are my preference; the rare Pacific or weather-vane scallop (similar to the sea scallop) has a short season in the Northwest; frozen scallops do well if properly handled
1	Opaque, slightly firm	Very soft, flaky	2 days for fillets	Sometime parasite carrier	Cod, haddock, hake	Sometimes mistaken for non-cod species; scrod is a young cod weighing less than 3 lbs.; not for sushi or sashimi
1	White; firm	Flakable	2–3 days whole, 2 days for fillets	-----	Grouper, black cod	Beautiful fish with excellent lean flesh; try to serve whole
3	Liver-colored; soft	Firm exterior, soft within	1–2 days	Must be very fresh	-----	Choose medium-size pairs; best cooked medium rare; wash well; to avoid spattering, make sure egg sacs are not torn

	SPECIES INCLUDE	WEIGHT/SIZE	MOST AVAILABLE FORM(S)	FAVORITE COOKING METHODS	PREFERRED DONENESS	FLAVOR 1-3 1=MILD
SHRIMP **a.k.a.** Prawns (for very large shrimp though incorrect when referring to any saltwater species; Dublin Bay prawns not shrimp but miniature lobsters), scampi ("shrimp scampi" restaurant redundancy)	Brown, blue prawn, Northern, pink, rock, spot, white shrimp	Per pound: colossal: 8–10; jumbo: 11–15; extra-large: 16–20; large: 21–30; medium: 31–35 small: 36–45 titi: 400	Head-off frozen or defrosted, raw or cooked, unshelled or peeled; IQF (instant quick frozen)	Broil, sauté, fry, stir-fry	Cooked 90% through	1
SOLE	Commercially available true sole is Dover or channel sole (not to be confused with lemon or gray sole or other flatfish commonly called sole)	14–18 ounces avg., up to 3 lbs.	Fillets	Sauté, grill	Cooked 90% through	1
SPANISH MACKEREL **a.k.a.** rock lobster, crawfish (though unrelatted)	-----	1½–3 lbs., avg., up to 20 lbs.	Whole	Seared, raw	Raw	2

LEANNESS 1-3 1=LEAN	FLESH COLOR AND TEXTURE RAW	TEXTURE WHEN COOKED	KEEPING PROFILE	HEALTH ISSUES	SUBSTITUTIONS, IF ANY	COMMENTS
1	Gray-white, gray-green, pinkish red; resilient	Firm	2 days fresh, 6 months frozen	Flesh deteriorates rapidly—avoid any that smell of ammonia	-----	Avoid overcooking; because of avail-ability, 16–20s and shrimp graded fewer than 12 per pound are best buys
1	Opaque, very firm	Fork-tender	2–3 days	-----	-----	True Dover or channel sole, taken from the North Sea, Channel Islands, and Bay of Biscay, is considered a great delicacy—flown from Europe, these fish may be found at "upscale" seafood markets
2	Light, reddish brown; soft	Long flakes, fork-tender	1–2 days whole, 1 day for fillets	Smaller fish less likely to carry parasites	-----	Smaller fish best as flesh not prone to gap-ing; excellent for sashimi; great seared

	SPECIES INCLUDE	WEIGHT/SIZE	MOST AVAILABLE FORM(S)	FAVORITE COOKING METHODS	PREFERRED DONENESS	FLAVOR 1-3 1=MILD
SQUID a.k.a. calamari; outtlefish	Long-finned or winter squid; short-finned or summer squid	Bodies 1–4 inches long avg., up to 30 feet	Whole cleaned and uncleaned, fresh and frozen	Fry, braise, stuffed, raw	Less than 2 minutes or more than 1½	1
STRIPED BASS a.k.a. Striper, rockfish	One member of the sea bass family, which includes black sea bass, giant sea bass; grouper	2–15 lbs. avg., up to 70 lbs.	Whole, fillets	Grill, sauté, broil	Cooked 80% through	1
SWORDFISH a.k.a. broadbill, spearfish	-----	150–350 lbs. avg., up to 1000 lbs.	Steaks	Grill, sear	Cooked 75% through	1
TILEFISH	Blackline tile, ocean whitefish, sand tile	2–50 lbs. avg., up to 60 lbs.	Whole, steaks, fillets	Sauté, raw	Cooked 90% through	1
TROUT	Brook, brown, Dolly Varden, lake, speckled, rainbow trout	6–12 ounces avg., up to 40 lbs.	Whole	Sauté, broil	Cooked 85% through	1

LEANNESS 1-3 1=LEAN	FLESH COLOR AND TEXTURE RAW	TEXTURE WHEN COOKED	KEEPING PROFILE	HEALTH ISSUES	SUBSTITUTIONS, IF ANY	COMMENTS
1	White; rubbery	Chewy, firm	1–2 days	-----	-----	If not cooked rapidly, squid toughens and will have to be cooked through firmness until tender again
1	White-opaque; firm	Flakes easily	2–3 days whole, 2 days for fillets	-----	Black sea bass, snapper	Fine firm flesh with exquisitely delicate taste; primarily because of overfishing, wild striped bass may be caught for a limited "season" only; great for sushi and sashimi
1	Brownish white, firm	Fork-tender	2–3 days	Can carry parasites	Marlin striped marlin	West Coast variety preferred; good for sashimi
1	White, very firm	Fork-tender	2 days whole, steaks and fillets	-----	Bass, snapper	Rainbow-colored fish suggest tropical origins but fish are caught from the Gulf of Mexico up the East Coast to Cape Cod; delicious but somewhat bland flesh; good for sushi and sashimi
1	Gray-white to pink-orange; soft	Long flakes	2 days	-----	-----	Most of the trout available to us commercially is farmed; deliciously delicate flesh invites the simplest preparations; not for sushi

	SPECIES INCLUDE	WEIGHT/SIZE	MOST AVAILABLE FORM(S)	FAVORITE COOKING METHODS	PREFERRED DONENESS	FLAVOR 1-3 1=MILD
TUNA	Albacore, bigeye, bluefin, bonito, yellowfin tuna	Depending on species 25–60 lbs. or 150–300 lbs. avg., up to 1,000 lbs.	Steaks, loins	Grill, sear, raw	Cooked 50% through	2
YELLOWTAIL a.k.a. hamachi		10–20 lbs. avg., up to 20 lbs.	Boneless sides	Raw	Raw	2
WHITEBAIT	Consists of small fish of various species including candlefish, silversides, smelt	1½–5 inches	Whole	Fry whole	Cooked 100% through	2

LEANNESS 1-3 1=LEAN	FLESH COLOR AND TEXTURE RAW	TEXTURE WHEN COOKED	KEEPING PROFILE	HEALTH ISSUES	SUBSTITUTIONS, IF ANY	COMMENTS
2	Ruby red; very firm	Firm, tender to the bite	2–3 days steaks and loins	Can carry parasites	-----	Outstanding for sushi and sashimi—choose firm dark red varieties. such as bluefin
3	Pale gray-white; very firm	-----	2 days	-----	-----	*The* fish for sashimi; be sure of freshness; the most outstanding fish come from Japan
2	Pale white, soft	Firm	2–3 days	-----	Minnows	Delicious fried whole and served with a dipping sauce

Index

CONVERSION CHART
Equivalent Imperial and Metric Measurements

American cooks use standard containers, the 8-ounce cup and a tablespoon that takes exactly 16 level fillings to fill that cup level. Measuring by cup makes it very difficult to give weight equivalents, as a cup of densely packed butter will weigh considerably more than a cup of flour. The easiest way therefore to deal with cup measurements in recipes is to take the amount by volume rather than by weight. Thus the equation reads:

1 cup = 240 ml = 8 fl. oz. $\frac{1}{2}$ cup = 120 ml = 4 fl. oz.

It is possible to buy a set of American cup measures in major stores around the world.

In the States, butter is often measured in sticks. One stick is the equivalent of 8 tablespoons. One tablespoon of butter is therefore the equivalent to $\frac{1}{2}$ ounce/15 grams.

Liquid Measures

Fluid Ounces	U.S.	Imperial	Milliliters
	1 teaspoon	1 teaspoon	5
$\frac{1}{4}$	2 teaspoons	1 dessert spoon	7
$\frac{1}{2}$	1 tablespoon	1 tablespoon	15
1	2 tablespoons	2 tablespoons	28
2	$\frac{1}{4}$ cup	4 tablespoons	56
4	$\frac{1}{2}$ cup or $\frac{1}{4}$ pint	110	
5	$\frac{1}{4}$ pint or 1 gill	140	
6	$\frac{3}{4}$ cup	170	
8	1 cup or $\frac{1}{2}$ pint	225	
9		250, $\frac{1}{4}$ liter	
10	$1\frac{1}{4}$ cups or $\frac{1}{2}$ pint	280	
12	$1\frac{1}{2}$ cups or $\frac{3}{4}$ pint	340	
15	$\frac{3}{4}$ pint	420	
16	2 cups or 1 pint	450	
18	$2\frac{1}{4}$ cups	500, $\frac{1}{2}$ liter	
20	$2\frac{1}{2}$ cups or 1 pint	560	
24	3 cups or $1\frac{1}{2}$ pints	675	
25	$1\frac{1}{4}$ pints	700	
27	$3\frac{1}{2}$ cups	750	
30	$3\frac{3}{4}$ cups or $1\frac{1}{2}$ pints	840	
32	4 cups or 2 pints or 1 quart	900	
35	$1\frac{3}{4}$ pints	980	
36	$4\frac{1}{2}$ cups	1000, 1 liter	
40	5 cups		
	2 pints or 1 quart or $2\frac{1}{2}$ pints	1120	
48	6 cups or 3 pints	1350	
50	$2\frac{1}{2}$ pints	1400	
60	$7\frac{1}{2}$ cups or 3 pints	1680	
64	8 cups or 4 pints or 2 quarts	1800	
72	9 cups	2000, 2 liters	

Solid Measures

U.S. and Imperial Measures			Metric Measures
Ounces	Pounds	Grams	Kilos
1		28	
2		56	
$3\frac{1}{2}$		100	
4	$\frac{1}{4}$	112	
5		140	
6		168	
8	$\frac{1}{2}$	225	
9		250	$\frac{1}{4}$
12	$\frac{3}{4}$	340	
16	1	450	
18		500	$\frac{1}{2}$
20	$1\frac{1}{4}$	560	
24	$1\frac{1}{2}$	675	
27		750	$\frac{3}{4}$
28	$1\frac{3}{4}$	780	
32	2	900	
36	$2\frac{1}{4}$	1000	1
40	$2\frac{1}{2}$	1100	
48	3	1350	
54		1500	$1\frac{1}{2}$
64	4	1800	
72	$4\frac{1}{2}$	2000	2
80	5	2250	$2\frac{1}{4}$
90		2500	$2\frac{1}{2}$
100	6	2800	$2\frac{3}{4}$

Oven Temperature Equivalents

Fahrenheit	Celsius	Gas Mark	Description
225	110	$\frac{1}{4}$	Cool
250	130	$\frac{1}{2}$	
275	140	1	Very Slow
300	150	2	
325	170	3	Slow
350	180	4	Moderate
375	190	5	
400	200	6	Moderately Hot
425	220	7	Fairly Hot
450	230	8	Hot
475	240	9	Very Hot
500	250	10	Extremely Hot

Equivalents for Ingredients

all-purpose flour—plain flour
cheesecloth—muslin
confectioners' sugar—icing sugar
cornstarch—corn flour

granulated sugar—castor sugar
shortening—white fat
sour cherry—morello cherry
unbleached flour—strong, white flour

vanilla bean—vanilla pod
zest—rind